LEGAL TRAIL SERIES®

INTELLECTUAL PROPERTY

Including

Copyright, Trademark & Patent Law

Mclaren Legal Publishers
New York

ALSO AVAILABLE IN THIS SERIES:

Civil Procedure
Constitutional Law
Contracts
Criminal Law
Criminal Procedure
Evidence
Intellectual Property
Professional Responsibility
Property
Secured Transactions
Torts

LEGAL TRAIL SERIES®

INTELLECTUAL PROPERTY

First Edition

Copyright, Trademark & Patent Law

Alexander P. Errico, Esq.

Elizabeth D. Hochberg, Esq.

Fabian M. Koenigbauer, Esq.

ISBN 0-9776210-7-3

Published by
Mclaren Legal Publishers LLC
136 West 21 Street, 8th Floor
New York, NY 10011

www.mclarenpublishing.com
Email: contact@mclarenpublishing.com

Printed in the United States of America

HOW TO USE THIS BOOK

This law school study aid is a non-keyed book. While it includes many of the key critical cases in the subject addressed, it is meant to provide an overall rigorous review of the topic indicated and convey key concepts and points of law for general study. For a keyed book linked to a specific casebook, please use our Legal Path Series® of keyed books.

"1-2-3 . . . Patents, Trademarks & Copyrights"
This Intellectual Property book contains an exhaustive review of Patent law, Trademark law and Copyright Law – in one publication. It includes critical case, were applicable, key points of law, federal statutes and more.

"All of what you need, none of what you don't"
Our law school study guides give you exactly what you need to understand the key principles of the subject, including the sometimes elusive Black Letter law. We are not a replacement for an in depth legal analysis of the subject matter covered; however, we do present what is absolutely critical in a very concise format.

Abbreviations used in this book

PTO – Patent & Trademark Office

® - Registered Trademark

TM - Trademark

© - Copyright

P - Plaintiff

D - Defendant

* Use of the word “his” in this book is gender neutral and encompasses both “his” and “her.”

TABLE OF CONTENTS

TABLE OF CONTENTS

TABLE OF CONTENTS

TABLE OF CONTENTS

TABLE OF CONTENTS

What Are Patents, Trademarks, Servicemarks and Copyrights?

(Excerpted from *General Information Concerning Patents* brochure)

Some people confuse patents, copyrights, and trademarks. Although there may be some similarities among these kinds of intellectual property protection, they are different and serve different purposes.

What Is a Patent?

A patent for an invention is the grant of a property right to the inventor, issued by the Patent and Trademark Office. The term of a new patent is 20 years from the date on which the application for the patent was filed in the United States or, in special cases, from the date an earlier related application was filed, subject to the payment of maintenance fees. US patent grants are effective only within the US, US territories, and US possessions.

The right conferred by the patent grant is, in the language of the statute and of the grant itself, "the right to exclude others from making, using, offering for sale, or selling" the invention in the United States or "importing" the invention into the United States. What is granted is not the right to make, use, offer for sale, sell or import, but the right to exclude others from making, using, offering for sale, selling or importing the invention.

What Is a Trademark or Servicemark?

A trademark is a word, name, symbol or device which is used in trade with goods to indicate the source of the goods and to distinguish them from the goods of others. A servicemark is the same as a trademark except that it identifies and distinguishes the source of a service rather than a product. The terms "trademark" and "mark" are commonly used to refer to both trademarks and servicemarks.

Trademark rights may be used to prevent others from using a confusingly similar mark, but not to prevent others from making the same goods or from selling the same goods or services under a clearly different mark. Trademarks which are used in interstate or foreign commerce may be registered with the Patent and Trademark Office. The registration procedure for trademarks and general information concerning trademarks is described in a separate pamphlet entitled "Basic Facts about Trademarks".

What Is a Copyright?

Copyright is a form of protection provided to the authors of "original works of authorship" including literary, dramatic, musical, artistic, and certain other intellectual works, both published and unpublished. The 1976 Copyright Act generally gives the owner of copyright the exclusive right to reproduce the copyrighted work, to prepare derivative works, to distribute copies or phonorecords of the copyrighted work, to perform the copyrighted work publicly, or to display the copyrighted work publicly.

The copyright protects the form of expression rather than the subject matter of the writing. For example, a description of a machine could be copyrighted, but this would only prevent others from copying the description; it would not prevent others from writing a description of their own or from making and using the machine. Copyrights are registered by the Copyright Office of the Library of Congress.

Chapter 1

COPYRIGHT BASICS

Reprinted from Circular 1, Library of Congress, www.copyright.gov

---

Sub-Table of Contents:

WHAT IS COPYRIGHT?

Copyright is a form of protection provided by the laws of the United States (title 17, U.S. Code) to the authors of "original works of authorship," including literary, dramatic, musical, artistic, and certain other intellectual works. This protection is available to both published and unpublished works. Section 106 of the 1976 Copyright Act generally gives the owner of copyright the exclusive right to do and to authorize others to do the following:

- ***To reproduce*** the work in copies or phonorecords;
- To prepare ***derivative works*** based upon the work;
- ***To distribute copies or phonorecords*** of the work to the public by sale or other transfer of ownership, or by rental, lease, or lending;
- **To perform the work publicly,** in the case of literary, musical, dramatic, and choreographic works, pantomimes, and motion pictures and other audiovisual works;
- ***To display the copyrighted work publicly***, in the case of literary, musical, dramatic, and choreographic works, pantomimes, and pictorial, graphic, or sculptural works, including the individual images of a motion picture or other audiovisual work; and
- In the case of ***sound recordings, to perform the work publicly*** by means of a ***digital audio transmission.***

In addition, certain authors of works of visual art have the rights of attribution and integrity as described in section 106A of the 1976 Copyright Act. For further information, request Circular 40, "Copyright Registration for Works of the Visual Arts."

It is illegal for anyone to violate any of the rights provided by the copyright law to the owner of copyright. These rights, however, are not unlimited in scope. Sections 107 through 121 of the 1976 Copyright Act establish limitations on these rights. In some cases, these limitations are specified exemptions from copyright liability. One major limitation is the doctrine of "fair use," which is given a statutory basis in section 107 of the 1976 Copyright Act. In other instances, the limitation takes the form of a "compulsory license" under which certain limited uses of copyrighted works are permitted upon payment of specified royalties and compliance with statutory conditions. For further information about the limitations of any of these rights, consult the copyright law or write to the Copyright Office.

WHO CAN CLAIM COPYRIGHT

Copyright protection subsists from the time the work is created in fixed form. The copyright in the work of authorship ***immediately*** becomes the property of the author who created the work. Only the author or those deriving their rights through the author can rightfully claim copyright.

In the case of works made for hire, the employer and not the employee is considered to be the author. Section 101 of the copyright law defines a "work made for hire" as:

- (1) a work prepared by an employee within the scope of his or her employment; or
- (2) a work specially ordered or commissioned for use as:
    - a contribution to a collective work
    - a part of a motion picture or other audiovisual work
    - a translation

- a supplementary work
- a compilation
- an instructional text
- a test
- answer material for a test
- an atlas

if the parties expressly agree in a written instrument signed by them that the work shall be considered a work made for hire....

The authors of a joint work are co-owners of the copyright in the work, unless there is an agreement to the contrary.

Copyright in each separate contribution to a periodical or other collective work is distinct from copyright in the collective work as a whole and vests initially with the author of the contribution.

Two General Principles

- Mere ownership of a book, manuscript, painting, or any other copy or phonorecord does not give the possessor the copyright. The law provides that transfer of ownership of any material object that embodies a protected work does not of itself convey any rights in the copyright.
- Minors may claim copyright, but state laws may regulate the business dealings involving copyrights owned by minors. For information on relevant state laws, consult an attorney.

COPYRIGHT AND NATIONAL ORIGIN OF THE WORK

Copyright protection is available for all unpublished works, regardless of the nationality or domicile of the author. Published works are eligible for copyright protection in the United States if ***any*** one of the following conditions is met:

- On the date of first publication, one or more of the authors is a national or domiciliary of the United States, or is a national, domiciliary, or sovereign authority of a treaty party,* or is a stateless person wherever that person may be domiciled; or

* A treaty party is a country or intergovernmental organization other than the United States that is a party to an international agreement.

- The work is first published in the United States or in a foreign nation that, on the date of first publication, is a treaty party. For purposes of this condition, a work that is published in the United States or a treaty party within 30 days after publication in a foreign nation that is not a treaty party shall be considered to be first published in the United States or such treaty party, as the case may be; or
- The work is a sound recording that was first fixed in a treaty party; or
- The work is a pictorial, graphic, or sculptural work that is incorporated in a building or other structure, or an architectural work that is embodied in a building and the building or structure is located in the United States or a treaty party; or
- The work is first published by the United Nations or any of its specialized agencies, or by the Organization of American States; or
- The work is a foreign work that was in the public domain in the United States prior to 1996 and its copyright was restored under the Uruguay Round Agreements Act (URAA). Request Circular 38b, "Highlights of Copyright Amendments Contained in the Uruguay Round Agreements Act (URAA-GATT)," for further information.
- The work comes within the scope of a Presidential proclamation.

WHAT WORKS ARE PROTECTED?

Copyright protects "original works of authorship" that are fixed in a tangible form of expression. The fixation need not be directly perceptible so long as it may be communicated with the aid of a machine or device. Copyrightable works include the following categories:

1. literary works;
2. musical works, including any accompanying words
3. dramatic works, including any accompanying music
4. pantomimes and choreographic works
5. pictorial, graphic, and sculptural works
6. motion pictures and other audiovisual works
7. sound recordings
8. architectural works

These categories should be viewed broadly. For example, computer programs and most "compilations" may be registered as "literary works"; maps and architectural plans may be registered as "pictorial, graphic, and sculptural works."

WHAT IS NOT PROTECTED BY COPYRIGHT?

Several categories of material are generally not eligible for federal copyright protection. These include among others:

- Works that have ***not*** been fixed in a tangible form of expression (for example, choreographic works that have not been notated or recorded, or improvisational speeches or performances that have not been written or recorded)
- Titles, names, short phrases, and slogans; familiar symbols or designs; mere variations of typographic ornamentation, lettering, or coloring; mere listings of ingredients or contents

- Ideas, procedures, methods, systems, processes, concepts, principles, discoveries, or devices, as distinguished from a description, explanation, or illustration
- Works consisting ***entirely*** of information that is common property and containing no original authorship (for example: standard calendars, height and weight charts, tape measures and rulers, and lists or tables taken from public documents or other common sources)

HOW TO SECURE A COPYRIGHT

Copyright Secured Automatically upon Creation

The way in which copyright protection is secured is frequently misunderstood. No publication or registration or other action in the Copyright Office is required to secure copyright (See following Note). There are, however, certain definite advantages to registration. See "Copyright Registration."

Copyright is secured ***automatically*** when the work is created, and a work is "created" when it is fixed in a copy or phonorecord for the first time. "Copies" are material objects from which a work can be read or visually perceived either directly or with the aid of a machine or device, such as books, manuscripts, sheet music, film, videotape, or microfilm. "Phonorecords" are material objects embodying fixations of sounds (excluding, by statutory definition, motion picture soundtracks), such as cassette tapes, CDs, or LPs. Thus, for example, a song (the "work") can be fixed in sheet music (" copies") or in phonograph disks (" phonorecords"), or both.

If a work is prepared over a period of time, the part of the work that is fixed on a particular date constitutes the created work as of that date.

PUBLICATION

Publication is no longer the key to obtaining federal copyright as it was under the Copyright Act of 1909. However, publication remains important to copyright owners.

The 1976 Copyright Act defines publication as follows:

"Publication" is the distribution of copies or phonorecords of a work to the public by sale or other transfer of ownership, or by rental, lease, or lending. The offering to distribute copies or phonorecords to a group of persons for purposes of further distribution, public performance, or public display constitutes publication. A public performance or display of a work does not of itself constitute publication.

> **NOTE:** Before 1978, federal copyright was generally secured by the act of publication with notice of copyright, assuming compliance with all other relevant statutory conditions. U. S. works in the public domain on January 1, 1978, (for example, works published without satisfying all conditions for securing federal copyright under the Copyright Act of 1909) remain in the public domain under the 1976 Copyright Act. Certain foreign works originally published without notice had their copyrights restored under the Uruguay Round Agreements Act (URAA). Request Circular 38b and see the "Notice of Copyright" section of this publication for further information. Federal copyright could also be secured before 1978 by the act of registration in the case of certain unpublished works and works eligible for ad interim copyright. The 1976 Copyright Act automatically extends to full term (section 304 sets the term) copyright for all works, including those subject to ad interim copyright if ad interim registration has been made on or before June 30, 1978.

A further discussion of the definition of "publication" can be found in the legislative history of the 1976 Copyright Act. The legislative reports define "to the public" as distribution to persons under no explicit or implicit restrictions with respect to disclosure of the contents. The reports state that the definition makes it clear that the sale of phonorecords constitutes publication of the underlying work, for example, the musical, dramatic, or literary work embodied in a phonorecord. The reports also state that it is clear that any form of dissemination in which the material object does not change hands, for example, performances or displays on television, is ***not*** a publication no matter how many people are exposed to the work. However, when copies or phonorecords are offered for sale or lease to a group of wholesalers, broadcasters, or motion picture theaters, publication does take place if the purpose is further distribution, public performance, or public display.

Publication is an important concept in the copyright law for several reasons:

- Works that are published in the United States are subject to mandatory deposit with the Library of Congress. See discussion on "Mandatory Deposit for Works Published in the United States."
- Publication of a work can affect the limitations on the exclusive rights of the copyright owner that are set forth in sections 107 through 121 of the law.
- The year of publication may determine the duration of copyright protection for anonymous and pseudonymous works (when the author's identity is not revealed in the records of the Copyright Office) and for works made for hire.
- Deposit requirements for registration of published works differ from those for registration of unpublished works. See discussion on "Registration Procedures."
- When a work is published, it may bear a notice of copyright to identify the year of publication and the name of the copyright owner and to inform the public that the work is protected by copyright. Copies of works published before March 1, 1989, must bear the notice or risk loss of copyright protection. See discussion on "Notice of Copyright" below.

NOTICE OF COPYRIGHT

The use of a copyright notice is no longer required under U. S. law, although it is often beneficial. Because prior law did contain such a requirement, however, the use of notice is still relevant to the copyright status of older works.

Notice was required under the 1976 Copyright Act. This requirement was eliminated when the United States adhered to the Berne Convention, effective March 1, 1989. Although works published without notice before that date could have entered the public domain in the United States, the Uruguay Round Agreements Act (URAA) restores copyright in certain foreign works originally published without notice. For further information about copyright amendments in the URAA, request Circular 38b.

The Copyright Office does not take a position on whether copies of works first published with notice before March 1, 1989, which are distributed on or after March 1, 1989, must bear the copyright notice.

Use of the notice may be important because it informs the public that the work is protected by copyright, identifies the copyright owner, and shows the year of first publication. Furthermore, in the event that a work is infringed, if a proper notice of copyright appears on the published copy or copies to which a defendant in a copyright infringement suit had access, then no weight shall be given to such a defendant's interposition of a defense based on innocent infringement in mitigation of actual or statutory damages, except as provided in section 504(c)(2) of the copyright law. Innocent infringement occurs when the infringer did not realize that the work was protected.

The use of the copyright notice is the responsibility of the copyright owner and does not require advance permission from, or registration with, the Copyright Office.

Form of Notice for Visually Perceptible Copies

The notice for visually perceptible copies should contain all the following three elements:

1. **The symbol** © (the letter C in a circle), or the word "Copyright," or the abbreviation "Copr."; and

2. **The year of first publication** of the work. In the case of compilations or derivative works incorporating previously published material, the year date of first publication of the compilation or derivative work is sufficient. The year date may be omitted where a pictorial, graphic, or sculptural work, with accompanying textual matter, if any, is reproduced in or on greeting cards, postcards, stationery, jewelry, dolls, toys, or any useful article; and

3. **The name of the owner of copyright** in the work, or an abbreviation by which the name can be recognized, or a generally known alternative designation of the owner.

Example: © 2002 John Doe

The "C in a circle" notice is used only on "visually perceptible copies." Certain kinds of works--for example, musical, dramatic, and literary works--may be fixed not in "copies" but by means of sound in an audio recording. Since audio recordings such as audio tapes and phonograph disks are "phonorecords" and not "copies," the "C in a circle" notice is not used to indicate protection of the underlying musical, dramatic, or literary work that is recorded.

Form of Notice for Phonorecords of Sound Recordings*

* Sound recordings are defined in the law as "works that result from the fixation of a series of musical, spoken, or other sounds, but not including the sounds accompanying a motion picture or other audiovisual work." Common examples include recordings of music, drama, or lectures. A sound recording is not the same as a phonorecord. A phonorecord is the physical object in which works of authorship are embodied. The word "phonorecord" includes cassette tapes, CDs, LPs, 45 r. p. m. disks, as well as other formats.

The notice for phonorecords embodying a sound recording should contain all the following three elements:

1. ***The symbol*** ℗(the letter P in a circle); and

2. ***The year of first publication*** of the sound recording; and

3. ***The name of the owner of copyright*** in the sound recording, or an abbreviation by which the name can be recognized, or a generally known alternative designation of the owner. If the producer of the sound recording is named on the phonorecord label or container and if no other name appears in conjunction with the notice, the producer's name shall be considered a part of the notice.

Example: ℗2002 A. B. C. Records Inc.

NOTE: Since questions may arise from the use of variant forms of the notice, you may wish to seek legal advice before using any form of the notice other than those given here.

Position of Notice

The copyright notice should be affixed to copies or phonorecords in such a way as to "give reasonable notice of the claim of copyright." The three elements of the notice should ordinarily appear together on the copies or phonorecords or on the phonorecord label or container. The Copyright Office has issued regulations concerning the form and position of the copyright notice in the Code of Federal Regulations (37 CFR Section 201.20). For more information, request Circular 3, "Copyright Notice."

Publications Incorporating U. S. Government Works

Works by the U. S. Government are not eligible for U. S. copyright protection. For works published on and after March 1, 1989, the previous notice requirement for works consisting primarily of one or more U. S. Government works has been eliminated. However, use of a notice on such a work will defeat a claim of innocent infringement as previously described provided the notice also includes a statement that identifies either those portions of the work in which copyright is claimed or those portions that constitute U. S. Government material.

Example: © 2002 Jane Brown. Copyright claimed in Chapters 7-10, exclusive of U. S. Government maps

Copies of works published before March 1, 1989, that consist primarily of one or more works of the U. S. Government ***should*** have a notice and the identifying statement.

Unpublished Works

The author or copyright owner may wish to place a copyright notice on any unpublished copies or phonorecords that leave his or her control.

Example: Unpublished work © 2002 Jane Doe

Omission of the Notice and Errors in Notice

The 1976 Copyright Act attempted to ameliorate the strict consequences of failure to include notice under prior law. It contained provisions that set out specific corrective steps to cure omissions or certain errors in notice. Under these provisions, an applicant had 5 years after publication to cure omission of notice or certain errors. Although these provisions are technically still in the law, their impact has been limited by the amendment making notice optional for all works published on and after March 1, 1989. For further information, request Circular 3, "Copyright Notice."

HOW LONG COPYRIGHT PROTECTION ENDURES

Works Originally Created on or after January 1, 1978

A work that is created (fixed in tangible form for the first time) on or after January 1, 1978, is automatically protected from the moment of its creation and is ordinarily given a term enduring for the author's life plus an additional 70 years after the author's death. In the case of "a joint work prepared by two or more authors who did not work for hire," the term lasts for 70 years after the last surviving author's death. For works made for hire, and for anonymous and pseudonymous works (unless the author's identity is revealed in Copyright Office records), the duration of copyright will be 95 years from publication or 120 years from creation, whichever is shorter.

Works Originally Created before January 1, 1978, but Not Published or Registered by That Date

These works have been automatically brought under the statute and are now given federal copyright protection. The duration of copyright in these works will generally be computed in the same way as for works created on or after January 1, 1978: the life-plus-70 or 95/120-year terms will apply to them as well. The law provides that in no case will the term of copyright for works in this category expire before December 31, 2002, and for works published on or before December 31, 2002, the term of copyright will not expire before December 31, 2047.

Works Originally Created and Published or Registered before January 1, 1978

Under the law in effect before 1978, copyright was secured either on the date a work was published with a copyright notice or on the date of registration if the work was registered in unpublished form. In either case, the copyright endured for a first term of 28 years from the date it was secured. During the last (28th) year of the first term, the copyright was eligible for renewal. The Copyright Act of 1976 extended the renewal term from 28 to 47 years for copyrights that were subsisting on January 1, 1978, or for pre-1978 copyrights restored under the Uruguay Round Agreements Act (URAA), making these works eligible for a total term of protection of 75 years. Public Law 105-298, enacted on October 27, 1998, further extended the renewal term of copyrights still subsisting on that date by an additional 20 years, providing for a renewal term of 67 years and a total term of protection of 95 years.

Public Law 102-307, enacted on June 26, 1992, amended the 1976 Copyright Act to provide for automatic renewal of the term of copyrights secured between January 1, 1964, and December 31, 1977. Although the renewal term is automatically provided, the Copyright Office does not issue a renewal certificate for these works unless a renewal application and fee are received and registered in the Copyright Office.

Public Law 102-307 makes renewal registration optional. Thus, filing for renewal registration is no longer required in order to extend the original 28-year copyright term to the full 95 years. However, some benefits accrue from making a renewal registration during the 28th year of the original term.

For more detailed information on renewal of copyright and the copyright term, request Circular 15, "Renewal of Copyright"; Circular 15a, "Duration of Copyright"; and Circular 15t, "Extension of Copyright Terms."

TRANSFER OF COPYRIGHT

Any or all of the copyright owner's ***exclusive*** rights or any subdivision of those rights may be transferred, but the transfer of exclusive rights is not valid unless that transfer is in writing and signed by the owner of the rights conveyed or such owner's duly authorized agent. Transfer of a right on a nonexclusive basis does not require a written agreement.

A copyright may also be conveyed by operation of law and may be bequeathed by will or pass as personal property by the applicable laws of intestate succession.

Copyright is a personal property right, and it is subject to the various state laws and regulations that govern the ownership, inheritance, or transfer of personal property as well as terms of contracts or conduct of business. For information about relevant state laws, consult an attorney.

Transfers of copyright are normally made by contract. The Copyright Office does not have any forms for such transfers. The law does provide for the recordation in the Copyright Office of transfers of copyright ownership. Although recordation is not required to make a valid transfer between the parties, it does provide certain legal advantages and may be required to validate the transfer as against third parties. For information on recordation of transfers and other documents related to copyright, request Circular 12, "Recordation of Transfers and Other Documents."

Termination of Transfers

Under the previous law, the copyright in a work reverted to the author, if living, or if the author was not living, to other specified beneficiaries, provided a renewal claim was registered in the 28th year of the original term.* The present law drops the renewal feature except for works already in the first term of statutory protection when the present law took effect. Instead, the present law permits termination of a grant of rights after 35 years under certain conditions by serving written notice on the transferee within specified time limits.

*The copyright in works eligible for renewal on or after June 26, 1992, will vest in the name of the renewal claimant on the effective date of any renewal registration made during the 28th year of the original term. Otherwise, the renewal copyright will vest in the party entitled to claim renewal as of December 31st of the 28th year.

For works already under statutory copyright protection before 1978, the present law provides a similar right of termination covering the newly added years that extended the former maximum term of the copyright from 56 to 95 years. For further information, see Circulars 15a and 15t.

INTERNATIONAL COPYRIGHT PROTECTION

There is no such thing as an "international copyright" that will automatically protect an author's writings throughout the entire world. Protection against unauthorized use in a particular country depends, basically, on the national laws of that country. However, most countries do offer protection to foreign works under certain conditions, and these conditions have been greatly simplified by international copyright treaties and conventions. For further information and a list of countries that maintain copyright relations with the United States, request Circular 38a, "International Copyright Relations of the United States."

COPYRIGHT REGISTRATION

In general, copyright registration is a legal formality intended to make a public record of the basic facts of a particular copyright. However, registration is not a condition of copyright protection. Even though registration is not a requirement for protection, the copyright law provides several inducements or advantages to encourage copyright owners to make registration. Among these advantages are the following:

- Registration establishes a public record of the copyright claim.
- Before an infringement suit may be filed in court, registration is necessary for works of U. S. origin.
- If made before or within 5 years of publication, registration will establish prima facie evidence in court of the validity of the copyright and of the facts stated in the certificate.
- If registration is made within 3 months after publication of the work or prior to an infringement of the work, statutory damages and attorney's fees will be available to the copyright owner in court actions. Otherwise, only an award of actual damages and profits is available to the copyright owner.

- Registration allows the owner of the copyright to record the registration with the U. S. Customs Service for protection against the importation of infringing copies. For additional information, request Publication No. 563 "How to Protect Your Intellectual Property Right," from: U.S. Customs Service, P.O. Box 7404, Washington, D.C. 20044. See the U.S. Customs Service Website at www.customs.gov for online publications.

Registration may be made at any time within the life of the copyright. Unlike the law before 1978, when a work has been registered in unpublished form, it is not necessary to make another registration when the work becomes published, although the copyright owner may register the published edition, if desired.

REGISTRATION PROCEDURES

Original Registration

To register a work, send the following three elements ***in the same envelope or package*** to:

Library of Congress
Copyright Office
101 Independence Avenue, S.E.
Washington, D.C. 20559-6000

1. A properly completed application form.
2. A nonrefundable filing fee of $30 for each application.

NOTE: Copyright Office fees are subject to change. For current fees, please check the Copyright Office Website at www.copyright.gov, write the Copyright Office, or call (202) 707-3000.

3. A nonrefundable deposit of the work being registered. The deposit requirements vary in particular situations. The general

requirements follow. Also note the information under "Special Deposit Requirements."

- If the work was first published in the United States on or after January 1, 1978, two complete copies or phonorecords of the best edition.
- If the work was first published in the United States before January 1, 1978, two complete copies or phonorecords of the work as first published.
- If the work was first published outside the United States, one complete copy or phonorecord of the work as first published.
- If sending multiple works, all applications, deposits, and fees should be sent in the same package. If possible, applications should be attached to the appropriate deposit. Whenever possible, number each package (e. g., 1 of 3, 2 of 4) to facilitate processing.

What Happens if the Three Elements Are Not Received Together

Applications and fees received without appropriate copies, phonorecords, or identifying material will not be processed and ordinarily will be returned. Unpublished deposits without applications or fees ordinarily will be returned, also. In most cases, published deposits received without applications and fees can be immediately transferred to the collections of the Library of Congress. This practice is in accordance with section 408 of the law, which provides that the published deposit required for the collections of the Library of Congress may be used for registration only if the deposit is "accompanied by the prescribed application and fee...."

After the deposit is received and transferred to another service unit of the Library for its collections or other disposition, it is no longer available to the Copyright Office. If you wish to register the work, you must deposit additional copies or phonorecords with your application and fee.

Renewal Registration

To register a renewal, send:

1. A properly completed application Form RE and, if necessary, Form RE Addendum, and
2. A nonrefundable filing fee of $60 without Addendum; $90 with Addendum for each application. (See Note above.) Each Addendum form must be accompanied by a deposit representing the work being reviewed. See Circular 15, "Renewal of Copyright."

NOTE: Complete the application form using black ink pen or type. You may photocopy blank application forms. **However,** photocopied forms submitted to the Copyright Office must be clear, legible, on a good grade of 8-1/2-inch by 11-inch white paper suitable for automatic feeding through a photocopier. The forms should be printed, preferably in black ink, head-to-head so that when you turn the sheet over, the top of page 2 is directly behind the top of page 1. **Forms not meeting these requirements may be returned resulting in delayed registration.**

Special Deposit Requirements

Special deposit requirements exist for many types of works. The following are prominent examples of exceptions to the general deposit requirements:

- If the work is a motion picture, the deposit requirement is one complete copy of the unpublished or published motion picture **and** a separate written description of its contents, such as a continuity, press book, or synopsis.
- If the work is a literary, dramatic, or musical work **published only in a phonorecord,** the deposit requirement is one complete phonorecord.

- If the work is an unpublished or published computer program, the deposit requirement is one visually perceptible copy in source code of the **first 25 and last 25 pages** of the program. For a program of fewer than 50 pages, the deposit is a copy of the entire program. For more information on computer program registration, including deposits for revised programs and provisions for trade secrets, request Circular 61, "Copyright Registration for Computer Programs."
- If the work is in a CD-ROM format, the deposit requirement is one complete copy of the material, that is, the CD-ROM, the operating software, and any manual(s) accompanying it. If registration is sought for the computer program on the CD-ROM, the deposit should also include a printout of the first 25 and last 25 pages of source code for the program.

In the case of works reproduced in three-dimensional copies, identifying material such as photographs or drawings is ordinarily required. Other examples of special deposit requirements (but by no means an exhaustive list) include many works of the visual arts such as greeting cards, toys, fabrics, oversized materials (request Circular 40a, "Deposit Requirements for Registration of Claims to Copyright in Visual Arts Material"); video games and other machine-readable audiovisual works (request Circular 61); automated databases (request Circular 65, "Copyright Registration for Automated Databases"); and contributions to collective works. For information about deposit requirements for group registration of serials, request Circular 62, "Copyright Registration for Serials."

If you are unsure of the deposit requirement for your work, write or call the Copyright Office and describe the work you wish to register.

Unpublished Collections

Under the following conditions, a work may be registered in unpublished form as a "collection," with one application form and one fee:

- The elements of the collection are assembled in an orderly form;

- The combined elements bear a single title identifying the collection as a whole;
- The copyright claimant in all the elements and in the collection as a whole is the same; and
- All the elements are by the same author, or, if they are by different authors, at least one of the authors has contributed copyrightable authorship to each element.

An unpublished collection is not indexed under the individual titles of the contents but under the title of the collection.

NOTE: A **Library of Congress Control Number** is different from a copyright registration number. The Cataloging in Publication (CIP) Division of the Library of Congress is responsible for assigning LC Control Numbers and is operationally separate from the Copyright Office. A book may be registered in or deposited with the Copyright Office but not necessarily cataloged and added to the Library's collections.

EFFECTIVE DATE OF REGISTRATION

A copyright registration is effective on the date the Copyright Office receives all the required elements in acceptable form, regardless of how long it then takes to process the application and mail the certificate of registration. The time the Copyright Office requires to process an application varies, depending on the amount of material the Office is receiving.

If you apply for copyright registration, you will not receive an acknowledgment that your application has been received (the Office receives more than 600,000 applications annually), but you can expect:

- A letter or a telephone call from a Copyright Office staff member if further information is needed or

- A certificate of registration indicating that the work has been registered, or if the application cannot be accepted, a letter explaining why it has been rejected.

Requests to have certificates available for pickup in the Public Information Office or to have certificates sent by Federal Express or another mail service cannot be honored. If you want to know the date that the Copyright Office receives your material, send it by registered or certified mail and request a return receipt.

CORRECTIONS AND AMPLIFICATIONS OF EXISTING REGISTRATIONS

To correct an error in a copyright registration or to amplify the information given in a registration, file a supplementary registration form - Form CA - with the Copyright Office. The filing fee is $100. The information in a supplementary registration augments but does not supersede that contained in the earlier registration. The supplementary registration is not a substitute for an original registration, for a renewal registration, or for recording a transfer of ownership.

MANDATORY DEPOSIT FOR WORKS PUBLISHED IN THE UNITED STATES

Although a copyright registration is not required, the Copyright Act establishes a mandatory deposit requirement for works published in the United States. See the definition of "publication." In general, the owner of copyright or the owner of the exclusive right of publication in the work has a legal obligation to deposit in the Copyright Office, within 3 months of publication in the United States, two copies (or in the case of sound recordings, two phonorecords) for the use of the Library of Congress. Failure to make the deposit can result in fines and other penalties but does not affect copyright protection.

Certain categories of works are exempt entirely from the mandatory deposit requirements, and the obligation is reduced for certain other categories. For further information about mandatory deposit, request Circular 7d, "Mandatory Deposit of Copies or Phonorecords for the Library of Congress."

USE OF MANDATORY DEPOSIT TO SATISFY REGISTRATION REQUIREMENTS

For works published in the United States, the copyright law contains a provision under which a single deposit can be made to satisfy both the deposit requirements for the Library and the registration requirements. In order to have this dual effect, the copies or phonorecords must be accompanied by the prescribed application form and filing fee.

WHO MAY FILE AN APPLICATION FORM?

The following persons are legally entitled to submit an application form:

- **The author.** This is either the person who actually created the work or, if the work was made for hire, the employer or other person for whom the work was prepared.
- **The copyright claimant.** The copyright claimant is defined in Copyright Office regulations as either the author of the work or a person or organization that has obtained ownership of all the rights under the copyright initially belonging to the author. This category includes a person or organization who has obtained by contract the right to claim legal title to the copyright in an application for copyright registration.
- **The owner of exclusive right(s).** Under the law, any of the exclusive rights that make up a copyright and any subdivision of them can be transferred and owned separately, even though the transfer may be limited in time or place of effect. The term

"copyright owner" with respect to any one of the exclusive rights contained in a copyright refers to the owner of that particular right. Any owner of an exclusive right may apply for registration of a claim in the work.

- **The duly authorized agent** of such author, other copyright claimant, or owner of exclusive right(s). Any person authorized to act on behalf of the author, other copyright claimant, or owner of exclusive rights may apply for registration. There is no requirement that applications be prepared or filed by an attorney.

APPLICATION FORMS

For Original Registrations

Form PA:	for published and unpublished works of the performing arts (musical and dramatic works, pantomimes and choreographic works, motion pictures and other audiovisual works)
Form SE:	for serials, works issued or intended to be issued in successive parts bearing numerical or chronological designations and intended to be continued indefinitely (periodicals, newspapers, magazines, newsletters, annuals, journals, etc.)
Form SR:	for published and unpublished sound recordings
Form TX:	for published and unpublished nondramatic literary works
Form VA:	for published and unpublished works of the visual arts (pictorial, graphic, and sculptural works, including architectural works)
Form G/DN:	a specialized form to register a complete month's issues of a daily newspaper when certain conditions are met

Short Form/ SE and Form SE/GROUP:	specialized SE forms for use when certain requirements are met
Short Forms TX, PA, and VA:	short versions of applications for original registration. For further information about using the short forms, request publication SL-7.
Form GATT and Form GATT/GRP:	specialized forms to register a claim in a work or group of related works in which U. S. copyright was restored under the 1994 Uruguay Round Agreements Act (URAA). For further information, request Circular 38b.

For Renewal Registrations

Form RE:	for claims to renew copyright in works copyrighted under the law in effect through December 31, 1977 (1909 Copyright Act) and registered during the initial 28-year copyright term
Form RE Addendum:	accompanies Form RE for claims to renew copyright in works copyrighted under the 1909 Copyright Act but never registered during their initial 28-year copyright term

For Corrections and Amplifications

Form CA:	for supplementary registration to correct or amplify information given in the Copyright Office record of an earlier registration

For a Group of Contributions to Periodicals

Form GR/CP:	an adjunct application to be used for registration of a group of contributions to

periodicals in addition to an application Form TX, PA, or VA

How to Obtain Application Forms

You must have Adobe Acrobat Reader ® installed on your computer to view and print the forms accessed on the Internet. Adobe Acrobat Reader may be downloaded free from Adobe Systems Incorporated through links from the same Internet site from which the forms are available.

FILL-IN FORMS AVAILABLE

All Copyright Office forms are available on the Copyright Office Website in fill-in version. Go to www.copyright.gov/forms and follow the instructions. The fill-in forms allow you to enter information while the form is displayed on the screen by an Adobe Acrobat Reader product. You may then print the completed form and mail it to the Copyright Office. Fill-in forms provide a clean, sharp printout for your records and for filing with the Copyright Office.

FEES

All remittances should be in the form of drafts, that is, checks, money orders, or bank drafts, payable to: **Register of Copyrights**. Do not send cash. Drafts must be redeemable without service or exchange fee through a U. S. institution, must be payable in U. S. dollars, and must be imprinted with American Banking Association routing numbers. International Money Orders and Postal Money Orders that are negotiable only at a post office are not acceptable.

If a check received in payment of the filing fee is returned to the Copyright Office as uncollectible, the Copyright Office will cancel the registration and will notify the remitter.

The filing fee for processing an original, supplementary, or renewal claim is nonrefundable, whether or not copyright registration is ultimately made.

Do not send cash. The Copyright Office cannot assume any responsibility for the loss of currency sent in payment of copyright fees. For further information, request Circular 4, "Copyright Fees."

Certain Fees and Services May Be Charged to a Credit Card

Some fees may be charged by telephone and in person in the office. Others may only be charged in person in the office. Credit card payments are generally authorized only for services that do not require filing of applications or other materials. An exception is made for fees related to items that are hand-carried into the Public Information Office.

Certifications and Documents Section: These fees may be charged in person in the office **or** by phone: additional certificates; copies of documents and deposits; searching, locating and retrieving deposits; certifications; and expedited processing.

Public Information Office: These fees may only be charged in person in the office, **not** by phone: standard registration request forms; special handling requests for all standard registration requests; requests for services provided by the Certifications and Documents Section when the request is accompanied by a request for special handling; search requests for which a fee estimate has been provided; additional fee for each claim using the same deposit; full term retention fees; appeal fees; Secure Test processing fee; short fee payments when accompanied by a Remittance Due Notice; in-process retrieval fees; and online service providers fees.

Reference and Bibliography Section: Requests for searches on a regular or expedited basis can be charged to a credit card by phone.

Records Maintenance Unit: Computer time on COINS, printing from the Optical Disk, and photocopying can be charged in person in the office.

Fiscal Control Section: Deposit Accounts maintained by the Fiscal Control Section may be replenished by credit card. See Circular 5, "How to Open and Maintain a Deposit Account in the Copyright Office."

NIE recordations and claims filed on Forms GATT and GATT/GRP may be paid by credit card if the card number is included in a separate letter that accompanies the form.

NOTE: Copyright Office fees are subject to change. For current fees, please check the Copyright Office Website at www.copyright.gov, write the Copyright Office, or call (202) 707-3000.

SEARCH OF COPYRIGHT OFFICE RECORDS

The records of the Copyright Office are open for inspection and searching by the public. Moreover, on request, the Copyright Office will search its records for you at the statutory hourly rate of $75 for each hour or fraction of an hour (See Note above.) For information on searching the Office records concerning the copyright status or ownership of a work, request Circular 22, "How to Investigate the Copyright Status of a Work," and Circular 23, "The Copyright Card Catalog and the Online Files of the Copyright Office." Copyright Office records in machine-readable form cataloged from January 1, 1978, to the present, including registration and renewal information and recorded documents, are now available for searching from the Copyright Office website at www.copyright.gov.

FOR FURTHER INFORMATION

Information via the Internet: Circulars, announcements, regulations, other related materials, and all copyright application forms are available from the Copyright Office Website at www.copyright.gov.

Information by telephone: For general information about copyright, call the Copyright Public Information Office at (202) 707-3000. The TTY number is (202) 707-6737. Information specialists are on duty from 8:30 a. m. to 5:00 p. m. Monday through Friday, eastern time, except federal holidays. Recorded information is available 24 hours a day. Or, if you know which application forms and circulars you want, request them from the Forms and Publications Hotline at (202) 707-9100 24 hours a day. Leave a recorded message.

Information by regular mail: Write to:

Library of Congress
Copyright Office
Publications Section, LM-455
101 Independence Avenue, S.E.
Washington, D.C. 20559-6000

For a list of other material published by the Copyright Office, request Circular 2, "Publications on Copyright."

> The Copyright Office provides a free electronic mailing list, *NewsNet,* which issues periodic email messages on the subject of copyright. The messages alert subscribers to hearings, deadlines for comments, new and proposed regulations, new publications, and other copyright-related subjects of interest. *NewsNet* is not an interactive discussion group. To subscribe, send a message to LISTSERV@LOC.GOV. In the body of the message say: SUBSCRIBE USCOPYRIGHT or fill in the subscription form online at www.copyright.gov/newsnet You will receive a standard welcoming message indicating that your subscription to *NewsNet* has been accepted.

The Copyright Public Information Office is open to the public 8:30 a.m. to 5:00 p.m. Monday through Friday, eastern time, except federal holidays. The office is located in the Library of Congress, James Madison Memorial Building, Room 401, at 101 Independence Avenue, S.E., Washington, D.C., near the Capitol South Metro stop.

Chapter

2

COPYRIGHT HISTORY

A Brief History of Modern Copyright Law

1710	Basis for modern copyright law is born with passage of Statue of Anne by British Parliament. The **Statute of Anne** (short title **Copyright Act 1709** 8 Anne c.19) was the first British copyright law, enacted in 1709 and entering into force on April 10, 1710. It is generally considered to be the first fully-fledged copyright law.
1786	12 of 13 original states had passed copyright laws based on the English legal system.
1790	U.S. Constitution creates law that books, maps and charts will be protected for a 14 year period with a 14 year renewal period. Based on English copyright law (Statue of Anne) and common law.
1802	Act passed that requires books to carry a notice of copyright. Designs, engravings and etchings were added protection.
1831	Act passed that extended protection to 28 years with a 14 year renewal. Music was added protection.
1856	Act passed protecting performance rights to dramatists.
1865	Act passed protecting photographs and negatives.
1870	Act passed to protect paintings, drawings, statues, models and other fine art.
1909	Act passed that extended protection to 28 years with a 28 year renewal. Jukeboxes were added protection.
1912	Act passed providing protection to motion pictures.

<table>
<tr><td>1976</td><td>Act marked a major change to copyright law.
<ul>
<li>Copyrightable works include published and unpublished.</li>
<li>Amended to cover original works of authorship fixed in any tangible medium of expression.</li>
<li>Work protected at creation.</li>
<li>Life of Author plus 50 years or Anonymous works 75 years from date of publication.</li>
<li>Computer programs and databases protected.</li>
</ul></td></tr>
<tr><td>1990</td><td>Copyright Act amended to ensure that state universities would not be immune from being sued for monetary damages in federal court. State and private universities are now subject to the same copyright regulations, and may be sued for copyright infringement. Architectural works protected.</td></tr>
<tr><td>1998</td><td>Sonny Bono Copyright Term Extension Act

For works created after January 1, 1978, copyright protection will endure for the life of the author plus an additional 70 years. In the case of a joint work, the term lasts for 70 years after the last surviving author's death. For anonymous and pseudonymous works and works made for hire, the term will be 95 years from the year of first publication or 120 years from the year of creation, whichever expires first. For works created but not published or registered before January 1, 1978, the term endures for life of the author plus 70 years, but in no case will expire earlier than December 31, 2002. If the work is published before December 31, 2002, the term will not expire before December 31, 2047. For pre-1978 works still in their original or renewal term of copyright, the total term is extended to 95 years from the date that copyright was originally secured. The act was named after the late Sonny Bono, who lobbied for extending the duration of copyrights. It was passed shortly after his death. Without it, Mickey Mouse would have entered the public domain between 2000 and 2004.</td></tr>
</table>

<table>
<tr>
<td>1998</td>
<td>

Digital Millennium Copyright Act (DMCA)

For the first time in US history, the DMCA applies criminal law, rather than fines or other civil penalties, to intellectual property. It states that circumventing technical anti-copying protections, or distributing a tool that could be used for these purposes, is illegal.

The Act is designed to implement the treaties signed in 1996 at the World Intellectual Property Organization (WIPO) Geneva conference, but also contains additional provisions. Internet Service providers are expected to remove material from users' web sites that appears to constitute copyright infringement, on request from the copyright holders. The law also requires that webcasters pay licensing fees to record companies. The act is widely supported by music and entertainment industries, but has met widespread opposition.

- Makes it a crime to circumvent anti-piracy measures built into most commercial software.
- Outlaws the manufacture, sale, or distribution of code-cracking devices used to illegally copy software.
- Provides exemptions from anti-circumvention provisions for nonprofit libraries, archives, and educational institutions under certain circumstances.
- Limits Internet service providers from copyright infringement liability for simply transmitting information over the Internet.
- Service providers, however, are expected to remove material from users' web sites that appears to constitute copyright infringement.
- Limits liability of nonprofit institutions of higher education -- when they serve as online service providers and under certain circumstances -- for copyright infringement by faculty members or graduate students.

</td>
</tr>
</table>

A. The Purpose of Copyright Law

The focus of copyright law is on the benefits derived by the public from the labors of authors. Under this view, reward to the copyright owner or author is a secondary concern.

B. The Concept of "Authorship"

1. Common Law

The common law meaning for "copyright" confers a negative right in the owner to prevent the copying of his work. In essence, the common law provided material support to an author who invests in producing a work - individual or otherwise (a corporate entity). The ultimate goal was the enhancement of the public's welfare; an essentially economic value.

2. Civil Law

The civil law tradition views the author's work as an extension of his or her personality which springs into existence by a personal act of creation. Under the civil law system, an author is deemed to have a moral entitlement to control and exploit the product of his or her intellect.

C. Historical Development of Anglo-American Copyright Law

1. Early Developments

a. The Statute of Anne

Parliament passed the first copyright act, the Statute of Anne, in 1710 which rewarded authors for their creations and recognized the importance of the public domain by limiting these rights to a specific number of years. For existing works, the Statute provided that "authors and their assigns" should have the sole right of publication (thereby seemingly breaking the stationers' historic monopoly) for 21 years. New books were given a first term of protection of 14 years for authors and their assigns, measured from the date of first publication, plus a second term of 14 years which reverted to the author if he lived to its commencement.

In *Donaldson v. Beckett*, the House of Lords established that the term of copyright is finite. Once that copyright term is exhausted, a work will fall into the "public domain."

The Statute of Anne defined a "copy" as being "the sale, liberty of printing, and reprinting of a book." Infringement occurred when a third party printed, reprinted, or imported the book without consent. The protection granted was basically no more than a prohibition against literal copying. To enforce his rights, an author had to register the title of the book with the Stationer's Company before publication.

b. United States Constitution

The Framers of the Constitution recognized the need for a uniform federal law for copyright and patents which was codified as Article I, § 8, cl. 8. It provides that "Congress shall have power . . . to promote the progress of science and useful Arts, by securing for limited Times, to Authors and Inventors, the exclusive Right to their respective Writings and Discoveries."

c. The Copyright Act of 1790

The Copyright Act of 1790 was passed pursuant to the new constitutional authority, and its provisions, and modeled on the Statute of Anne. It secured to authors and their assigns the rights to exploit maps, charts and books for two 14-year terms, an original term and a renewal term.

2. The 1909 Act

a. General Provisions of the 1909 Act

Under the 1909 Act, copyrightable subject matter was expanded to include "all the writings of an author." *See* 17 U.S.C. § 4 (1909 Act). The 1909 Act included a system consisting of a first term of 28 years from publication, plus a second 28-year renewal term, allowing copyright protection for a possible total of 56 years. *See* 17 U.S.C. § 24 (1909 Act).

Under the 1909 Act, federal copyright protection began the moment of publication (assuming affixation of a proper copyright notice), *see* 17 U.S.C. § 10 (1909 Act), not from the time the title of the work was filed for registration. Unpublished works were not covered by the 1909 Act, resulting in a dual system of state common law copyright for unpublished works and federal protection for published works.

b. The Berne Convention

The Berne Convention is the decisive treaty governing international copyright relations.

What it did: The Berne Convention made notice permissive instead of mandatory for copyright protection; even though registration was still a prerequisite for infringement suit for U.S. works but not foreign works. If you are registered, then that is *prima facie* evidence - **no** summary judgment allowed.

If you are not registered you automatically lose the right to collect attorney fees and statutory damages. Two of the more prominent impediments were:

i. The 1909 Act's insistence on compliance with certain formalities as a prerequisite for copyright protection or work will fall into the public domain, *see* 17 U.S.C. § 10 (1909 Act); and
ii. The 1909 Act's shorter term of copyright (minimum requirement of the life of the author plus 50 years).

United States adherence to the Berne Convention means that failing to place a copyright notice on the work is not automatically fatal to copyright protection.

c. Legislative Attempts to Revise the 1909 Act

From 1909 until the passage of the 1976 Act, changing technologies forced Congress to amend the 1909 Act:

i. Motion pictures were added as a subject matter category.
ii. Performance right for profit was provided for non-dramatic literary works (1952).United States ratified the Universal Copyright Convention (U.C.C.) which provides nondiscriminatory protection to nationals of all member nations for works published within their borders (1954).
iii. No formalities are required for unpublished works.
iv. Published works must bear a prescribed copyright.

3. The Copyright Act of 1976

a. Important Changes Made by the 1976 Act

i. ***Subject Matter*:** The 1976 Act established broad categories of subject matter. *See* 17 U.S.C. § 102(a) (amended in 1990 to include architectural works as an eighth category).

ii. ***The "exclusive rights"*** *and their limitations*: § 106 of the 1976 Act enumerates five exclusive rights of copyright ownership. A new provision, § 106A, was added in 1990 to delineate rights in works of visual art. The sections immediately following § 106A impose various limitations on the exclusive rights. *See* 17 U.S.C. §§ 107-20.

iii. ***Ownership***: Ownership of copyright is divisible under the 1976 Act, thus permitting the copyright owner to license or assign parts of the copyright "bundle of rights" to third parties, who can then exploit those rights themselves and bring suits for their infringement against others. *See* 17 U.S.C. § 201(d).

iv. ***General preemption of common law copyright***: Every original work of authorship fixed in a tangible medium of expression is federally protected from the moment of creation. *See* 17 U.S.C. § 301.

v. ***Duration***: For works created after it took effect, a basic single term of the life of the author plus 70 years. *See* 17 U.S.C. § 302(a). An alternate term of 95 years from publication or 120 years from creation, whichever is less, is provided for anonymous and pseudonymous works, and works made for hire. *See* 17 U.S.C. § 302(c).

vi. ***Termination rights***: Inalienable option to terminate transfers of interest after specified periods of time. *See* 17 U.S.C. §§ 203, 304(c).

vii. ***Formalities***: Initially, under the 1976 Act, notice was required for all published works, and it was possible to forfeit copyright by failure to affix notice. As of March 1, 1989, the use of copyright notice ceased to be mandatory. *See* 17 U.S.C. §§ 401(a) and 405. Registration of copyright and recordation of transfers of copyright were also a condition to bringing suits for infringement of these works until amendments, which took effect in 1989, eliminated the latter requirement and modified the former. *See* 17 U.S.C. § 411. These formalities have been modified by the Berne Convention Implementation Act of 1988. *See* 17 U.S.C. §§ 205, 411.

viii. ***Fair use*:** § 107 codifies the broadest exception to the § 106 exclusive rights: the judicially developed

ix. ***Compulsory licenses*:** The 1976 Act increased the number of compulsory licenses, which allow access to copyrighted works upon payment of the statutory fees and compliance with formalities. (Cable television (§ 111), mechanical recording (§ 115), jukebox (§ 116), public broadcasting (§ 118), and satellite home viewing (§ 119).)

x. ***Entry into Berne*:** It was not until the Berne Act amendments of 1988 that the impediments (formalities of notice and registration) to U.S. adherence were overcome. The amendments are as follows:

- The notice requirement was invalidated. *See* 17 U.S.C. § 401
- For works published after March 1, 1989, notice is permissive and a copyright owner can no longer forfeit copyright by omitting notice of publicly distributed copies of the work. *See* 17 U.S.C. § 405.
- One no longer needs registration to bring an infringement suit against works originating from a Berne country.
- Recordation in the Copyright Office is no longer a prerequisite to bring an infringement suit. *See* 17 U.S.C. § 205(d).

b. Subsequent Developments under the 1976 Act

In 1980, § 117 was completely amended providing protection for and establishing the scope of rights in computer programs. Since 1978, the enactment of the Semiconductor Chip Protection Act of 1984 is a major development in copyright.

c. The Continuing Importance of the 1909 Act

Neither the 1976 Act nor any subsequent copyright legislation is retroactive. Thus, copyrighted works which entered the public domain under the 1909 Act are not revived by these Acts.

D. Justifications for Copyright Law

1. In General

There are two approaches to copyright, one based on the natural rights of the author and the other on utilitarian principles (the economic rationale of copyright) which are the foundations of a system of copyright, are sometimes at cross purposes.

Arguments for establishing property rights are justified on two fundamental grounds:

a. A person's moral right to reap the fruits of his or her own labor (an idea based on natural law philosophy, including the ideology of authorship); and
b. The utilitarian rationale that views copyright law as an incentive system designed to produce an optimum quantity of works of authorship and thereby enhance the public welfare.

2. The Natural Law Justification

The natural law justification for recognizing property rights in works of authorship is based on the rights of authors to reap the fruits of their creations, to obtain rewards for their contributions to society, and to protect the integrity of their creations as extensions of their personalities.

John Locke's Theory: Copyright law, which confers an exclusive property right in an author's work, vindicates the natural right of individuals to control their works and be justly compensated for their contributions to society.

Criticism of the natural law justification:

i. How much control should the author have? How long should that control last? Who should benefit from the copyrighted work?
ii. The goal of fair compensation is at best a vague concept. No one can show what the "fair" price for any commodity, service, or work of authorship is.

3. The Incentive Rationale for Copyright Law

a. Generally

Rather than encouraging production of works by government subsidy, awards, or prizes, the author is given, through the limited monopoly of copyright law, a private property right in her creation, whose worth ultimately will be determined by the market. The underlying policy of this constitutional scheme is to promote the public welfare through private market incentives.

b. An Economic Argument for Rights in Intellectual Property

Intellectual property can be a great value, as well as costly to produce; without a legal regime protecting such products, the public welfare would suffer.

Free market economics disfavor the creation of monopolies unless there is an economic justification.

If an author cannot exclude others from her work, the result will be either non-production or non-disclosure. Viewed in this way, copyright law represents an economic trade-off between optimal creation of works of authorship and their optimal use.

* On one hand, copyright provides the incentive to create new products and a shelter to develop and protect them.
* On the other hand, a copyright owner's monopoly right is limited in time and scope by such doctrines as originality, the idea/expression dichotomy, and fair use.

In the absence of copyright protection, self-help through market head start is the traditional means by which an author or inventor can obtain a return on investment. But a head start advantage is only as good as the length of time it takes another to copy your product.

c. Copyright and "Interest Analysis"

Functionally, publishers, movie studios, record companies, and other entities which are not "authors" can best be understood as "distributors" or "disseminators" firms (or occasionally individuals) in the business of bridging the gap between individual creative workers and the ultimate consumers of their work.

4. The Future of Copyright

What seemed to be a farsighted, intelligently drafted statute is already obsolete in some ways. The reason is the time lag between technological and legal change. Perceived threats posed by the new technology should not overshadow the fact that a copyright is a monopoly, whose basic term lasts the life of the author plus 50 years.

E. Related Bodies of Federal Law

- Copyright law protects "original works of authorship."
- Patent law provides a limited monopoly for new and inventive products, processes and designs.
- Trademark law prohibits product imitators from passing off their goods or services as the products of others.

All three areas of intellectual property law recognize property rights in intangible products:

- Copyright (expression)
- Patent (technology)
- Trademark (symbolic information).

These bodies of law, because they concern federally recognized rights, generally are governed by federal statutes and administered by federal agencies (except in the case of trademarks, as to which state law also may apply.

F. State Intellectual Property Law

In addition to federal law, a diverse system of state intellectual property law also plays a significant role in protecting intangible property.

1. Trade Secret

Trade secret law protects much of the same technological information as patent law; however, trade secret subject matter is even broader, extending to customer lists, marketing plans, and other information not included within patentable subject matter. In addition, a trade secret does not have to meet the rigorous standards of inventiveness required by patent law. A valid trade secret exists only if it is substantially "secret" within the trade secret's owner's industry; absolute secrecy is not required. Unlike a patent, a trade secret can potentially last forever.

2. Unfair Competition

Defined two ways:

a. A general area of law covering various commercial torts.
b. An action brought when one company passes off its goods or service as someone else's (narrower preferred sense).

3. Common Law Copyright

Common law copyright is almost entirely preempted by federal law. Although federal preemption casts a long shadow, state common law copyright might play a role when a work is not fixed in a tangible medium of expression. In practice, however, few courts have even considered copyright protection for oral works, but they have recognized its possibility.

4. The Right of Publicity

The right of publicity prohibits appropriation for commercial benefit of a celebrities' name, likeness, picture, or voice, for the celebrity has been deprived of a property right in the fruit of his labors (i.e., the ability to exploit commercially her name, likeness, picture, or voice). The right of publicity prohibits appropriation for commercial benefit of a person's name, likeness, picture or voice. The right of privacy relates to dignity harm, whereas the right to publicity involves commercial harm.

The right of publicity is a more absolute right than either trademark or general unfair competition rights, and is based on a theory of unjust enrichment.

5. Misappropriation

Misappropriation doctrine is the broadest, and also the vaguest, theory protecting intangible property under state law. Causes for action for misappropriation have been successful where the traditional forms of intellectual property protection do not apply, but where a need for protection exists. Some courts have expressed hostility toward the misappropriation doctrine, claiming that it conflicts with the policy underlying federal patent and copyright law and is therefore preempted under the Supremacy Clause of the Constitution.

Chapter

3

SUBJECT MATTER OF COPYRIGHT LAW

Originality and fixation are two fundamental prerequisites for copyright protection under § 102(a). Section 102(b), on the other hand, denies protection to works otherwise satisfying the Act's requirements if the copyright is claimed for any "*idea, procedure, process, system, method of operation, concept, principle, or discovery. . . .*"

A. Fixation

A work is incapable of protection under federal law unless it is "fixed" in a "tangible meaning of expression." Only works which qualify as writings may claim federal copyright protection. The Supreme Court has construed the "writings" requirement to mean any physical rendering of the fruits of intellectual activity. A copyright comes into existence when both a work of authorship and a material object merge through the act of fixation.

A work would be considered "fixed in a tangible medium of expression" if there has been an authorized embodiment in a copy or phonorecord and if that embodiment "is sufficiently permanent or stable" to permit the work "to be perceived, reproduced, or otherwise communicated for a period of more than transitory duration."

As a basic condition of copyright protection, the work must be fixed in a "tangible medium of expression," and this medium may be one "now known or later developed," and that the fixation is sufficient if the work "can be perceived, reproduced, or otherwise communicated, either directly or with the aid of a machine or device."

The concept of fixation is important not only because it determines whether the provisions of the statute apply to a work, but it also represents the dividing line between common law and statutory protection.

An unfixed work of authorship would continue to be subject to protection under State common law or statute, but would not be eligible for Federal statutory protection under § 102.

1. Perception by Machine or Device

The fixation requirement is satisfied if the work as fixed can be perceived either directly or with the aid of a machine or device existing now or developed at a later time.

White-Smith Music Publishing Co. v. Apollo Co.,
209 U.S. 1, 28 S. Ct. 319, 52 L. Ed 655 (1908). The Supreme Court held that a piano roll was not a copy of the musical composition embodied on it and therefore did not qualify for copyright because there must be a printed record in intelligible notation, readable to the eye. (Doctrine applied to both phonorecords and magnetic tape, neither of which embody intelligible, eye-readable written notation.) Thus, what is readable is copyrightable while what is audible is not. Language of statute does not cover perforated rolls of music. Perhaps the drafters never thought about this technology.

Today, the White-Smith doctrine is inapplicable and its holding ***overruled*** under the Copyright Act. The Act allows for the copyrighting of sound recordings, computer programs, motion pictures, and other works embodied on objects which cannot be read without a machine or device.

The majority in *White-Smith* was telling Congress that they made a mistake under strict language of the statute and that Congress needed to expand its definition.

In reaction, Congress added the following language:

- § 102(a): "now known or later developed;" also "either directly or with the aid of a machine or device."
- § 101: See definition of "copies" and "fixed" (still room for interpretation).

2. The Videogame Cases

The fixation requirement was tested in certain specific cases involving actions for infringement of copyrighted video games, where the game's visual images and sounds are produced by computer programs and stored in various memory devices. When the game is not being played, the images are repetitive. During play, however, they are subject to variation by human intervention. The defendants in several cases have claimed that they were free to copy the plaintiff's games because they were not fixed in a tangible medium of expression but were rather transitory projections on a cathode ray tube.

Midway Manufacturing Co. v. Arctic Int'l., Inc., 704 F.2d 1009 (7th Cir. 1982). The court rejected the claim that the player's participation prevents the fixing of the audiovisual patterns, concluding that there is always a repetitive sequence of a substantial portion of the sights and sounds of the game. Many aspects of the display remain constant from game to game regardless of how the player operates the controls.

Holding: The fixation requirement does not require that the work be written down or recorded exactly as it is perceived by the eye - all that is necessary is that the work is capable of being perceived with the aid of a machine or device.

B. Originality

There are two aspects of originality developed by the courts and embodied in § 102(a):

i. Independent creation by the author; and
ii. A modest amount of creativity.

Copyright protects an author's expression of his idea, but not the idea itself.

"Original, as the term is used in copyright, means only that the work was independently created by the author (opposed to copied from other works), and that it possesses at least some minimal degree *(de minimis)* of creativity *(See Feist Publications, Inc. v. Rural Telephone Service Co., Inc.). Feist* focuses on the law of authorship; however, the court's definition of "originality" applies equally to claims of copyright protection for works of all descriptions. Originality requires independent creation plus a modicum of creativity such that reproductions are copyrightable.

Under U.S. copyright law, all that is required for protection is independent creation - not significant uniqueness, ingenuity or novelty.

Alfred Bell & Co. v. Catalda Fine Arts, Inc., 191 F.2d 99 (2d Cir. 1951) (Mezzotint engravings of old masters.) In general, an artistic reproduction which merely makes an exact copy of a prior work would lack sufficient originality. If the copy, however, entails the independent creative judgment of the artist in its production, those aspects will render the work original. A modest grade of originality is all that is required for copyrightability.

Atari Games Corp. v. Oman, 888 F.2d 878 (D.C. Cir. 1989) (Breakout - bricks (various colors), ball, and paddle). In determining whether a work meets the quantum of originality, the work must be evaluated as a whole, not dissected as to its individual components. The Copyright Office improperly denied registration to a videogame screen because it focused on the independent components of the screens made up of simple geometric shapes.

Holding: The Office should have evaluated the work as a whole because even simple geometric shapes, when selected and combined in a distinctive manner, may meet the modest standard for creative authorship. Originality can be bringing together of mundane objects (series of audio-visual protected). One needs to look at the totality of the work.

Burrow-Giles Lithographic Co. v. Sarony, 111 U.S. 53, 4 S. Ct. 279, 28 L. Ed. 349 (1884) (Photograph of Oscar Wilde). Oscar Wilde was subject of photograph. The photographer dressed and positioned his pose. One gets protection for mechanical reproductions because a photograph is a natural moment captured. Thus, separate from the mechanical part there is a separate copyright for the express vision, graphic, and artistic elements.

Bleistein v. Donaldson Lithographing Co., 188 U.S. 239, 23 S. Ct. 298, 47 L.Ed. 460 (1903) (Copyrightability of Wallace's circus ad). Although the requirement of creative authorship entails a certain *de minimis* amount of originality, it embodies no conception of artistic merit or beauty. Thus, the court should not sit and judge, "what is art?"

Since *Bleistein*, both courts and the Copyright Office have avoided aesthetic decisions in deciding questions of originality. This case involved the question of whether a copyright could be claimed for a work intended for advertising purposes. The earlier view was that copyright protection was denied for advertisements. However, some non-artistic works, such as maps or ledgers, were protected. Today, however, so long as the work contains the required original elements, courts will not look to the intended purpose of the work or the audience to whom it is directed.

Judges evaluate work compared to a countless number of possible works (in essence, they judge art). Thus, originality requires some evaluation by the court. Just because something is an advertisement and the public cannot see the value of it now, courts are afraid to deny protection because it might be valuable later.

1. The Idea/Expression Dichotomy

Section 102(b) of the Copyright Act codifies the principle that copyright protects the expression of an idea but not the idea itself. Thus, copyright protection will be denied to any idea, procedure, process, system, method of operation, concept, principle, or discovery, regardless of the form in which it is described, explained, illustrated, or embodied in such work.

Once an author reveals his work to the public, he injects the idea into the public domain and must be content to maintain control only over the form in which the idea is expressed.

To create new works, future authors must have access to a well-endowed pubic domain – a repository where the fundamental building materials concepts, discoveries, and technological solutions reside and are freely available for those wishing to embellish them with their own original expression.

As in the case of originality, the idea-expression distinction is left undefined in the Copyright Act. Separating an idea from its expression is an ad hoc process, and how broadly a court defines what constitutes the idea as compared to the expression depends on the nature of the subject matter at issue.

- If the idea is defined too broadly, it will impede the production of future works.
- On the other hand, if the idea is defined too narrowly, future authors will not have sufficient economic incentive to create new work.

Baker v. Selden, 101 U.S. 99, 11 S. Ct. 99, 25 L. Ed. 841 (1880) Selden published Selden's Condensed Ledger of Bookkeeping Simplified with forms and explanations of use. Because functional works often closely integrate idea and expression, they tend to conflict with copyright law's protection of original expression. Interests of utility will frequently compel expression in functional works "to hew closely to the underlying and unprotectable idea, procedure, process, system or method of operation that it expresses."

Result: When encountering a functional work, the courts will limit protection to avoid conferring a de facto monopoly over the unprotectable, utilitarian aspects of the work. Distinguishing between idea and expression is a difficult but necessary task because of the policies that differentiate copyright from patent law.

The Supreme Court reversed a judgment for the plaintiff, reasoning that the system could not be used absent the methods and diagrams in the book. According to the Court, the ledger was actually a utilitarian object rather than an expressive work. Unless copyright was denied in this instance, a monopoly could in effect be granted over the underlying idea of the system. We should not allow a creator of inherently patentable subject matter, i.e., a system or process, to use copyright law to circumvent the patent system.

2. Merger Doctrine

There are some instances where the use of a system or process necessitates the identical copying of the author's expression of the system or process. In other words, if the underlying idea (or system, process, or method of operation) can effectively be expressed in only one way, the idea and expression are said to have "merged." When this occurs, the work cannot receive protection under copyright law. To allow copyright protection in such an instance would undermine the distinction between copyright and patent law.

Kern River Gas Transmission Co. v. Coastal Corp., 899 F.2d 1458 (5th Cir. 1990) (Map created and given out in public domain.) The plaintiff's depiction of its proposed natural gas pipeline route on government survey maps was not copyrightable. The maps may have been original, but, according to the court, they expressed the idea of the location of the pipeline in the only effective way possible. Thus, when idea and expression are inseparable they merge, precluding copyright protection. If copyright protection were granted, suppression of the expression as well as idea would occur. Under the Merger Doctrine, expressions of certain ideas are not copyrightable because there exists only a very limited number of ways of expressing each idea.

C. Works of Authorship

One should always make the distinction between the copyright on the work of authorship and the object in which the work is fixed.

The list of categories of works of authorship in § 102(a) of the 1976 Act is meant to be illustrative, rather than limitative. The categories are not only broad, but also overlapping. Of the eight categories listed, four are defined in § 101. Three of the undefined categories "musical works," "dramatic works," and "pantomimes and choreographic works" have fairly settled meanings.

The four items defined in § 101 are;

i. Literary works;
ii. Pictorial, graphic, and sculptural works;
iii. Motion pictures and audiovisual works; and
iv. Sound recordings.

In each of these cases, definitions are needed not only because the meaning of the term itself is unsettled but also because the distinction between "work" and "material object" requires clarification.

<u>The definition of "pictorial, graphic, and sculptural works" carries with it no implied criterion of artistic taste, aesthetic value, or intrinsic quality</u>.

In the Supreme Court's decision *Mazer v. Stein*, (*infra*) works of "applied art" encompass all original pictorial, graphic, and sculptural works that are intended to be or have been embodied in useful articles, regardless of factors such as mass production, commercial exploitation, and the potential availability of design patent protection.

<u>The declaration that "pictorial, graphic, and sculptural works" include "works of artistic craftsmanship insofar as their form but not their mechanical or utilitarian aspects are concerned" is classic language</u>.

<u>A "useful article" is defined as "an article having an intrinsic utilitarian function that is not merely to portray the appearance of the article or to convey information</u>."

The test of separability and independence from "the utilitarian aspects of the article" does not depend upon the nature of the design that is, even if the appearance of an article is determined by aesthetic (as opposed to functional) consideration, only elements, if any which can be identified separately from the useful article as such are copyrightable.

Copyrightable "sound recordings" are original works of authorship comprising and aggregate of musical, spoken, or other sounds that have been fixed in tangible form. The copyrightable work comprises the aggregation of sounds and not the tangible medium of fixation.

Deciding whether a writing will be considered a work of authorship is a two-step process:

i. One must determine whether the legislative history has expressly excluded it. Examples of express exclusion are industrial design and typeface design, which Congress has explicitly indicated are not to be considered works of authorship.
ii. Even absent express exclusion, one must determine whether the writing has been historically excluded. This determination requires a return to the case law under the 1909 Act. Examples of writings

which have been historically excluded and which have not been expressly included by the Copyright Act or the legislative history are literary characters and titles.

Ultimately, a court would decide whether a work fits into one category or another. However, the Copyright Office has an influential role in determining into which category a work falls.

Explanations of Levels:

i. House/Senate statement made on floor following enactment; President statement during signing (has spin on it, not very reliable).
ii. Failure of action = (legislature approve of action) or (that they didn't get act together to meet).
iii. Public statements to press; not there to serve best interest of entire country; *Special interest written to persuade. (All copyright legislation written by non-legislative drafters)*
iv. Congress operates as a rubber stamp; they will not modify or amend.
v. For © legislation, we have no legislative drafters.
vi. Debate about meeting or purpose, not in writing, no connection to writing of Act.
vii. Will know what proposal doesn't mean, rejection usually.
viii. Outside interest brought legislation and why.
ix. Especially Joint Reports.

D. The Categories of Original Works

Notice also that the § 102(a) list, as indicated by the definition of "including" in § 101, is "illustrative and not limitative," so as to allow the courts as much flexibility as possible to adapt the law to new technologies and media. Furthermore, each enumerated category is liberal defined.

Congress in 1976 purposely chose the phrase "original works of authorship" to describe what it wanted to protect, after the courts had found it necessary to limit judicially the seemingly more expansive language of the 1909 Act, "all the writings of an author."

It is consistent in separating works of authorship from the material objects, (i.e., the copies or phonorecords) in which they might be embodied. But regardless of the media in which they are embodied, the novel remains a literary work and the ballad remains a musical work.

1. Literary Works

Literary works are defined by the 1976 Act as "works, other than audiovisual works, expressed in words, numbers, or other verbal or numerical symbols or indicia, regardless of the nature of the material objects, such as books, periodicals, manuscripts, phonorecords, film, tapes, disks, or cards, in which they are embodied."

This category encompasses all works written in words or symbols of any kind, regardless of the material objects in which they are embodied. The word "literary," in this context, implies no idea of literary merit. A literary work can be a computer program, a catalog, a data base, or a poem, written on a piece of paper or recorded on cassette. Copyright in computer programs is one form of literary work which has caused much controversy in recent years.

***Miller v. Universal City Studios, Inc.*,** 650 F.2d 1365 (5th Cir. 1981). Plaintiff spent 2,500 hours in the preparation of a book involving a notorious Georgia kidnapping in which the victim was imprisoned in an underground coffin. Despite some pronouncements in the case law that historical research in itself can be the basis of copyright, the recent trend in the case law, even before *Feist*, was to refuse copyright protection based on the industrious effort of the researcher.

Here, the kidnapping victim and the reporter collaborated on the book. Universal Studios, after unsuccessful attempts to secure movie rights, nevertheless made a movie based entirely on the book.

The District Court declared itself in favor of the copyrightability of research. Its justification was based on a rationale similar to the telephone directory compilation cases: to reward the effort and ingenuity involved in giving expression to facts and to the effort required to unearth the facts.

The Court of Appeals for the Fifth Circuit reversed the District Court decision because it was unable to identify any appropriation of original expression. The court distinguished the telephone directory cases as constituting a category in of themselves rather than extending their questionable logic to another setting.

According to the Fifth Circuit, copyright should be based only on the resulting writing and the original elements of authorship expressed in the work. The court could find "no rational basis for distinguishing between facts and the research involved in obtaining facts."

If the historian holds out the events as factual matter, they enter into the public domain, despite the strangeness or the improbability of their occurrence.

If one is allowed to copyright research, then everyone is going to have to start from ground zero (not efficient). Protection is not granted because the courts would rather only one person does the research and have other expand and build on existing work.

Apple Computer, Inc. v. Franklin Computer Corp., 714 F.2d 1240 (3d Cir. 1983) (Defendant Franklin copied Apple's O/S program to manufacture an Apple compatible computer.)

The court was confronted with three basic issues about the scope of protection for computer programs:

i. Whether copyright can exist in a computer program expressed in object code;
ii. Whether copyright can exist in a computer program embedded in a ROM; and
iii. Whether copyright can exist in an O/S program.

The court answered all three issues affirmatively, both reaffirming and expanding the scope of protection for computer programs:

i. The court had little trouble in concluding that a work written in object code unintelligible to humans would qualify as a literary work. Section 102(a) states that copyright protection extends to works fixed in any tangible means of expression "from which they can be perceived . . . with the aid of a machine or device," and does not require that they be intelligible to humans.
ii. The court had no difficulty repeating that the statutory requirement of fixation was satisfied because the ROM computer chip constituted the material object in which the copyrighted work, i.e., the program, was embedded.
iii. Franklin claimed that the O/S was per se uncopyrightable under *Baker v. Selden* (merger doctrine). This argument states the doctrine of "merger" in which a work is uncopyrightable if its idea and expression merge, or are so closely related that one cannot be used without the other. Here, the Third Circuit found that the trial court had made insufficient findings as to whether idea and expression had merged, and remanded the case on this issue.

The court, however, unequivocally upheld the copyrightability of computer programs, whether application or O/Ss. Franklin has established the copyrightability of O/S programs and the illegality of copying the programmer's expression manifested in the program.

The court did not define the difference between idea and expression as applied to computer programs. In the computer program context, one can equate idea with the accomplishment of a given task or function. Thus, if there are other ways to achieve the same result, there are alternative means of expression, and the doctrine of merger does not apply. Copyright should not be used to monopolize a result: the very essence of § 102(b).

The *Franklin* court, however, fell short of establishing 100% compatibility as the uncopyrightable "idea." In addition, it did not indicate either what degree of compatibility or how this compatibility could be achieved.

2. Computer Software Protection

In the United States, original works become protected under copyright laws when it is "fixed in a tangible medium." In most circumstances an original piece of software becomes "fixed" when the data is stored on a hard or floppy disk. However, the problem of registering is another issue that is later discussed.

The group of cases of which *Apple v. Franklin* is the most important sometimes is referred to as the "first generation" of software protection decision. Once that choice had been made in favor of protection, there arose a whole set of additional dilemmas, often referred to as "second generation" software protection issues: the fact that a work is protected by copyright does not mean that every element of that work is protected, not that every protected element is protected completely.

There are many ways to infringe the copyright in a conventional "literary work" without copying it word-for-word in its entirety.

Traditionally, where conventional works are concerned, experts have been barred from contributing to this inquiry into so-called "substantial similarity." But the *Whelan* court *(see e.g. Whelan Assoc. Int'l. v. Jaslow Dental Laboratory, Inc., 797 F. 2d 1222 (3d Cir. 1983))* stated that it would join "the growing number of courts which do not apply the ordinary observer test in copyright cases involving exceptionally difficult materials, like computer programs.

Ultimately, the *Whelan* court's conclusion that "copyright protection of computer programs may extend beyond the programs' literal code to their structure, sequence, and organization" is based, in principal part, on an analogy drawn between programs and other, more traditional copyrightable works.

In ***Computer Associates International, Inc. v. Altai, Inc.***, 982 F.2d 963 (2d Cir. 1992) the court approves a three-step procedure (Abstraction-Filtration-Comparison) for evaluating claims of substantial similarity in such cases:

The plaintiff's work is first put through processes of "abstraction" and "filtration," designed to "sift out all elements of the allegedly infringed program which are 'ideas' or are dictated by efficiency or external factors, or taken from the public domain;"

i. Then, and only if "there [remains] a core of copyrighted material," this "golden nugget" is put through the final process;
ii. Finally, make a "Comparison" with the allegedly infringing work.

The implications of the *Computer Associates* approach for copyright protection of computer screen display formats remain uncertain. One line of cases treat the screen display which function as "user interfaces" as separate works, whether or not subject to separate copyright registration, and in particular as "compilations" of terms and symbols. In the decision which forms the other groups, screen display formats are treated as protected aspects of the computer program work. Either way, we must deal with the argument that the software developer's unprotected "idea" is merged with its expression where screen display formats are concerned, and the related argument that, in any event, a "user interface" display is a "useful article" and therefore not subject to copyright protection where its utilitarian (as distinct from merely decorative) features are concerned.

The order in which commands are listed in a menu has a very limited functional value and is protectable.

The "reverse engineering" issue: to what extent should software developers be permitted, as a matter of copyright doctrine, to manipulate their competitors' products so as to discover the basic, unprotectable programming ideas on which those products are based? Two important Court of Appeals decisions have indicated that a solution to the "reverse engineering" problem may lie in the doctrine of "fair use."

3. Musical Works

The legislative history to the 1976 Copyright Act states that the term "musical works" (treated in § 102(a) (2)) is left undefined because they have "fairly settled meaning."

Musical works include both the instrumental component of the work and any accompanying words. Taking either the lyrics or the music alone infringes a musical work. Where musical works are concerned, one of the most valuable exclusive rights of the copyright owner is the right to prepare and distribute what used to be called "musical reproductions" - a category which, over time, has included recordings in forms ranging from piano rolls to "digital audio tapes." The 1976 Act refers to these as "phonorecords" and recognizes the rights of the musical work copyright owner in § 106.

The Copyright Act was amended in 1971 to create a new category of protected works, "sound recordings," which arise out of the joint "authorship" of those who participate in the phonogram production process generally as employees of production companies which acquire the resultant copyrights by virtue of assignment or by operation of the "work for hire" doctrine.

4. Dramatic Works

The legislative history to the 1976 Copyright Act states that the term "dramatic works"(§ 102(a) (3)) is left undefined because they have "fairly settled meaning". Dramatic works category illustrates how various categories in the § 102(a) list may overlap one another. Music accompanying a dramatic work could be copyrighted separately rather than under the dramatic works category. The script for a dramatic work could be protected as a literary work.

A film dramatization of a screenplay is protected as a motion picture. Since the list of § 102(a) is illustrative and not limitative, it serves the minimal purpose of making it clear that plays, screenplays and other dramatizations of works are protectable.

5. Pantomimes and Choreographic Works

The legislative history to the 1976 Copyright Act states that the terms "pantomimes and choreographic works" (§ 102(a) (4)) are left undefined because they have "fairly settled meaning."

Pantomimes and Choreographic Works were added to the statutory catalogue of copyrightable works for the first time in the 1976 Act.

These works may be protected if the necessary prerequisites are met:

i. The work must be fixed in a tangible medium; and
ii. The work must contain original routines or original arrangements of preexisting routines.

6. Pictorial, Graphic, and Sculptural Works

"Pictorial, graphic, and sculptural works" is listed in §102(a)(5) and defined in § 101 by means of an illustrative list, which includes "two-dimensional and three-dimensional works of find, graphic, and applied art, photographs, prints and art reproductions, maps, globes, charts, technical drawings, diagrams, and models."

The term "pictorial, graphic, and sculptural works" encompasses works of fine as well as applied art and implied no criteria of aesthetic value or taste. The aspect of this category which has engendered the most controversy is the role of copyright in protecting artistic creations embodying utilitarian objects.

The key issue - originality rather than fixation.

To meet the standard of originality, the creator of a map must engage in at least a modicum of direct observation. Case law under the 1976 Act has tended to reject the "sweat of the brow" requirement for copyrightability in maps, treating the standard the same as for other factual compilations.

Mazer v. Stein, 347 U.S. 201, 74 S. Ct. 460, 98 L. Ed 630 (1954) (Copyrightability of statuettes of Balinese dancers used for bases of lamps) Copyright protection was limited to works of artistic craftsmanship insofar as their form, but not as to their mechanical or utilitarian aspects, as in jewelry, enamels, glassware, and tapestries.

The Supreme Court upheld the Copyright Office's regulation allowing copyright for works embodied in useful objects as to their form, but not as to their mechanical or utilitarian features. In addition, the Court also held that protection by design patent did not bar copyright protection.

After *Mazer v. Stein*, the use to which a work of art was put became irrelevant, but the question remained whether the whole range of industrial design in useful articles could qualify for copyright. In addition to these mass-produced objects, graphic designs for textiles were also included within copyrightable subject matter. While the statuettes were copyrightable, we do not allow copyrightability of an automobile, a toaster, or a modernistic lighting fixture because their artistic aspects are of an abstract nature often fused with the functional attributes of the object. Unless the shape of an automobile, airplane, lady's dress, food processor, television set, or any other industrial product contains some element that, physically or conceptually, can be identified as separable from the utilitarian aspects of the article, the design would not be copyrighted under the bill. A work is creative if aesthetic element is primary and utilitarian element is secondary.

Carol Barnhart Inc. v. Economy Cover Corp., 773 F.2d 411 (2d Cir. 1985) (Plaintiff produced human torsos used to display articles of clothing). The court found that the claimed artistic features, the life-size breast form and the width of the shoulders, were inextricably related to their utilitarian function, i.e., the display of clothes. The majority granted summary judgment for the defendant because the torsos utilitarian articles are not separate works of art. Therefore, they're not copyrightable.

The dissent was troubled with result and by its absence of a unifying test for conceptual separability. It proposed a test: for design features to be conceptually separate from the utilitarian aspects of the useful article that embodies the design, the article must stimulate in the mind of the beholder a concept that is entirely separable from the utilitarian functions.

7. Motion Pictures and Other Audiovisual Works

§ 102(a) (6) of the 1976 Act specifically includes among the subject matter of copyright the category described as "motion pictures and other audiovisual works." Notice, however, that in § 102(a) (6), motion pictures are treated as a subcategory of audiovisual works.

The key language in the statutory definition ("series of related images") raises several issues:

i. Is it necessary that the images be presented serially sequentially, in a fixed, invariable order? NO.
ii. What is meant by the requirement that the image be related?
iii. What is the proper approach to be adopted in determining whether a work satisfies the quantum-of-originality requirement? Clearly, a work can qualify as an audiovisual work even though it consists of images

which, individually, qualify for protection as pictorial, graphic or sculptural works.

Soundtracks of motion pictures are specifically included in the definition of "motion pictures," and excluded in the definition of "sound recordings." To be a "motion picture," as defined, requires three elements:

i. A series of images;
ii. The capability of showing the images in certain successive order; and
iii. An impression of motion when the images are thus shown.

It does not include:

i. Unauthorized fixation of live performances or telecasts;
ii. Live telecasts that are not fixed simultaneously with their transmission; or
iii. Filmstrips and slide sets which, although consisting of a series of images intended to be shown in succession, are not capable of conveying an impression of motion.

8. Sound Recordings

Sound recordings are defined in § 101 as "works that result from the fixation of a series of musical, spoken, or other sounds, but not including the sounds accompanying a motion picture or other audiovisual work, regardless of the nature of the material objects, such as discs, tapes, or other phonorecords, in which they are embodied." Sound recordings, however, archetypically involve musical works.

It is easy to confuse the sound recording with the musical work. The musical work is the "tune," plus any accompanying lyrics, as created by the composer. The sound recording is the "rendition" of the song as embodied in the phonorecord, including such components as the way the song is sung by the vocalist, played by the instrumentalists, arranged by the musical director, mixed by the recording engineer, and so on. The vocalist, instrumentalist, musical director and engineer, in other words, are the creators of the work, and their expression is the sound recording, not the song which is the composer's expression, and a separately copyrighted work. § 102(a) (7) protects the particular aggregate of sounds collected in the copyrighted work called the "sound recording," not the song being recorded (the "musical work") nor the physical object in which the sound recording and the musical work are embodied (the "phonorecord").

A sound recording must satisfy the ordinary prerequisites for a copyright: originality and fixation.

9. Architectural Works

The current U.S. Copyright Act expressly includes "diagram, models, and technical drawings, including architectural plans" as a species of protected "pictorial, graphic, and sculptural work."

The Committee concluded that the design of a work of architecture is "a writing" under the Constitution and fully deserves protection under the Copyright Act.

Under the "Architectural Works Copyright Protection Act of 1990," an "architectural work" is defined as "the design of a building as embodied in any tangible medium of expression, including a building, architectural plans, or drawings."

The work includes "the overall form as well as the arrangement and composition of spaces and elements in the design, but does not include individual standard features."

* "Design" includes the overall form as well as the arrangement and composition of spaces and elements in the design.
* "Arrangement and composition of spaces and elements" recognizes that:
    i. Creativity in architecture frequently takes the form of a selection, coordination, or arrangement of unprotectable elements into an original, protectable whole;
    ii. An architect may incorporate new, protectable design elements into otherwise standard, unprotectable building features; and
    iii. Interior architecture may be protected.

The definition makes clear that protection does not extend to individual standard features. Architectural work is deliberately not encompassed as pictorial, graphic, or sculptural works; therefore, the copyrightability of architectural works shall not be evaluated under the separability test applicable to pictorial, graphic, or sculptural works embodied in useful article.

A Two step analysis is envisioned:

i. An architectural work should be examined to determine whether there are original design elements present, including overall shape and interior architecture;

ii. Examine whether the design elements are functionally required.

Determinations of infringement of architectural works are to be made according to the same standard applicable to all other forms of protected subject matter.

A new § 120 of Title 17, U.S.C., limiting the exclusive rights in architectural works, provides that state and local landmark, historic preservation, zoning, or building codes relating to architectural works protected under § 102(a)(8) are not preempted by the Copyright Act.

The bill is prospective, protecting:

i. "Architectural works created on or after the date of enactment"; These works will be governed by § 302 of title 17, United States Code: that is, works created by individuals will have a copyright measured by the life of the author plus 70 years; works created under a work-made-for-hire arrangement anonymously, or under a pseudonym will have a copyright measured from 120 years from creation or 95 years from publication, whichever occurs first. (see discussion infra regarding Copyright Term Extension Act)

ii. "Architectural works that on the date of enactment are unconstructed and embodied in unpublished plans or drawings." In order to encourage authors of architectural works to construct their unpublished creations, a provisional cut-off date of December 31, 2002, has been provided: works that would ordinarily be eligible for a term of protection continuing past that date will lose protection on the date if the architectural work has not been constructed.

* Works created by individuals. These works will be governed in the first instance by the life plus 70 years *post mortem auctoris* term in § 302 of Title 17, U.S.C.
* Works created under work-made-for-hire. These works will be governed in the first instance by the term set forth in § 302 of Title 17, U.S.C.: 120 years from the date of creation; the 95 year term

for published works made-for-hire will not apply, since the provisions of § 6 of the proposed legislation are limited to architectural works that are unconstructed on the date of enactment.

E. What is not Protected

1. Ideas, systems, processes, discoveries, methods, procedures, or devices as distinguished from a description, explanation or illustration.
2. Works not in a fixed tangible form such as improvisational speeches or performances not in written form.
3. Works containing information that is entirely public domain or common property and containing absolutely no original authorship.

Names, phrases, titles, slogans, coloring, or listings of ingredients.

F. Derivative Works and Compilations Under § 103

The fixation and originality requirements apply to all works described by §§ 102(a) and 103(a).

Under § 102, "first generation" works are composed essentially (although not, of course, exclusively) of materials created by their authors.

Under § 103, derivative works and compilations are fundamentally are "second generation" works based on preexisting matter.

So long as the author of a derivative work or compilation incorporates preexisting matter and satisfies both the fixation and originality requirements, the work qualifies for copyright protection under § 103(a).

§ 103(a) states that no copyright can be claimed for any part of a derivative or collective work that has used the pre-existing material unlawfully.

According to § 103(b): The copyright in a compilation or derivative work extends only to the material contributed by the author of such work, as distinguished from the preexisting material employed in the work, and does not imply any exclusive right in the preexisting material. The copyright in such work is independent of, and does not affect or enlarge the scope, duration, ownership, or subsistence of, any copyright protection in the preexisting material.

A "compilations" results from a process of selecting, bringing together, organizing, and arranging previously existing material of all kinds, regardless of whether the individual items in the materials have been or ever could have been subject to copyright.

A "derivative work" requires a process of recasting, transforming, or adapting "one or more preexisting works;" the "preexisting work" must come within the general subject matter of copyright set forth in § 102, regardless of whether it is or was ever copyrighted.

1. Derivative Works.

A derivative work would be an infringement of the work on which it is based. To avoid infringement, the derivative work author of a translation, musical arrangement, or art reproduction must either base his work on one in the public domain or obtain permission from the author of the preexisting copyrighted work. Any recasting, reforming, abridgment, or editorial revision can be copyrighted as a derivative work so long as the standard of originality is met.

Tiffany Design, Inc. v. Reno-Tahoe Specialty, Inc., 55 F. Supp.2d 1113 (D. Nev. 1999) (Tiffany Design created and copyrighted a computer-enhanced image of the Las Vegas strip. Reno-Tahoe Specialty created its own digitally altered photographic image of the Las Vegas Strip. In its production, a Reno-Tahoe employee scanned at least part of a Tiffany Design computer-enhanced photograph of the Las Vegas strip to create a "precursor image." From the precursor image, six architectural works were cut, "manipulated" and placed within the Reno-Tahoe image. The employee claims the image was 85% complete before the Tiffany Design image was even seen.)

The district court found that the act of creating a "precursor image" violated the plaintiff's copyright and awarded partial summary judgment. Such a "precursor image" was a fixed work as soon as it was loaded into the computer's RAM. In deciding the issue of whether the Reno-Tahoe's work violated plaintiff's right to produce derivative works, the court denied summary judgment, finding that there still remained questions of fact as to whether Reno-Tahoe used a substantial amount of the recognizable elements of plaintiff work to constitute "substantial use" (i.e., an infringing derivative work).

Mirage Editions, Inc. v. Albuquerque A.R.T. Co., 856 F.2d 1341 (9th Cir. 1988) (cut out photographs of works of art from a commemorative book and transferred them to individual ceramic tiles for resale as a new product.)

OTHER CIRCUITS DO NOT FOLLOW THIS DECISION

The court incorrectly found this to be an infringement of the derivative right, chiefly because defendant's work supplanted the demand for the underlying work. From these facts, it is difficult to understand how the derivative right was infringed. He remounted copies without recasting, transforming, or adapting the copyrighted work in any significant way. This case illustrates a tendency of some courts to push the derivative right beyond reasonable limits to achieve an "equitable" result.

Gracen v. Bradford Exchange, 698 F.2d 300 (7th Cir. 1983) (7th Circuit refused © to an artist's rendering of a photograph of Judy Garland's Dorothy for lack of substantial variation.)

The originality standard, particularly for derivative works such as artistic reproductions, should be higher than for preexisting works, to prevent potential overlapping claims and harassment by claimants of derivative work copyrights. Without requiring a quantum of originality, it may be very difficult to determine whether a third part has copied from a public domain source or copied from the copyrighted work. Thus, too liberal construction of the originality standard may paradoxically inhibit rather than promote the creation of works based on those in the public domain. Therefore, additions to derivative works must be original.

2. Compilations

The compilation differs from the derivative work in one significant way. Unlike the derivative work author, the creator of a compilation does not recast, reform or change the underlying materials but rather compiles (or assembles) them in his own manner. Thus, a compilation can include the selection, coordination, and arrangement of facts, data, or materials that are in the public domain.

Copyright law does not protect facts *per se*, nor the talent that went into discovering them. Rather, copyright protects original works of authorship. One cannot author a fact because facts simply exist, even if they sometimes have to be discovered at great effort and expense. This principle is embodied in § 102(b) of the 1976 Act which denies copyright to any "discovery, regardless of the form in which it is described. . . ."

A compilation must be independently created and display a *de minimis* amount of creative, intellectual, or aesthetic labor.

Feist Publications, Inc. v. Rural Telephone Service Co., Inc., 499 U.S. 240, 111 S. Ct. 1282, 113 L. Ed. 358 (1991) (Feist used Rural's telephone listings without permission, copying about 1,300 names and numbers from Rural's white pages, including four fictitious listings that Rural had inserted to detect copying.)

The Supreme Court found that Rural's copyright in its telephone directory did not protect the names and numbers copied by Feist. It's a constitutional principle that a protectable work must be original with the author. "Original" in the copyright sense means that the work was independently created and possessed at least some minimal degree of creativity. In sum, protection of a factual work extends only to its original selection or arrangement. Thus, even though Feist took a substantial amount of factual information from Rural's directory, it did not take anything that amounted to original authorship. Accordingly, Feist's copying did not constitute copyright infringement.

Feist is unequivocal on one point: an alphabetical listing of telephone subscribers and their numbers cannot be protected as a compilation under copyright unless the selection, coordination, or arrangement of the facts is original.

The Supreme Court specifically discarded industrious effort ("sweat of the brow") as standard for copyrightability separate from the effort's embodiment in the creative arrangement, selection, and coordination of the subject matter in the work.

The yellow pages are a compilation of grouping of ads. Each ad is copyrightable by individual company/person. If there was no copyright for the Yellow Pages, there was no incentive to improve the groupings of information. The white pages do not get copyright protection because they are facts. They do not owe their origin to an act of authorship. In addition, originality is a constitutional requirement (can't amend statute to protect facts).

Originality has two parts: **SOURCE** and **CREATIVITY**. The "Sweat of the brow" theory no longer exists, we only look for originality.

West Publishing Co. v. Mead Data Central, Inc., 799 F.2d 1219 (8th Cir. 1986) (Copyrightability of West's arrangement of legal decisions (the star pagination system) in its National Reporter System; Lexis was not allowed to use star pagination because the arrangement of the cases is copyright and there is originality in the page numbers.)

In favor of denying protection - Page numbers are mechanical or accidental. **In favor of granting protection** - West chose cases and designated a unique order. Thus, West did determine or choose the page numbers and this would satisfy the originality requirement.

Chapter 4

EXCLUSIVE RIGHTS

A. Fundamental Rights

The five fundamental rights given to copyright owners are the exclusive rights of reproduction, adaptation, publication, performance, and display, which is stated generally in § 106.

These exclusive rights, which comprise the so-called "bundle of rights" are copyrightable, are cumulative and may overlap in some cases. Each of the five enumerated rights may be subdivided indefinitely and may be owned and enforced separately.

Everything in § 106 is made subject to §§ 107-20.

B. Compulsory Licenses

To use a copyrighted work, normally one must obtain from the copyright owner a license whose terms are determined through private bargaining. In four instances, the Copyright Act supersedes the normal market mechanism for negotiating a license and replaces it with a compulsory license. (Cable television license (§ 111); mechanical license (§ 115); public broadcasting license § 118 and satellite retransmission license (§ 119)).

Under a compulsory license, a third party can use a copyrighted work without the copyright owner's permission, so long as he complies with the statutory procedure and pays the established royalties.

C. Moral Rights

American copyright law is based on the principle that the public benefits by the incentive given to authors to produce copyrighted work. A number of other countries recognize a "moral right" that treats the author's work not as just an economic interest, but rather as an inalienable, natural right and an extension of the artist's personality. Moral rights are:

i. The right of integrity: the right to insist that the work not be mutilated or distorted;

ii. The right of attribution: the right to be acknowledged as the author of the work and to prevent others from naming anyone else as the creator; and
iii. The right of disclosure: the right to decide when and in what form the work will be presented to the public.

The concept of moral rights has made its way into American law in 3 ways:

i. An author's integrity and attribution rights have been protected piecemeal by various bodies of state and federal law;
ii. About a dozen states have passed statutes explicitly recognizing the moral rights of visual artist;
iii. With the Visual Artists Rights Act of 1990, federal law has followed the lead of state law in protecting the integrity and attribution rights of visual artists.

Boosey Hawkes Music Pubs. Ltd. v. Walt Disney Co., 53 U.S.P.Q.2d 2021 (S.D.N.Y. 2000) (Walt Disney Co. and Buena Vista Home Video ("Disney") distributed the Disney video "Fantasia," which includes in its soundtrack a substantial portion of Igor Stravinsky's "Rites of Spring." Boosey, Stravinsky's assignee, argued that such sales infringed Stravinsky's copyright and that the video was "morally offensive," claiming "moral rights damages.")

The court granted Disney's motion *in limine* to exclude all evidence relating to moral rights. Moral rights are inalienable and unassignable, and thus can only be asserted by the author/composer or his heirs. Therefore, since Boosey is the successor-in-interest to Stravinsky, it did not have standing to bring the claim for moral rights damages.

Gilliam v. American Broadcasting Co., 538 F.2d 14 (2d Cir. 1976) (Plaintiff's right to prevent distortion of his work was protected under both the copyright and unfair competition laws.

ABC obtained a license from the BBC to broadcast Monty Python programs in their entirety except for minor editing to insert commercials. ABC substantially abridged the programs, cutting twenty-four of ninety minutes from them. An additional problem: The BBC didn't have editorial control, so it could not then sell editorial control to ABC.)

The court held that the unauthorized editing of the underlying work constituted an infringement of the copyright by creating an unauthorized derivative work. Thus, a prospective user of a copyrighted work should negotiate, in the appropriate situation, a license to adapt, as well as the rights to reproduce and perform the work. Court should have said no right to make derivative work was passed on and that would have been the end of the case. This case has never been followed.

Wojnarowicz v. American Family Association,
745 F. Supp. 130 (S.D.N.Y. 1990). This case deals with New York law, not VARA. The New York Artists' Authorship Rights Act prevents unauthorized public display, publication, or reproduction of an altered, defaced or mutilate work where such display would reasonably damage the artist's reputation. The New York Art provides that "the artist shall retain at all times the right to claim authorship." While one violates the New York Act by displaying the defaced art work (focuses on the artist's reputational interest), one violates the California Act by defacing a work of art (emphasizes a broad personal interest in the integrity of cultural preservation). Both statutes are limited in their application to works of fine art. These state moral right acts present serious questions of federal preemption under § 301 of the Copyright Act and the Visual Artists Rights Act of 1990.

One has the right to criticize an author's work under the First Amendment, but to get out of problem would be to add language to say it's only a portion of work. Court awarded nominal damages of $1.

D. The Visual Artists Rights Act of 1990 (VARA) § 106A

The VARA protects both the reputations of certain visual artists and the works of art they create. It provides these artists with the rights of "attribution" and "integrity."

These rights are analogous to those protected by Article 6 of the Berne Convention, which are commonly known as "moral rights."
Only the author of the work of visual art can claim protection (whether or not artist is copyright owner).

Work made for hire not included.
- § 106A (a)(3)(A): Mutilation that is prejudicial to his or her honor or reputation that is intentional.
- § 106A (a)(3)(B): Intentional or grossly negligent destruction of work.
- § 504: Only give statutory damages for VARA
- § 501: Can get an injunction? (But the work is already destroyed what good would it do?).

The point of VARA is to act as window dressing to comply with Berne Convention. Moral rights are inevitable. Moral rights are being diluted in Europe instead of being built in USA.

Summary of Provisions of Visual Artists Rights Act of 1990

The major provisions of the Act are:

1. **Works protected**. The Act does not cover all possible visual art works, but instead is limited to works of visual art. Qualified works include paintings, drawings, prints, sculptures and still photographic images produced for exhibition purposes only, and existing in single copies or in limited editions of 200 or fewer copies, signed by the artist. Works not covered include reproductions of qualifying works and works destined for commercial purpose. Works made for hire are excluded specifically. (§ 101, "work of visual art").

2. **Rights of attribution and integrity**. The rights of attribution includes the artist's rights:
   a. to claim authorship of the work;
   b. to prevent the use of her name as the author of any work of visual art which she did not create; and
   c. to prevent the use of her name as the author of the work in the event of a distortion, mutilation or other modification of the work which would be prejudicial to her honor or reputation.

   (§106A(a), "recognized stature" has been defined in the case law as describing a work that is meritorious and acknowledged as such by art experts and other member of the artistic community, or by some cross-section of society.)

3. **Scope and exercise of rights**. The author of a work of visual art has the rights provided in § 106A, whether or not she owns the copyright in the work and whether or not the work qualifies for protection under the national origin provisions of § 104. (§ 106A (b)).

   Exceptions. There are three exceptions:
   i. A work is not destroyed, distorted, mutilated or otherwise objectionably modified, for purposes of the integrity right, if the modification is the result of the passage of time or the inherent nature of the materials;
   ii. The integrity right is not violated when a modification is the result of conservation measures or of public

presentation, including lighting or placement, unless the modification is caused by gross negligence; and

iii. The integrity and attribution rights do not apply to reproductions or other uses of protected works in forms not themselves protected by VARA. (§106A(c)).

Removal of works from buildings. The Act amends § 113 to establish conditions under which a work of art incorporated as a part of a building may be removed from the building. If the work cannot be removed without being mutilated or destroyed, the owner of the building can remove if the artist consented to the installation before June 1, 1991, or if thereafter she consented to the eventuality of mutilation or destruction in a signed instrument. If work can be removed without mutilation or destruction, the work automatically is subject to the artist's attribution and integrity rights unless the owner has tried and failed to notify the artist. If notice succeeds, the artist has 90 days to remove the work or pay for its removal. (§ 113(d)).

4. **Duration of rights.** With respect to works of visual art created on or after June 1, 1991, the effective date of the Act, the § 106A rights endure for the life of the artist. If the work of visual art was created before June 1, 1991 and the artist has not parted with title to the copy/copies of the work, the artist receives the life-plus-70-years term for both the § 106 rights and the § 106A rights. If the work was created before June 1, 1991 and the artist has sold the copy/copies to others, no §106A rights arise at all. § 106A (d)).

5. **Transfer and waiver.** The artist's attribution and integrity rights cannot be transferred.

6. **Infringement.** The Act subjects violators of the new attribution and integrity rights in works of visual art to the normal liabilities for infringement, but not to criminal penalties. (§§ 501, 506).

7. **Preemption.** The statute amends § 301 by preempting any legal or equitable rights at state law that are equivalent to those created by the Act's new provisions. (§ 301(f)).

Chapter

5

OWNERSHIP AND TRANSFERS

When thinking about ownership and transfers of rights, asks and answers the following questions: Who owns the copyright in the work, once created, and how is ownership transferred by persons, subsequent to the initial owner, who are interested in exploiting the copyright?

Two Basic Principles

i. Mere ownership of a copy or phonorecord does not give the owner a copyright.
ii. Minors may claim copyright protection, but state laws may regulate dealings with minors.

A. Initial Ownership

Initial ownership of copyright is easy to determine when an individual creates a work at his own instance and expense. However, many works are created as the result of an employment relationship ("work made for hire", in the language of the 1976 Act) or through the combined efforts of several persons ("joint works").

Initial Ownership

Two basic and well-established principles of copyright law are restated in § 201(a): that the source of the copyright ownership is the author or the work, and that, in the case of a "joint work," the co-authors of the work are likewise co-owners of the copyright.

Under § 101, a work is "joint" if the authors collaborated with each other, or if each of the authors prepared his or her contribution with the knowledge and intention that it would be merged with the contributions of other authors as "inseparable or interdependent parts of a unitary whole." The touchstone here is the intention, at the writing is done, that the parts be absorbed or combined into an integrated unit, although the parts themselves may be either "inseparable" or "interdependent."

Work made for hire

§ 201(b): In the case of works made for hire, the employer is considered the author or the work and is regarded as the initial owner of copyright unless there has been an agreement otherwise. Any agreement under which the employee is to own rights must be in writing and signed by the parties.

The basic problem is how to draw a statutory line between those works written on special order or commission that should be considered as "works made for hire" and those that should not.

Contributions to collective works

§ 201(c) deals with the troublesome problem of ownership of copyright in contributions to collective works, and the relationship between copyright ownership in a contribution and in the collective work in which it appears.

- Under § 101, a "collective work" is a species of "compilation" and, by its nature, must involve the selection, assembly, and arrangement of "a number of contributions."
- Unlike the contents of other types of "compilations," each of the contributions incorporated in a "collective work" must itself constitute a "separate and independent" work, therefore ruling out compilations of information or other non-copyrightable material and works published with editorial revisions or annotations.

The second sentence of § 201(c), in conjunction with the provisions of § 404 dealing with copyright notice, will preserve the author's copyright in a contribution even if the contribution does not bear a separate notice in the author's name, and without requiring any unqualified transfer of rights to the owner of the collective work.

1. Works Made for Hire

In order to be considered a work made for hire:

i. Employee within scope of employment or work ordered or commissioned for use as a collective work, as a translation, as part of a motion picture, as an atlas, as a compilation, or as a test.
ii. Full time employee;
iii. No agreement needs to be signed to get this;
iv. This can be altered in writing separate agreement.

Therefore, employee will negotiate for employer to assign back rights in a work which he creates.
Employer now is the author, not the employee.

Before *Community for Creative Non-violence v. Reid,* the issue which has divided the case law is whether the clause "employee within the scope of his or her employment" in subdivision (1) can encompass an independent contractor in some circumstances.

Two views emerged:

i. Broadly reading statute to include independent contractor; or
ii. Narrowly reading statute, limiting it to the master-servant relationship in agency law.

Neither "employee" nor "independent contractor" is defined by the 1976 Act.

Community for Creative Non-Violence v. Reid, 490 U.S. 730, 109 S. Ct. 2166, 104 L. Ed. 2d 811 (1989). The Supreme Court limited the definition of employee in subdivision (1) to the master-servant relationship as understood by the common law of agency. A charitable organization dedicated to eliminating homelessness claimed copyright ownership of a statute called "Third World America." CCNV had commissioned the sculptor, Reid, to create a sculpture dramatizing the plight of the homeless for a Christmas pageant in Washington, D.C. CCNV supplied the plans and sketches, ultimately executed by Reid. On that basis, CCNV claimed ownership of the copyright in the sculpture as an employer for hire. The Supreme Court ruled for Reid and found that the work could not be a work made for hire. Four bases for a work made for hire emerged in the case law:

i. A work made for hire comes into existence when the hiring party retains the right to control the work;
ii. A work made for hire comes into existence when the hiring party actually retains control in the creation of the work;
iii. The term "employee" applies only to those persons so defined under agency law; and

The term "employee" only refers to formal salaried employees. After *CCNV*, contractual arrangements creating a work made for hire are more difficult. Employers will adopt a rule of thumb: when in doubt, insist on an assignment of copyright from the prospective employee. Although an assignment of copyright provides a somewhat shorter duration of copyright ownership than a work made for hire, it may satisfy the needs of most employers. Grants of rights in works for hire, unlike most other types of grants (an assignment can be terminated between the thirty-fifth and fortieth years of the grant), are immune from termination by operation of law under the provisions of the current statute. §§ 203 and 304(c).

The Court looked at the statute as follows:

§ 201(b): It is possible for employer to give back some rights to employee.
§ 101(a)(1) "work made for hire": If Reid is an employee, then it is work made for hire.
§ 101(a)(2) "work made for hire": Not applicable as commission work for hire since not a signed agreement which you need.

CCNV paid salary, gave much direction, control, supervision and generated the idea, concept and analysis of the work. Thus, under an instance and expense test, *CCNV* argued that the court should consider the reason for creation and the financial backing for the creation. Also, it stated that because it paid Reid's taxes and benefits, he should be afforded full-time employer status.

Court stated that if you fail categories of commission work, you cannot then claim employee status. Court used commonly understood definition of employee. Thus, if statute uses a work defined in another statute and commonly understood, then that is definition if same basic context.

2. Joint Works

§ 101 defines a "joint work" as a work prepared by two or more authors with the intention that their contributions by merged into inseparable or interdependent parts of a unitary whole. What counts is that the authors intended their respective labors to be integrated into one work. The contributions of the individual authors do not have to be equal in quantity and quality.

Courts have unanimously denied joint authorship claims where an individual contribution is not itself copyrightable. Thus, a joint author must not only intend that his contribution be part of a joint work but must contribute more than *de minimis* authorship to the resulting work.

Why this insistence upon copyrightable contributions from all joint authors?

i. Seems more consistent with the spirit of copyright law.
ii. Prevents spurious claims by those who might otherwise try to share the fruits of the efforts of a sole author; and

iii. It may encourage those with non-copyrightable contributions to protect heir rights through contract, because if they neglect to do so, the copyright will remain with the one or more persons who created the copyrightable material.

Childress v. Taylor, 945 F.2d 500 (2d Cir. 1991). Defendant Taylor contacted Childress to write a play based on the life of the legendary comedian "Moms" Mabley. Although Taylor, a professional actress, wrote none of the script, she provided Childress with her research of "Moms" Mabley's life, and suggested that certain scenes be included in the play. The relationship between the two parties deteriorated before the rights were specified by contract. Taylor then had another author modify the script and shortly thereafter, using this new version, she performed the work publicly. In response to Childress's suit for copyright infringement, Taylor contended she was a joint author and shared with Childress the rights to the play.)

The Second Circuit rejected Taylor's claim of joint authorship because her efforts lacked the two basic elements needed to create a joint work. First, she only supplied ideas and research, and did not contribute the requisite degree of authorship. Second, even if Taylor's contribution was independently copyrightable, a joint work was not created due to a lack of intent.

One needs intent to be joint authors to avoid slippery slope (i.e., overhearing someone talking about a dog on the subway and writing a story about it). Circuits are split as to whether each contribution must be copyrightable. The Supreme Court has not answered question yet.

3. Collective Works

According to § 101, a "collective work" is a work, such as a periodical issue, anthology, or encyclopedia, in which a number of contributions, constituting separate and independent works in themselves, are assembled into a collective whole. <u>Unlike other types of compilations, however, a collective work consists of separate and independent works capable of copyright themselves</u>.

Under § 201(c), one should distinguish copyright in the contribution to the collective work from copyright in the collective work. The individual contributors to the collective work retain the copyrights in their works, absent a written agreement stating the contrary.

B. Transfer of Rights

Ownership of Copyright
Under § 201(d)(1), the ownership of a copyright, or of any part of it, may be transferred by any means of conveyance or by operation of law, and is to be treated as personal property upon the death of the owner.

The term "transfer of copyright ownership" is defined in § 101 to cover any "conveyance, alienation, or hypothecation, including assignment, mortgages, and exclusive licenses, but not including nonexclusive licenses . . ."

§ 201(d) (2) recognizes the principle of divisibility of copyright. The principle of divisibility applies whether or not the transfer is "limited in time or place of effect." The term "copyright owner," with respect to any one exclusive right, refers to the owner of that particular right and is entitled "to all of the protection and remedies accorded to the copyright owner."

§ 201(e) provides that when an individual author's ownership or a copyright have not previously been voluntarily transferred, no action by any governmental body or other official or organization purporting to seize, expropriate, transfer, or exercise rights of ownership with respect to the copyright, or any exclusive rights under a copyright, shall be given effect under this title. . . ."

Distinction between Ownership of Copyright and Material Object:
Copyright ownership and ownership of a material object in which the copyrighted work is embodied are entirely separate things.

1. Execution and Recordation of Transfers

Under § 204(a), a transfer of copyright ownership is valid only if there exists an instrument of conveyance, or alternatively a "note or memorandum or the transfer," which is in writing and signed by the copyright owner "or such owner's duly authorized agent."

§ 204(b) makes clear that a notarial or consular acknowledgment is not essential to the validity of any transfer, whether executed in the United States or abroad.

§ 205(c) makes clear that the recorded document will give constructive notice of its contents only if two conditions are met:

i. The document or attached material specifically identifies the work to which it pertains sot that a reasonable search under the title or registration number would reveal it, and
ii. Registration has been made for the work.

Under § 205(c), a nonexclusive license in writing and signed, whether recorded or not, would be valid against a later transfer, and would also prevail as against a prior unrecorded transfer if taken in good faith and without notice.

The Bundle of Rights

A copyright is independent of both its physical manifestation and the very thing that is copyrighted.

Under the 1909 Act, a copyright was perceived as an indivisible bundle of rights incapable of being broken up into smaller rights and exercised by multiple owners. Under the 1976 Act, however, there is an explicit statutory recognition of the principle of divisibility of copyrights.

Effects Associates v. Cohen, 908 F.2d 555 (9th Cir. 1990)
The writing requirement is a flexible one; it must be signed by the copyright owner. Although the "writing" may take many forms, it can be viewed as a simple, straightforward, and absolute requirement for a valid transfer of copyright. Accordingly, courts have not relaxed the writing requirement to allow for industry practices (movie industry), where written contracts are not the way business is done.

Cohen v. Paramount Pictures Corp., 845 F.2d 851 (9th Cir. 1988)
An example of the stricter approach to construing contractual language, one that would take a more literal reading of the contractual terms. The issue was whether a license conferring the right to exhibit a film "by means of television" included the right to distribute videocassettes of the film. When executed in 1969, the videocassette was not envisaged.

The court found for Cohen (who wished to prevent distribution of the videocassettes). The court scrutinized the contractual terms of the Cohen-Paramount license and found that it lacked broad enough language to encompass distribution by videocassette (other contracts included language like "the right to exhibit films by methods yet to be invented"). The purposes of the Act would be frustrated if the court construed this license with its limiting language as granting a right in a medium that had not been introduced to the domestic market at the time the parties entered into the agreement.

C. Recordation

§ 205 permits recordation in the Copyright Office of all documents of copyright ownership, whether assignment, exclusive licenses, or nonexclusive licenses. To enjoy fully the benefits of the 1976 Act, an owner of any such interest should accompany the recordation with a registration of the subject work, if it is not already registered.

What should be recorded?

§ 204(a) provides that a transfer of ownership may be accomplished by a signed "instrument of conveyance, or a note or memorandum of the transfer."

Why record?

For causes of action arising before March 1, 1989, recordation of a copyright interest is a prerequisite to bringing a suit for copyright infringement. For causes of action arising on or after March 1, 1989, recordation is no longer required as a prerequisite to bring a copyright infringement suit. However, it is highly recommended. Also, recordation establishes priority of ownership between conflicting transfers of copyright, as well as between conflicting transfers and nonexclusive licenses.

Priority between conflicting transfers

Under § 205(d), if A transfers a copyright to B, and then later to C (C takes without knowledge), the first to record owns the copyright. However, the transferee has a one-month grace period (two-month if outside country) to record from the date of execution of the agreement.

These priority rules apply only if the work is registered in addition to being recorded.

Priority between transfers and nonexclusive licenses

Under § 205(e), a nonexclusive license will prevail over an assignment or exclusive license if:

i. The nonexclusive license must be evidenced in a written instrument signed by the copyright owner and have been take before execution of the transfer; and

ii. If the nonexclusive license was taken after the transfer, it will prevail if it is evidence in writing and was taken in good faith before recordation of the transfer without notice thereof.

Chapter

6

DURATION OF COPYRIGHT

How long does ownership last?

1790 Act: 14 years + 14 years (if author survives to end).
1909 Act: 28 years + 28 years.
1976 Act: Life + 70 years.

Work made for hire = 120 years from creation or 95 years from publication whichever shorter (also anonymous & pseudonymous works).

Note, effective October 27, 1998, under the Sonny Bono Copyright Term Extension Act (CTEA), copyright terms were extended by 20 years. This term extension was challenged by Eric Eldred in *Eldred v. Ashcroft 123 S. Ct. 769 (2003)*. In *Eldred*, the petitioner argued that the CTEA violated the "limited times" prescription of the Copyright Clause and that it failed First Amendment inspection under the heightened judicial scrutiny appropriate for such regulations. The Supreme Court held that the CTEA did not violate the First Amendment or the Copyright and Patent Clause of the United States Constitution.

Also note, this legislation does not restore copyright protection to any works that are in the public domain.

A. Duration and Renewal

It is impossible to determine the minimum duration sufficient to encourage the optimum amount of investment for the enormous range and variety or works of authorship.

A copyright term consists of the life of the author and 70 years after his death. Under the 1909 Act, protection begins on the date of publication (registration for unpublished works) and continues for 28 years from that date; it may be renewed for a second 28 years, making a total of 56 years.

Arguments for changing this system to one based on the life of the author:

i. The present 56-year term is not long enough to insure an author and his dependents the fair economic benefits from his works.
ii. The tremendous growth in communications media has substantially lengthened the commercial life of a great many works.
iii. Although limitations on the term of copyright are obviously necessary, too short a term harms the author without giving any substantial benefit to the public.
iv. A system based on the life of the author would go a long way toward clearing up the confusion and uncertainty involved in the vague concept of "publication," and would provide a much simpler, clearer method for computing the term.
v. One of the worst features of the present copyright law is the provision for renewal of copyright. Under a life-plus-70 system the renewal device would be inappropriate and unnecessary.
vi. Under the preemption provisions of § 301 and the single Federal system they would establish, authors will be giving up perpetual, unlimited exclusive common law rights in their unpublished works, including works that have been widely disseminated by means other than publication.

A very large majority of the world's countries have adopted a copyright term of the life of the author and 50 years after the author's death. Since American authors are frequently protected longer in foreign countries than in the United States, the disparity in the duration of copyright has provoked considerable resentment and some proposals for retaliatory legislation. A change in the basis of our copyright term would place the United States in the forefront of the international copyright community. The advantages of a basic term of copyright enduring for the life of the author and for 70 years after the author's death outweigh any possible disadvantages.

B. Basic copyright term

Under § 302(a), a work "created" on or after the effective date of the revised statute would be protected by statutory copyright "from its creation" and, with exceptions, "endures for a term consisting of the life of the author and 70 years after the author's death."

1. Joint works
Since by definition a "joint work" has two or more authors, the term of copyright is measured from the death of the last survivors of a group of joint authors, no matter how many there are. Therefore, under the Sonny Bono Copyright Term Extension Act, the copyright will endure for 70 years after the last surviving joint author's death.

2. Anonymous works, pseudonymous works & works for hire

§ 302(c) provides a special term for anonymous works, pseudonymous works, and works made for hire: 95 years from publication or 120 years from creation, whichever expires first.

§ 302(c) provides that the 95- and 120-year terms for an anonymous or pseudonymous work can be converted to the ordinary life-plus-70 term if "the identity of one or more authors . . . is revealed" in special records maintained for this purpose in the Copyright Office.

The alternative terms established in § 302(c), 95 years from publication or 120 years from creation, whichever expires first, are necessary to set a time limit on protection of unpublished material.

3. Records and presumption as to author's death

§ 302(d) and (e) together furnish an answer to practical problems of how to discover the death dates of obscure or unknown authors.

4. Preexisting Works under Common Law Protection

Every "original work of authorship" fixed in tangible form that is in existence would be given statutory copyright protection as long as the work is not in the public domain in this country. § 303 provides protection for works created but not published or registered before January 1, 1978. § 303 provides that under no circumstances would copyright protection expire before December 31, 2002. The copyright term will not expire before December 31, 2047 (this provides for 45 years of more protection - - 25 years plus 20 years as a result of the Sonny Bono Copyright Term Extension Act). This also attempts to encourage to encourage publication by providing 25 years more protection (through 2027) if the work were published before the end of 2002.

5. Duration of Subsisting Copyrights
The statute's approach is to increase the present 56-year term to **95** years in the case of copyrights subsisting in both their first and their renewal terms.

The total term has been extended to **95** years (previously 75 years) from the date the copyright was secured as a result of the Sonny Bono Copyright Term Extension Act.

6. Copyrights in their first term

§ 304(a) reenacts and preserves the renewal provision, previously in § 24 of the statute, for all works presently in their first 28-year term. Renewal registration will be required during the 28th year of the copyright but the length of the renewal term will be increased from 28 to 47 years. Under the most recent Sonny Bono Copyright Term Extension Act, the total term is extended to 95 years from the date the copyright was secured

7. Copyrights in their renewal term

Renewal copyrights that are subsisting in their second term at any time during the period between December 31, 1976 and December 31, 1977, inclusive, would be extended under

§ 304(b) to run for a total of 95 years. This provision would add another 19 years to the duration of any renewed copyright whose second term started during the 28 years immediately preceding the effective date of the act

(January 1, 1978):
§ 304(b) also extends the duration of renewal copyrights whose second 28-year term is scheduled to expire during 1977.

§ 304(b) also covers the special situation of a subsisting first-term copyright that becomes eligible for renewal registration during the year before the act comes into effect.

If a renewal registration is not made before the effective date, the case is governed by the provisions of § 304(a).

If a renewal registration is made during the year before the new law takes effect, however, the copyright would be treated as if it already existed in its second term and would be extended to the full period of 95 years without the need for further renewal.

Provided the work did not fall into the public domain prior to October 27, 1998, the total copyright term is extended to 95 years from date copyright is secured.

8. Year End Expirations of Terms
Under § 305, the term of copyright protection for a work extends through December 31 of the year in which the term would otherwise

have expired. § 305 applies only to "terms of copyright provided by §§ 302- 04," which are sections dealing with duration of copyright.

Since all copyright terms under the bill expire on December 31, and since § 304(a) requires that renewal be made "within one year prior to the expiration of the original term of copyright," the period for renewal registration in all cases will run from December 31 through December 31 at the ending year.

Fred Fisher Music Co. v. Witmark & Sons, 318 U.S. 643, 63. S. Ct. 773, 87 L. Ed. 1055 (1943). The Supreme Court held that an assignment by an author of the renewal term, before that right had vested, was binding on the author. It soon became industry practice to require an assignment of the author's renewal rights in the initial contract.

In order to sell their works, authors were pressured into conveying their renewal rights in the second copyright term. The renewal rights may be assigned before their vesting, whereby the right to terminate cannot be assigned away in advance.

Epoch Producing Corp. v. Killiam Shows, Inc., 522 F.2d 737 (2d Cir. 1975). Demonstrates some of the difficulties involved in the retroactive application to determine who, is anyone, owns the renewal term in a copyrighted work. Plaintiff Epoch asserted ownership as an employer for hire of Griffith's Birth of a Nation, and argued that is had the right to claim the renewal term in the work. Epoch had renewed the work in 1942 and brought its suit for infringement against Killiam in 1969. The defendant argued that Epoch had no right to claim the renewal term because it did not qualify as an employer for hire. Thus, according the defendant, the work had entered the public domain because it had not been renewed by the proper party. The court agreed that no work for hire was created and that, unlike an original registration of copyright, a renewal registration carried no presumption of validity. In addition, Griffith nowhere explicitly stated his intent to convey the renewal right. Thus, the work had entered the public domain after the first 28-year term of copyright.

9. Copyright Term Extension Act (Sonny Bono Act)

Effective October 27, 1998, under the Copyright Term Extension Act (Sonny Bono Act), copyright terms were extended by 20 years. This applies to all existing works currently protected by copyright on the effective date. It does not, however, restore copyright protection to any work that is in the public domain.

Eldred v. Reno, 239 F.3d 372 (D.C. Cir. 2001) (Copyright Term Extension Act of 1998 (CTEA) retroactively lengthened the terms of copyrights. Plaintiffs asserted that CTEA violated the First Amendment as well as the "originality" and "limited times" constitutional requirements.)

The D.C. Circuit Court of Appeals determined that neither the First Amendment nor the Copyright Clause prohibits Congress from changing the duration of existing copyrights. While the court upheld familiar idea/expression doctrine, the Court did not find any First Amendment right to commercially use the works of others. Regarding the "originality" challenge, the Court determined that existing copyrights do not have to re-satisfy the originality requirement to be extended. The Court also rejected the "limited times" argument pointing out that the preamble "is not a substantive limit" on Congress' power. Therefore, the statutory extension of copyright duration was not unconstitutional and the decision dismissing plaintiffs' action was affirmed.

C. COPYRIGHT RENEWAL ACT OF 1992

***Permissive renewal*:** For works whose copyright was secured between 1964 and 1977, the Renewal Act confers renewal automatically when the first term ends. On the other hand, pre-1964 works are not affected by the 1992 legislation.

***Clarifying the vesting date*:** If a renewal application is filed during the 28th year by the person entitled to the renewal, the renewal term will vest, at the beginning of the 29th year, in that person, even if that person dies before the renewal term begins. If no application is made, the renewal term will vest in whoever is the appropriate renewal claimant on December 31st of the initial term's 28th year.

The incentive to register: Thanks to automatic renewal, the renewal term will no longer be lost for failure to comply with renewal formalities. If a timely renewal is filed, the author's first-term grants of renewal rights to exploit such derivative works are nullified if the author dies before the renewal term. If registration is made during the last year of the first term, the certificate of renewal registration shall constitute *prima facie* evidence as to the validity of the facts stated in the certificate. Remedies for copyright infringement are narrowed for authors who fail to file a timely renewal registration and disallows statutory and actual damages, attorney's fees, and seizure and forfeiture (§§ 504, 505, and 509) for all infringements that commence before registration.

Stewart v. Abend, 495 US 207, 110 S. Ct. 1750, 109 L. Ed. 2d 184 (1990). The Supreme Court held that the assignment of renewal rights by an author does not defeat the right of the author's statutory successor(s) to those rights if the author dies before the renewal right vests. In other words, when the grant of rights in the preexisting work lapses, the right to use parts of it in the derivative work ceases, and its continued use will infringe the preexisting work. This case involved the film right to a short story, first published in 1942. The author, Woolrich, assigned the film rights to the short story to a production company and agreed to renew the copyright and assign the rights to the second term. Stewart and Hitchcock acquired theses rights and released the film version, Rear Window, in 1954. Woolrich died in 1968 before he could renew his copyright. In the 1969, the executor of Woolrich's estate renewed the copyright and assigned the renewal term to Abend. On the re-release of the film in various media, Abend sued for copyright infringement, claiming that the right to use the film version terminated when Woolrich died before renewing the copyright.

The Supreme Court agreed with Abend, holding that the derivative work film could not be exploited without the permission of the owner of the underlying work. One may exploit only such copyrighted material as one owns or is authorized to use. Under this principle, a derivative work author cannot escape his obligations to the owner of the renewal copyright merely because he created a new version under an assignment or license that ended with the first copyright term.

Simply stated, Stewart denies continued exploitation during the renewal term of derivative work prepared during the initial term, unless rights during the renewal term were properly obtained. Of course, the derivative work author owns the original elements added to the underlying work and can continue to use them as he wished, unless this use would infringe the underlying work.

If no registration is filed, a derivative work made pursuant to the grant can still be exploited but no new derivative work can be made after the new term begins.

If the renewal right vests in the author (author is alive at the renewal time), he is bound by the grant, and the assignee will own the renewal rights.

If the author dies before renewal vest, the author's statutory beneficiaries can prevent the assignee from exploiting the derivative work, but only if renewal registration is timely claimed.

Without timely renewal registration, an authorized derivative work prepared under the grant can continue to be exploited under the terms of the grant.

The renewal term creates an entirely new right, one that reverts automatically to the author and his family, unencumbered by assignment and licenses granted during the initial term. This suggests that a license to prepare a derivative work would terminate at the end of the initial term, as would the right to exploit the derivative work prepared under that license.

A derivative work may be individually copyrighted, and the derivative work author will own the copyright in the original elements added to the underlying work.

D. Termination

1. Termination of Transfers

Authors who assign their copyright interests to others should be able, after a reasonable time, to regain those interests, i.e., to "terminate" their transfers.

§ 203 applies to transfers made on or after January 1, 1978 and permits termination at a specified interval after the date of the grant.

§ 304(c) applies to works that were in their renewal term on January 1, 1978, and allows the author or her surviving family to terminate transfers made before that date, so as to recover the 19-year "bonus" period appended by the 1976 Act to the 1909 Act's 28-year renewal term.

If work is not in the public domain as of October 27, 1998, the Sonny Bono Copyright Term extension Act grants an additional 20 years of protection, thereby allowing a 39-year "bonus" period.

Termination Is Not Automatic: If the author or her family fails to take the necessary steps within the statutory time period, the transfer continues in accordance with the terms of the grant itself. 35 years following a grant, the author can go back to assignee and renegotiate.

Termination rights are INALIENABLE

(Cannot be bought or sold).

2. Termination Under § 203

Termination of transfers under § 203 apply to grants made after 1977. Another way to state the same important point is this: when the copyright came into existence is irrelevant for determining whether § 203 applies. All that matters is the date of the transfer.

A provision of this sort is needed because of the unequal bargaining position of authors, resulting in part from the impossibility of determining a work's value until it has been exploited.

The termination of a transfer or license under § 203 would require the serving of an advance notice within specified time limits and under specified conditions. The scope of the right would extend not only to any "transfer of copyright ownership," as defined in § 101, but also to non-exclusive licenses.

a. Who can terminate a grant?

Two issues emerged from the disputed over § 203 as to the persons empowered to terminate a grant:

i. The specific classes of beneficiaries in the case of joint works; and
ii. Whether anything less than unanimous consent of all those entitled to terminate should be required to make a termination effective.
    a) In the case of joint works, majority action by those who signed the grant, or by their interests, would be required to terminate it.
    b) There are three different situations in which the shares of joint authors, or of a dead author's widow or widower, children, and grandchildren, must be divided under the statute:
        (1) The right to effect a termination;
        (2) The ownership of the terminated rights; and
        (3) The right to make further grants of reverted rights.

The respective shares of the authors, and of a dead author's widow or widower, children, and grandchildren, would be divided in exactly the same way in each of these situations. The term "widow," "widower," and "children" are defined in § 101 in an effort to avoid problems and uncertainties that have arisen under the present renewal section.

Consistent with the *per stirpes* principle, the interest of a dead child can be exercised only as a unit by majority action of his surviving children.

b. When a grant can be terminated

§ 203(a)(3) provides, as a general rule, that a grant may be terminated during the 5 years following the expiration of a period of 35 years from the execution of the grant.

As an exception to this basic 35-year rule, the bill also provides that "if the grant covers the right of publication of the work, the period begins at the end of 35 years from the date of publication of the work under the grant or at the end of 40 years from the date of execution of the grant, whichever term ends earlier."

The effective date of termination, which must be stated in the advance notice, is required to fall within the 5 years following the end of the applicable 35- or 40-year period, but the advance notice itself must be served earlier. Under § 203(a) (4) (A), the notice must be served "not less than two or more than ten years" before the effective date stated in it.

c. Effect of termination

§ 203(b) makes clear that, unless effectively terminated within the application 5-year period, all rights covered by an existing grant will continue unchanged.

Under the bill, termination means that ownership of the rights covered by the terminated grant reverts to everyone who owns termination interests on the date the notice of termination was served, whether they joined in signing the notice or not.

3. Termination under § 304(c)

§§ 304(a) and 304(b) add 39 years to the second or renewal term of protection for works copyrighted under the 1909 Act.

Through § 304(c), Congress created a "second chance" for such persons to benefit from the exploitation of commercially valuable works by permitting them to terminate, at least with respect to the 39-year extension, virtually all grants of renewal term interests. They receive an opportunity to regain their interest in the copyright during 39-year extension if they comply with certain carefully prescribed procedures.

If the work is not in the public domain as of October 27, 1978, the previous 19-year term is increased by 20 additional years under the Copyright Term Extension Act, thereby adding 39 years to the second or renewal term of protection.

The reach of § 304(c) is not limited to assignments of renewal expectancies; it also extends to a variety of other grants, including both exclusive and nonexclusive licenses.

In the case of either a first-term or renewal copyright already subsisting when the new statute becomes effective, any grant of rights covering the renewal copyright in the work, executed before the effective date, may be terminated under certain conditions and limitation.

The 5-year period during which termination could be made effective would start 56 years after copyright was originally secured.

4. Comparison of Termination under §§ 203 and 304(c)

§ 203 deals with transfers of copyright, or interests in copyright, made on or after January 1, 1978, whether or not the copyright itself existed on that date.

§ 304(c) deals with assignment executed prior to the effective date of the new Act.

To understand §§ 203 and 304(c), think initially in terms of three categories: (1) copyright interests obtained and transferred after 1977; (2) copyrights obtained and assigned before 1978; and (3) copyrights obtained before 1978 but transferred in whole or in part after 1977.

5. Copyright Interests Obtained and Transferred After 1977

For copyrights arising after 1977, the new Act replaces its predecessor's complicate durational provisions with a life-plus-70-year term, at least in the typical case of a single creator not working for hire.

Under § 203, a transfer of a copyright or any interest therein, if made by the author, may be terminated by qualified person at any time within a 5-year "termination window" that typically opens 35 years after the transfer is executed.

Termination is effect by giving notice between 2 and 10 years prior to a date within the window.

6. Copyrights Obtained and Assigned Before 1978

For copyrights which came into being prior to 1978, the new Act leaves intact the durational period created under the 1909 Act, namely, a 28-year initial term with the possibility of a 28-year renewal term.

The 1976 Act extends this period, however, by tacking on an additional 39-year term. Thus, the focus of the § 304(c) termination right is not the first 56 years of a copyright obtained under the 1909 Act, but rather the 39 years added onto that period by the 1976 Act.

This previous 19 year term is increased to 39 years, unless the work entered the public domain prior to October 27, 1998. Post-1977 Transfers of Pre-1978 Interests

The duration of copyrights obtained before 1978 is an augmented 1909 Act period (28+28+19+ 20 = 95 years), which approximated the period anticipated by the drafters of the 1976 Act under its life-plus-70-years term.

a. Transfers Covered

Unlike § 203, the language of § 304(c) specifically applies not only to grants made by the author, but also to those made by the author's widow, widower or children, and his/her next of kin. § 304(c) applies to grants covering the renewal term for copyrighted works. § 203 applies to any interest in copyright.

b. Persons Qualified to Terminate

The persons who qualify to claim the extra 19 years granted by § 302(a) are set out in § 304(c) (1) and (2). Under § 203(a) (1) and (2), a somewhat different list of persons is empowered to terminate grants made after 1977, although the provisions for the exercise of the right by a deceased author's survivors are identical.

c. Beginning of the Termination Window

Under § 304(c), reclamation of the extra 39 years granted to copyrights subsisting on the effective date of the new Act and subject to pre-1978 grants of the renewal term must be accomplished within a 5-year window beginning with the start of the 39-year period.

Under § 203, termination of a transfer made after 1977 must be done within the 5-year period beginning 35 years after the transfer.

d. Persons Who Make Further Grants

Under § 304(c)(6), each owner of a right which has reverted after termination of a transfer made by an author's successor becomes a tenant in common entitled to deal separately with the right. Under § 203(b), the situation is different. There is no tenancy in common. Instead, one the right in a post-1977 grant has been recovered, a majority of the owners thereof, voting in the statutorily prescribed fashion, may make further grants that bind the other owners as well.

7. Case Law

Burroughs v. Metro Goldwyn-Mayer, Inc., 683 F.2d 610 (2d Cir. 1982). This case involved an attempt to terminate a 1931 nonexclusive license to film rights with use of certain Tarzan characters. The nonexclusive license in question was given by a family-owned corporation, ERB, Inc., to MGM's predecessor in title. The author's heirs served notice of termination on the family-owned corporation, but not on MGM, in 1977, before the effective date of the 1976 Act. The plaintiffs contend that the Tarzan grant was effectively terminated and that a 1981 remake of Tarzan by MGM infringed their rights.

The District Court held that the character, Tarzan, was sufficiently delineated to be a copyrightable interest and as such could be terminated. The termination was ineffective, however, because it was premature (the Act was not yet in effect in 1977) and because it was served on the family-owned corporation (the original grantee) and not on the "current successor in title," MGM, as it should have been.

The Second Circuit affirmed the decision, but on different grounds, stating that the Copyright Office regulations require that notice of termination be accompanied by a short statement as to the grants covered. The plaintiffs, however, failed to list five titles of works in their notice of termination. The court concluded that this omission rendered the termination ineffective because the grant gave the right to use the Tarzan character for each of these titles. Thus, the grant remained intact because, to be effective, a notice of termination must clearly identify the grant to which the notice applies.

Mills Music v. Albuquerque A.R.T. Co., 469 U.S. 153, 105 S. Ct. 638, 83 L. Ed.2d 556 (1985) (A derivative work prepared under a grant can continue to be used under its terms even after termination of the grant).

Issue: whether an author's termination of a music publisher's interest in a copyright also terminated the publisher's contractual right to share in the royalties from those whom he had sublicensed to make derivative works.

Result: The Supreme Court, reversing a decision in favor of Snyder, held that the use of the term "grant" three times in § 304(c)(6)(A) revealed a legislative intent to cover not only the original grant but he sublicense made under that grant as well. The Court acknowledged that the principal purpose of § 304 was to benefit authors, but recognized that his was not its sole rationale. Its other purpose was to enable continued public accessibility to derivative works after termination. The Court concluded that upholding the status quo did justice to both policies.

Chapter 7

PUBLICATION AND FORMALITIES

Before the 1976 Act took effect, unpublished works were protected by the "common law" copyright of the states; published works were protected only by "statutory" copyright under federal law.

A. Publication

The dividing line between protection and non-protection is creation (that is, the fixation of an original work).

1. Works fixed on or after January 1, 1978

Before March 1, 1989, publication without attending to the statutory formalities, particularity notice, still effects a forfeiture or abandonment.

After March 1, 1989, observation of notice formalities in connection with publication may enhance significantly the remedies available to a copyright owner bringing an action for infringement.

2. Works in their first (or original) term as of January 1, 1978

If the copyrights in such works arose prior to 1964 and were not properly renewed under old § 304(a), the works fell into the public domain.

If the copyrights were properly renewed, they acquired an additional 67 (47 + 20) years of protection.

3. Works in their second (or renewal) term as of January 1, 1978 (works published with notice prior to January 1, 1950)

Under the 1909 Act, the total of the original and renewal term would have been 56 years.

Under the 1976 Act, the total duration of such a copyright is 95 years, which the drafters of the Act thought approximated the "life plus 70" duration typical for works fixed after January 1, 1978. Total term is now 95 years, unless work was in the public domain prior to October 27, 1998.

4. **Works created but not federally copyrighted prior to January 1, 1978** (At least at one time had a common law copyright, but which had not obtained a statutory copyright prior to January 1, 1978.)

If the work had a subsisting state law copyright on that date, it was transmuted into a federal copyright by operation of § 303 of the 1976 Act.

If, however, the work had been the subject of a general publication without notice prior to January 1, 1978, it was divested of its common law copyright without being invested with statutory copyright, and has fallen into the public domain; it is not protected by any subsisting copyright and cannot be made the basis of an action for infringement.

5. Federal Preemption of Rights Equivalent to Copyright

Under § 301, a work would obtain statutory protection as soon as it is "created" or, as that term is defined in § 101, when it is "fixed in a copy or phonorecord for the first time."

<u>Main arguments for a single Federal system</u>:

i. Promote national uniformity.
ii. Help give a clear interpretation of "publication."
iii. § 301 will implement the "limited times" provision of the Constitution.
iv. Need for effective international copyright relations.

B. Limited Publication versus General Publication

A limited publication is a non-divestive publication which communicates the contents of a work to a narrowly selected group for a limited purpose, without transferring the rights of diffusion, reproduction, distribution, or sale. A limited publication is one in which circulation of the work is restricted both as the person who receive it and the purpose for its distribution. Otherwise, it is a general publication.

Because it focuses on the copyright owner's purpose in publishing the work, the limited publication doctrine contradicts the general rule that a person's subjective intent is irrelevant in deciding whether a publication has taken place.

Estate of Martin Luther King, Jr. v. CBS, 194 F.3d 1211 (11th Cir. 1999) (King's estate sued CBS for copyright infringement for using 60% of King's "I Have a Dream" speech in a video-documentary. CBS maintained that King had delivered the speech into the public domain and refused to pay royalties to King's estate. The district court declared that King's speech was a general publication, thereby entering it into the public domain, and granted summary judgment for CBS. King's estate appealed.)

The court analyzed this case using the Copyright Act of 1909, instead of the 1976 Act, because King received his copyright for the speech in 1963.

Under the 1909 Act, state common law protection automatically began when the speech was created and continued until general publication. General publication occurred: (a) if the work was distributed to the public in a format allowing public control over the work or (b) presented to the public in a format which would allow unrestricted copying. "The case law indicates that distribution to the news media, as opposed to the general public, for the purpose of enabling the reporting of a contemporary newsworthy event, is only a limited publication." Therefore, despite the fact that King's speech had a large radio and television audience; it was distributed to news agencies as a limited publication.

C. What is Publication?

If been distributed, a general use is usually for money (meant to distribute) while a limited use (sent to mom) will not give effect to § 10 under the 1909 Act. Under 1909 Act, § 10 deals with publication of work with notice; under the Copyright Act of 1976, "a public performance or display of a work does not of itself constitute publication."

Forfeiture typically occurs through publication without proper notice and is accomplished by operation of law.

Abandonment requires intent, usually evidenced by an overt act such as a statement appearing on copies of the work that anyone who wishes to reproduce, perform or display the work is free to do so.
The statutory definition of publication in § 101 of the 1976 Act says nothing about where the relevant "sale or other transfer of ownership, or . . . rental, lease or lending" must take place.

Academy of Motion Pictures Arts & Sciences v. Creative House Promotions, Inc., 944 F.2d 1446 (9th Cir. 1991). The Academy had distributed 158 copies of its famed Oscar statuette to award winners between 1929 and 1941, without notice of copyright and without any express restriction on the recipient's right to sell or dispose of their Oscar. In 1941, the Academy registered their claim to copyright, and from that time, all Oscars have borne notice of copyright. In 1976, the defendant commissioned a trophy sculptor to create a sculpture strikingly similar to the Oscar, which it sold to various corporate buyers.

The district court ruled that the Oscar had entered the public domain in 1941, because the Academy's divestive and general publication, without notice, triggered the loss of copyright.

The Court of Appeals reversed because the Oscars were distributed to a select group of persons for a limited purpose. Although there was no express restrictions on the use or distribution of the Oscar before 1941, the Ninth Circuit held that such restrictions were implied (no one ever offered to sell Oscar; each Oscar personalized; Academy never gave the recipients the permission to sell, distribute, or make other copies of their Oscars).

D. Notice

Under the 1909 Act, terms of copyright ran from the date of publication, so that notice had an obvious utility. Under the 1976, most works are protected for fixed terms related to the length of their authors' lives, making calculation of the term on the basis of the date of the copyright notice impossible.

As of March 1, 1989, the use of copyright notice ceased to be mandatory under American law.

The U.S. Copyright Office has not spoken on the issue of whether work first published with notice before March 1, 1989, and reprinted after March 1, 1989 should bear the copyright notice.

Under the present law the copyright notice serves four principal functions:

i. It has the effect of placing in the public domain a substantial body of published material that no one is interested in copyrighting;
ii. It informs the public as to whether a particular work is copyrighted;

iii. It identifies the copyright owner; and
iv. It shows the date of publication.

§401(b) sets out the form of notice to appear on visually-perceptible copies ("Copyright," "Copr.," or "©"; the year of first publication; and the name of the copyright owner) A minority of courts have allowed the use of "©" as a copyright symbol. This is because in computer programs (ASCII) there is no © symbol available. However, very few courts have allowed this symbol to protect the author's rights. In the case of ASCII it is recommended that the author use "copyright" or "Copr.".

§401(b) (2) - in the case of a derivative work or compilation, it is not necessary to list the date of publication of all preexisting material incorporated in the work.

§401 (b) (3) - Recognizable abbreviation or a generally known alternative designation may be used instead of the full name of the copyright owner.

§401(c) provides that the notice "shall be affixed to the copies in such manner and location as to give reasonable notice of the claim of copyright."
Example: © 1999 Acme Publishing Corporation

1. Notice on Phonorecords of Sound Recordings

In general, the form of the notice specified by § 402(b) consists of the symbol "P"; the year of first publication of the sound recording; and the name of the copyright owner or an admissible variant. There are three reasons for prescribing use of the symbol "P" rather than "©":

i. Avoid confusion between copyright in the sound recording and in the musical or literary work embodied in it;
ii. Distinguishing between copyright claims in the sound recording and in the printed test or art work appearing on the record label, album cover, etc.; and
iii. Symbol "P" has been adopted as the international symbol for the protection of sound recordings.

2. Position of Notice

The notice should be placed on the copy or phonorecord in such a manner and location as to "glue reasonable notice of the claim of copyright." Notice on a phonorecord may be on a label or container as long as it gives reasonable notice.

3. Notice for Publications Incorporating United States Works

Requires that when the copies or phonorecords consist "preponderantly of one or more works of the United States Government," the copyright notice (if any) identify those parts of the work in which a copyright is claimed.

Example: © 1999 Acme Corporation. Copyright claimed in Sections 2-5, exclusive of U.S. Government maps.

4. Notice for Contributions to Collective Works

Basic approach:

i. To permit but not require a separate contribution to bear its own notice;
ii. To make a single notice, covering the collective work as a whole, sufficient to satisfy the notice requirement for the separate contributions it contains, even if they have been previously published or their ownership is different; and
iii. To protect the interests of an innocent infringer of copyright in a contribution that does not bear its own notice, who has dealt in good faith with the person named in the notice covering the collective work as a whole.

§ 404(b) - A separate contribution that does not bear its own notice, and that is published in a collective work with a general notice containing the name of someone other than the copyright owner of the contribution, is treated as if it has been published with the wrong name in the notice.

5. Omission of Copyright Notice

Under the proposed law, a work published without any copyright notice will still be subject to statutory protection for at least 5 years, whether the omission was partial or total, unintentional or deliberate. Section 405(a) provides that omission of notice, whether intentional or unintentional, does not invalidate the copyright:

i. If "no more than a relatively small number" or copies or phonorecords have been publicly distributed without notice; **or**
ii. If registration for the work has already been made, or is made within 5 years after the publication without notice, and a reasonable effort is made to add notice to copies

or phonorecords publicly distributed in the United States after the omission is discovered. (** unlike the 1909 Act, which didn't allow for curing of omissions of notice.)

Current notice requirements are unchanged for works first published before the effective date of the Act. These works will fall into the public domain if published without notice, and registration is not made before or within 5 years of publication.

6. Case Law

Hasbro Bradley, Inc. v. Sparkle Toys, Inc., 780 F.2d 189 (2d Cir. 1985). (The plaintiff, a toy manufacturer, brought an action to enjoin an admitted copyist from distributing its Transformer brand robot toys in the United States. The defendant claimed that copyright was forfeited by the Japanese company, the assignor to Hasbro and the originator of the toys, in deliberately omitting notice from 213,000 of the toys sold in Asia.)

The court held that the assignor's deliberate omission of notice was indeed discovered by the assignee who was then attempting to cure the omission.

In addition to registration, § 405(a) (2) requires that the copyright owner make a reasonable effort to add notice to all copies or phonorecords that are publicly distributed before March 1, 1989. By this provision, the copyright owner does not have to make a reasonable effort to add notice to copies already possessed by members of the public. On the other hand, the copyright owner has a clear duty to affix notice to copies still in his possession awaiting distribution. The reasonable effort requirement is a question of fact to be worked out under the circumstances of each case. The general rule is that a copyright owner who can establish impracticality is excused.

Whether Hasbro cured Takara's omission of notice is determined by looking at § 405(a) (2):

i. Register within 5 years after publication without notice.
ii. Reasonable effort is made to add notice to copies or phonorecords publicly distributed in the United States after the omission is discovered.

Berne Convention prohibits the imposition of formalities. A defendant cannot use the benefit of innocent infringement in mitigation of actual or statutory damages.

Chapter 8

INFRINGEMENT ACTIONS

§ 501(a) identifies a copyright infringer as someone who "violates any of the exclusive rights of the copyright owner as provided by §§ 106 - 20" of the bill, or who imports copies or phonorecords in violation of § 602.

§ 501(b) enables the owner of a particular right to bring an infringement action in that owner's name alone, while at the same time insuring to the extent possible that the other owners whose rights may be affected are notified and given a chance to join the action.

A "beneficial owner" for this purpose would include, for example, an author who had parted with legal title to the copyright in exchange for percentage royalties based on sales or license fees.

§ 501(b) is intended to allow a court to permit or compel joinder of the owners of rights in works upon which a derivative work is based.

To be held a related or vicarious infringer in the case of performing rights, a defendant must either actively operate or supervise the operation of the place wherein the performances occur, or control the content of the infringing program, and expect commercial gain from the operation and either direct or indirect benefit from the infringing performance.

A. Jurisdiction

28 U.S.C. § 1338(a) gives federal courts exclusive jurisdiction for action arising under the Copyright Act. To determine that an action arises under the 1976 Copyright Act requires distinguishing between an action based primarily on a right conferred by the 1976 Copyright Act, and an action incidentally involving issues of copyright law. A suit for statutory copyright infringement is the classic example of an action expressly conferred by copyright, where federal jurisdiction is exclusive.

By comparison, an action brought to enforce an assignment of copyright is essentially an action under contract law. Here, the state court jurisdiction would be exclusive, even though the state court may have to interpret aspects of copyright law to determine whether to enforce the assignment. Similarly, an action brought to enforce royalties under a licensing agreement would lie essentially in the domain of state law, as would a will conveying a copyright and an action to foreclose a statutory copyright mortgage.

Even where the action does not involve statutory copyright infringement, exclusive jurisdiction will be conferred if the complaint necessitates construction or application of provisions of the 1976 Copyright Act.

Often a complaint will include both federal as well as non-federal claims. Under 28 U.S.C. § 1338(a), the federal court must determine whether it has jurisdiction to decide the case under the copyright laws. Under 28 U.S.C. § 1338(b), a district court has the power to decide the nonfederal claim if three jurisdictional requirements are met:

i. The basis of the nonfederal claim must be "unfair competition," and the federal claim to which it is attached must be both;
ii. Substantial; and
iii. Related.

As for the requirement that the state claim constitute "unfair competition," the courts have broadly construed them to include claims of passing off, misappropriation, misrepresentation, conversion, trade secret misappropriation, and breach of contract.

As for the "substantiality" of the claim, the courts will deny jurisdiction over the state cause of action if the federal claim is denied on a pretrial motion.

Two views exist on the meaning of "related" for the purpose of pendent jurisdiction.

i. The more restrictive view holds that the two claims are related only if they rest on substantially identical facts.
ii. The more liberal view, which appears to be the current trend, holds that the two claims are related if they have the same "factual nucleus," even though they might not derive from identical facts.

T.B. Harms Co. v. Eliscu, 339 F.2d 823 (2d Cir. 1964). This case is about "arising under" jurisdiction of 28 U.S.C. § 1338. There is no federal jurisdiction if only arguing over state claim. One needs "arising under" jurisdiction to get into federal court. If there is a contract question (interpretation), the cause of action is out of federal court's jurisdiction. However, if there is a federal statutory question, then federal court can decide.

The parties are not fighting about the length of the renewal, the procedure of the renewal, or whether the widow has a claim, but rather the contract they entered into. Thus, state law applies and case should be heard in state court. Attorney tried to get into federal court by making question look like a federal question.

Once you get into federal court under either federal question or diversity jurisdiction, you can bring in other non-federal claims provided both claims are arise out of the same transaction or occurrence.

Friedman, Eisensteink, Raemer & Schwartz v. Afterman, 599 F. Supp 902 (N.D. Ill. 1984). Plaintiff published "Practitioners Technical Bulletin;" Defendant, who formerly worked for plaintiff, published "Accounting & Auditing Update Services;" Defendant breached covenant of non-competition.

The issue in the case is whether the plaintiff's state law claims and the copyright claim are derived from a common nucleus of operative facts. The federal law issue is whether under the work-for-hire doctrine the defendant was an employee at the time of he wrote the copyrighted material. If he was, then the plaintiff owns the work. The state law issue is whether the defendant breached his covenant not to compete.

The case was properly decided in federal court because both issues derive from a common nucleus of operative facts. Thus, under the theory of pendent claim jurisdiction if jurisdiction lies in federal court, non-federal issues as well as federal claims may be heard in federal court.

1. Procedure and Remedies §§ 500's

Possible Remedies:

i. Injunctions
ii. Damages
iii. Profits
iv. Statutory damages
v. Attorney's fees

Swarovski America Ltd. v. Silver Deer Ltd., 537 F. Supp 1201 (D. Colo. 1982) (Plaintiff alleges that the defendants infringed the plaintiff's copyright in certain crystal figurines by authorizing their manufacture and by distributing them to the public.)

§ 205 of the Copyright Act of 1976 allows recordation in the Copyright Office of all documents of copyright ownership whether assignment, exclusive licenses, or nonexclusive licenses. To fully enjoy the benefits of the 1976 Act, an owner of a copyright interest should accompany the recordation with a registration of the underlying work.

An owner of an exclusive license to perform a copyrighted work cannot defend his rights in a court of law without recording his exclusive license in the Copyright Office.

For causes of action arising on or after March 1, 1989, recordation as a prerequisite to bringing a copyright infringement suit is no longer required. However, one should still record because:

i. Recordation specifically identifying the work will give notice to the world of the terms set forth in the document; and
ii. Recordation establishes priority of ownership between conflicting transfers of copyright as well as conflicts between a transfer and a nonexclusive license.

The author is not required to be joined because it may be hard to join everyone in the case. The author would later be estopped from suing because of *res judicata*. Thus, under § 501(b) this is permissive joinder not compulsive.

The statute says that non-exclusive licensee may not sue because of unjust enrichment, *res judicata*, and it would discourage oral contracts. Thus, there is no federal remedy, but there might be a state remedy. If have exclusive license, you may sue in federal court.

Cortner v. Israel, 732 F.2d 267 (2d Cir. 1984) (1984) Plaintiff composed music for the "ABC, Monday Night Football" theme. ABC and plaintiff were the copyright owners. They had a contract for royalties; ABC commissioned defendant to write a new, similar theme song and ABC held the copyright under the work-made-for-hire doctrine. Plaintiff sued defendant for copyright infringement.

Court held that it lacks diversity jurisdiction and affirmed the district court's decision.

§ 501(b) states that the legal or beneficial owner of a copyright has an exclusive right. Beneficial owner not defined in § 101, but from legislative history it is an author who had parted with legal title to the © in exchange for % royalties based on sales or license fees. Therefore, appellants have standing of infringement under either act as beneficial owner. ABC is not liable because it is the copyright owner and Israel and Score are not liable because they were commissioned by the copyright right owner to create a work-made-for-hire.

Demetriades v. Kaufmann, 690 F. Supp 289 (S.D.N.Y. 1988) The court concluded that infringement could be found if they had copied in whole or in part the floor plans from the brochures in making their own architectural plans, even if these same plans would give the copyright owner no claim over the features they detail. However, these limitations on copyright for architecture have been removed by the 1990 amendments.

The Second Circuit has noted that vicarious liability is "when the right and ability to supervise [the infringer] coalesce (unites) with an obvious and direct financial interest in the exploitation of copyrighted materials," a third party may be held liable for the direct infringement by another. However, the doctrine of "vicarious liability" is inapplicable in this case.

2. Burden of Proof

The plaintiff in a copyright action is responsible for proving:

i. His or her ownership of the pertinent exclusive right(s) in the accusing work; and
ii. A *prima facie* case of infringement of the right(s) in suit by the defendant.

Once a *prima facie* case has been established by the plaintiff, the defendant bears the burden of rebutting that case, including any of the limitations found in §§ 107-20, which act as affirmative defenses.

As to ownership, the principal matters to be proved include: the copyrightability of the work; its authorship by the plaintiff; the plaintiff's citizenship status; compliance with any statutory formalities; and the basis of the plaintiff's claim to ownership if he or she obtained title to the right in suit subsequent to registration of the copyright.

While the *prima facie* presumption of ownership, once established by the plaintiff, is rebuttable, "defendant must meet a very high burden of proof to overcome that presumption.

B. Substantive Aspects

Proof of infringement has two components:

i. The plaintiff must demonstrate that the defendant did, in fact, copy material from the copyrighted work.

ii. The plaintiff must show that the defendant's copying constitutes an improper appropriation.

"Copying" almost always is proved by indirect i.e., circumstantial evidence of the defendant's infringing activity, simply because direct evidence is not available. Accordingly, the courts are forced to presume copying upon proof that the defendant had "access" to the copyrighted work, usually coupled with proof of some degree of similarity between that work and the alleged infringing work.

"Improper appropriation" is a separate matter. Even if the defendant cannot rebut the plaintiff's case on copying, he or she still may escape liability if the plaintiff fails to show that the taking was impermissible as to both kind and amount.

i. The plaintiff must demonstrate that what the defendant appropriated from the copyrighted work was protected expression.
ii. The plaintiff must show that the intended audiences for the two works will find "substantial similarity" between the defendant's work and the plaintiff's protected expression.

In short, if both copying and improper appropriation are demonstrated, the plaintiff has made out a *prima facie* case.

1. Copying

Bright Tunes Music Corp. v. Harrisongs Music, Ltd.,
420 F.Supp 177 (S.D.N.Y. 1976). Access has been inferred where the work was in possession of a third party which had done business with both plaintiff and defendant, or where the work was available to employees in defendant corporation's files. Alternatively, evidence of access was insufficient to support a claim for infringement where nothing more could be shown other than the work was available in defendant's city of residence.

In this case, access to a famous, widely-disseminated work may also be inferred where facts suggest that defendant had a reasonable opportunity to view or copy it.

The court found that defendant had access to the copyrighted work because of its popularity as a hit in the United States and abroad. And even though defendant may have unintentionally copied it through subconscious processes, unintentional copying does not constitute a defense against an action for copyright infringement.

To prove access, plaintiff must show that defendant had a reasonable opportunity to view or copy the work. Generally, the evidence must be sufficient for the trier of fact to infer a reasonable probability of access. On the other hand, a mere possibility of access, based on conjecture or speculation, is not enough to make the circumstantial case.

Strikingly Similar: When two works are so strikingly similar that independent creation is not reasonably possible. To infer access in this situation, plaintiff must show similarities that could only be explained by copying rather than by coincidence, independent creation, or use of a prior common source. The nature of the copyrighted work is the essential factor in making the circumstantial case in this situation.

Selle v. Gibb, 741 F.2d 896 (7th Cir. 1984). The question involved in this case was whether the Bee Gee's international hit song "How Deep Is Your Love" was so strikingly similar to defendant's prior song that proof of access could be inferred. The court held that even strikingly similarity is not enough to infer access unless there is some evidence making it reasonably possible that plaintiff's work was available to the infringer. Some courts feel that if two works are strikingly similar, then the subsequent author must have had access and will therefore find infringement. Here the reasonable possibility does not exist. The Bee Gee's song was written in France, while the plaintiff's song was limited to play in the Chicago area. Moreover, the songs did not involve the kind of striking similarity sufficient to overcome the need to show reasonable opportunity to copy.

When the works are trite or commonplace and resemble available public sources, the fact that they are similar does not support the inference that the work was copied, and other proof of access showing a reasonable opportunity to view the work will be required.

2. Improper Appropriation

Subtractive Approach to Substantial Similarity:
After the unprotected elements are "subtracted," so to speak, the finder-of-fact proceeds to ask whether there are significant similarities between what remains of the allegedly infringed work, on the one hand, and the various components and characteristics of the allegedly infringing work, on the other.

Three Boys Music Corp. v. Bolton, 212 F.3d 477 (9th Cir. 2000) (The Isley Brothers, a popular 60's group, created and copyrighted the song "Love is a Wonderful Thing." In early 1990, Michael Bolton released a song "Love is a Wonderful Thing." The Isley Brothers sued Bolton for copyright infringement. The district court found that the Bolton song was substantially similar to the 1966 Isley release and that Bolton had subconsciously copied the song. Bolton appealed.)

Especially in music cases, the proof of copyright infringement is highly circumstantial. To prove copyright infringement, the plaintiff must prove ownership of a valid copyright and infringement (e.g., that the defendant copied protected elements of the plaintiff's work), which is proven by access and substantial similarity. The court affirmed the jury's holding, finding that despite this being a "weak case of access and a circumstantial case of substantial similarity," the verdict should not be second-guessed because it is supported by substantial evidence. Although the inverse ratio rule requires a lesser showing of substantial similarity if there is a stronger proof of access or vice versa, it does not inversely mean that a weak showing of access requires a stronger showing of substantial similarity.

Totality Approach. Under this "total concept and feel" approach, the ultimate role of the finder-of-fact is to determine whether the accused and complaining works would have the same appeal to the relevant audience for the works.

Nichols v. Universal Pictures Corp., 45 F.2d 229 (1930)
Judge Learned Hand made a famous attempt to draw the line between taking idea and taking expression. Plaintiff-author of the play "Abie's Irish" Rose sued defendant for its motion picture "The Cohens and the Kelleys". The issue was whether the play and the movie were substantially similar, given the obvious similarity of the storylines of the two shows. The court concluded that "[T]he only matter common to the two is a quarrel between a Jewish and an Irish father, the marriage of their children, the birth of grandchildren and reconciliation.

The abstractions test (formulated by, Judge Learned Hand) provides insight into how to separate copyrightable expression from non-infringing public domain ideas to determine substantial similarity. The test may be viewed as a continuum with pure idea at one end and pure expression at the other. As the idea travels along continuum (uninterrupted), it gathers concrete details and becomes more complex. No longer a vague set of generalities, it cannot be summed up in a few words. A taking at this point is a taking of the author's expression.

Although the abstractions test is a useful conceptualization of the problem, it does not clearly indicate where on the continuum an undue amount of plaintiff's expression has been taken. Perhaps all that can be said is that there comes a point where defendant's use of the general theme combines with similarities in details, scenes, sequence of events, characterization, and interplay of characters to constitute infringement.

***Scenes a fair*:** Scene must be essential to play and commonly associated. Exclude stock characters and certain character relationships. One can get copyright protection for arrangement, which is similar to the compilation statute.

Each circuit have general trend (analytic or "look and feel" approach") (Supreme Court never said either one must be used.) One can overcome the presumption of access by disproving access.

Peter Pan Fabrics, Inc. v. Martin Weiner Corp., 274 F.2d 487 (2d Cir. 1960). Graphic designs for textiles were also included within copyrightable subject matter of pictorial, graphic, and sculptural works (implied). A flexible approach was taken to notice of copyright placed on the selvage of a fabric design which would either be cut off from the fabric or rendered undetectable on a dress.

Commercial impairment test (adopted by Judge Learned Hand) in which, at least in the case of deliberate copyist, the defendant has the burden to show that notice could have been embodied in the design without impairing it market value.

Laureyssens v. Idea Group, Inc., 964 F.2d 131 (2d Cir. 1992) (Two foam rubber puzzles were created that looked similar.) What test do you apply (standard) to determine if substantial similarity? Lay observer.

Court concluded that the puzzles were similar. The copyright was for the pieces, not for puzzle as a whole. But nothing in statute tells you to look at pieces themselves instead of overall effect.

The idea of a flat-to-cube puzzle is not copyrightable because one cannot protect this idea. Can protect expression of idea (pieces), but may not protect structure together. If the court used the total concept and feel test, it would have come out with a different result. The court used the Abstraction/Filtration analytical test.

Lay-observer test can be used for analytical test or total concept test.

One will be told what test to apply and what standard to use. Music industry has been good about using expert standard (but still can be applied to either test). See both types of standards and observers in copying and unlawful appropriation (more helpful in unlawful appropriation).

Jury instructions are usually challenged, law unclear in this area. Likely to get copyright infringement when have some similarity and ask lay observer to compare total-concept. (Judge may award smaller damages though). Normally, Judge decides copying, not jury. Some works get opinion letter from © office, can block registration. Go to court.

3. Computer Programs

Under § 101, a computer program is "a set of statements or instructions to be used directly or indirectly in a computer in order to bring about a certain result".

a. **Similarity between computer programs:**
Computer program may be considered a literary work under § 102(a) (1), but it does not appear in § 117. However, the term "include" is illustrative and not limitative.

If a computer program is considered a procedure, process, system, then it is not copyrightable.

Baker v. Selden, 101 U.S. 99, (1880) is the closed case to computer program. Thus, absent a merger problem, one could have ©. The test used depends on the circuit:

- Second Circuit in *Altai* used the total concept or analytical approach.
- Third Circuit in *Whalen* looked at the structure, sequence, organize to determine copying.

Now that computer programs are copyrightable subject matter and are protected against verbatim copying, the difficult question is to what extent programs are protected against non-literal copying. The question is whether copyright protection will extend beyond the written code itself to the structure of the program and its user interface.

To determine how far computer programs should be protected against non-literal copying should ultimately depend on whether the particular approach encourages the optimal production and dissemination of computer programs. Inadequate protection will undermine the incentive to create computer programs, whereas too much protection will unduly impede their dissemination and deprive creators of basic material on which they build their own works.

Computer Associates International, Inc., v. Atlai, Inc., 982 F.2d 963 (2d Cir. 1992). Both plaintiff and defendant marketed a computer program that performed similar functions on IBM mainframe computers. Although the defendant's first version of the program had directly used significant parts of the code structure, the second version contained no program code in common with the plaintiff's software. The defendant conceded liability for copyright infringement for the first version of the program while denying that the second version infringed the plaintiff's copyright. The similarity between the programs, however, raised the question of how far copyright should go to protect the non-literal elements of a program.

b. Analysis

The court developed *three stages of analysis*: abstraction, filtration, comparison:

i. ***Abstraction***: One must abstract the program into various layers of generality. Here, in a manner similar to reverse engineering, a court should dissect the copyrighted program's structure and isolate each level of abstraction in it.

ii. ***Filtration***: The merger doctrine can be used to filter out those elements of the program dictated by efficiency or by factors external to the program itself, e.g., mechanical specification, compatibility requirements or those taken from the public domain.

iii. ***Comparison***: Compare the remaining elements with the corresponding elements of defendant's work.

Result: The court agreed with the district court that the program contained protectable elements similar to plaintiff's program. These similarities, however, were not sufficiently material to the overall program to uphold a finding of infringement. This holding clearly narrows the scope of protection for non-literal components of computer program.

3 PART TEST FOR UNLAWFUL APPROPRIATION:

Abstraction: Expression can turn into idea the more vague it is:

i. ***Conceptual separation test*** does expression embody an idea that may appear in a different expression; Stock and trade elements are segments that are used segment over and over again, and therefore are not copyrightable. Computer programs get thin protection because they use a lot of stock and trade elements. Repetition turns expression into idea; being driven to patent law standard.

ii. ***Filtration***: Go through pieces and see what the scope of plaintiff's copyright is. Unlawful appropriation standard is used and test is similar to analytical test. Don't protect the elements that are necessary to run program.

iii. ***Comparison:*** Compare the remaining elements with the corresponding elements in defendant's work.

C. Damages

1. **Injunctive Relief**
   Under U.S.C. § 502, a court can grant temporary and permanent injunctions.

2. **Infringer Liability:** Under 17 U.S.C. § 504, an infringer of copyright is liable for either:

   i. the copyright owner's actual damages and any additional profits of the infringer; or
   ii. statutory damages.

Thus, if the copyright owner (or Plaintiff(s)) wants to seek actual damages and profits under 504(b), he/she is entitled to recover actual damages suffered as a result of the infringement (lost profits) and any profits of the infringer attributed to the infringement that were not taken into account in computing the actual damages. In establishing the infringer's profits, the copyright owner is only required to prove the infringer's gross revenue. After this is established, the burden shifts to the infringer to show what portion of total profits is attributable to deductible expenses, if any, and any non-infringing elements.

3. **Monetary Relief -- Statutory Damages**
Pursuant to § 504(c), the copyright owner may elect at any time before final judgment is rendered to recover in lieu of actual damages and profits an award of statutory damages for all infringements involved in the action with respect to any one work for which any one infringer is liable. Thus, under the current law, a copyright owner may elect to recover "a sum of not less than $500 or more than $20,000 as the court considers just" for each work that is infringed (rather than the number of infringements, as was the case under the 1909 Act). Although the term "work" is not defined in the statute, "all parts of a compilation or derivative work constitute one work."

These monetary limits imposed for statutory damages under §504(c) (1) have two exceptions under §504(c) (2):

i. **Willful infringement** - the court has discretion to increase the maximum award of damages to $100,000.

ii. **Innocent infringement** - the court has discretion to decrease the minimum award of damages to $200.

4. **Cost and Attorney's Fees**
§ 505 gives the court discretion to award the prevailing party of an action recovery of its full costs and/or attorney's fees.

5. **Prerequisite for Statutory Damages and Attorney's Fees**
§ 412 states that the election of statutory damages or recovery of attorney's fees is not available if:

i. the copyright infringement of an unpublished work began before the effective date of its registration; or
ii. the copyright infringement began after first publication of the work and before the effective date of its registration, unless the registration is made 3 months of the first publication of the work.

Chapter 9

FAIR USE

Fair use is an affirmative defense that allows someone to lawfully copy another usually for educational purposes, reviews, comments, criticisms, etc. Fair use finds its way in through legal misappropriation. Fair use is a defense to © infringement. Every fair use case assumes copying. To determine whether the use was a "fair use," the court looks at:

i. Purpose or character of the use;
ii. Nature of the copyrighted work;
iii. Amount and substantial portion of the underlying work that was used in relation to the copyrighted work as a whole; and
iv. Effect of the use upon the potential market.

The determination of fair use is fact specific - there is no bright line test.

Sony Computer Entertainment v. Connectix, 203 F.3d 596 (9th Cir. 2000) (Connectix developed a video game system known as Virtual Game Station for personal computers, which is capable of using the Sony products that are designed for the Sony PlayStation. While developing the software, Connectix reverse engineered the Sony BIOS system. The district court granted Sony a preliminary injunction and Connectix appealed.)

The appellate court reversed the district court and determined that Connectix reverse engineering constituted fair use. The appellate court pointed out that software engineers often had to reverse engineer products to access functional elements. Such reverse engineering might necessitate copying the copyrighted program into a computer's RAM. In concluding that the Connectix acts of reverse engineering were a fair use as a matter of law, the court analyzed and weighed the four statutory factors of the fair use doctrine:

i. *Purpose and Character* – Connectix's Virtual Game Station was "modestly transformative," as it dealt with a new platform, the personal computer. When this was weighed against the other factors, including commercialism, Connectix's commercial use was only "indirect or derivative. Thus, this factor favored Connectix.

ii. *Nature of Use* – Connectix needed to copy the protected elements of the Sony BIOS system to access the non-protected elements. When such copying is "necessary," it constitutes fair use.

iii. *Amount and Substantial Portion of Underlying Work* – Connectix disassembled and made numerous copies of the Sony BIOS system. While this factor favors Sony, the court pointed out that when none of the intermediate work is incorporated into the final product, this factor carries "very little weight."

iv. *Effect on the Potential Market* – Connectix Virtual Game Station was a "legitimate" competitor with the Sony PlayStation. While Sony may suffer economic losses, copyright did not extend monopolistic protection to all platforms that play Sony games and devices.

Sony Corp. of America v. Universal City Studios, Inc., 464 U.S. 417, 104 S .Ct. 774, 748 L. Ed.2d 574 (1984) (People using betamax to tape TV and use TIME-SHIFTING. Universal sued Sony because this deep pocket furnished people with device to copy.) Time shifting used by people who are not able to watch a TV show during its original time slot. Time shifting allows them to watch the TV program and then erase it when they're finished watching it; that is, they can "tape it" and watch it at a more convenient time but do not "tape" the show in order to create a library of tapes.

The U.S. Supreme Court held that the instant action was a non-commercial use because it was a private activity done in the home and because the users were not using them ("the recordings") for resale. If this was an infringement, then the police would have to go into the private homes of the users to make a determination - an illegal search and seizure. Europe has addressed this issue by charging a fee on all blank tapes, which is similar in concept to a copyright royalty.

Chapter 10

THE INTERNET AND CYBERLAW

A. Introduction

The Internet has raised many challenging copyright issues, but the most important rules to remember are the basic doctrines of copyright law.

After studying the preceding chapters, you should have a good idea of what constitutes a copyright and how it can be infringed. The intricacies of Internet copyright law arise from tensions in three areas:

i. New technologies and the degree of copyright protection (i.e., hyperlinking)
ii. New uses of traditionally copyrighted materials (i.e., music, books)
iii. New enforcement issues in copyright law (i.e., chat room owner liability)

To the layperson these cyberspace tensions seem new, but keeping copyright law abreast of new technologies is the perennial objective of copyright law.

1. New technologies

New technologies that are protected include:

a. Web sites including text and pictures
b. Software source/object codes
c. Internet products

Although protecting these new technologies may seem intuitive (i.e., a web page is similar to an audiovisual work), as the Internet evolves, new issues regarding these technologies arise.

One of the more recent technology cases involves hyperlinking, which allows a user browsing one web site to be transferred directly to a web page within another web site.

Ticketmaster Corp. v. Tickets.com Inc., 54 U.S.P.Q.2d 1344 (C.D. Cal. 2000) (Both Ticketmaster and Tickets.com provide information on events and ticket sales online. Ticketmaster sued Tickets.com for copyright infringement, basing its complaint on: (a) Tickets.com copied Ticketmaster web pages to the Tickets.com web site to gather event information such as event, place, date, time, and price of ticket; (b) the factual information was then used on the Tickets.com web pages in a different format; and (c) Tickets.com also provided hyperlinks to the Ticketmaster web site but bypassed the Ticketmaster homepage.)

The court dismissed points (b) and (c), finding that neither the use of the factual information from another's web page nor hyperlinking to another's web page constitutes copyright infringement. The court, however, did not dismiss point (a) because it was based on actual copying of the web page.

2. New uses of traditionally copyrighted materials

Some web sites and service providers may be passive in contributing to copyright infringement, as they merely provide the medium or gateway for sharing and distributing copyrighted material. If these web sites and service providers are held liable for the copyright infringement of third parties, however, many people worry that the Internet will be stunted. Since the copyrighted works posted on these web sites still need to be protected, the courts are beginning to distinguish these cases and discuss the policies behind them.

National Basketball Association v. Motorola, 105 F.3d 841 (2nd Cir. 1997) (Motorola developed the SportsTrax pager, which delivered real-time information on NBA games including score, possession, and time. Reporters provide the SportsTrax pager information by entering data into a personal computer while watching/listening to the broadcast. This data is subsequently transmitted to the Sports Team Analysis and Tracking Systems' (STATS) "host computer," and then retransmitted in a standard format to the pager. NBA brought several charges including copyright infringement. The district court granted a permanent injunction and Motorola appealed.)

In vacating the permanent injunction, the court first considered whether the games themselves are copyrightable. Since the underlying basketball games do not fall within any of the enumerated categories of "works of authorship" covered by § 102(a), the court found these athletic events are not copyrightable. The court next considered whether SportsTrax infringed on the copyrighted broadcasts of the game. Pointing out that SportsTrax and the America On-line web site only used the facts from the broadcasts, the court found that this does not constitute copyright infringement. Turning to the crux of the dispute, the court found that a narrow state law "hot-news" misappropriation claim based on

International News Service v. Associated Press could survive preemption by the federal Copyright Act. In evaluating a "hot-news" misappropriation claim, the following factors are considered:

i. Cost to plaintiff to gather information
ii. Time-sensitivity of information
iii. Whether D's use constitutes "free riding" on P's efforts
iv. Whether competition between plaintiff and defendant is direct
v. If there were free riding, would the amount of individuals free-riding constitute a disincentive to continued service?

However, since each party is bearing its own costs in gathering the information and the NBA has not shown any damages based on "free-riding" by Motorola, the NBA's claim for misappropriation is dismissed as well.

UMG Recordings, Inc. v. MP3.com, Inc., 92 F. Supp.2d 349 (S.D.N.Y. 2000) (MP3 technology enables users to store music from a CD into a computer medium. MP3.com bought about 45,000 CDs, copied the songs contained on the CDs, and stored them as MP3 files. MP3.com then provided a service entitled "My.MP3.com," which enables users to listen to these MP3 files through the Internet. After initially demonstrating that a user owned a given CD, which can be done by placing it within their hard drive or buying it through one of MP3's preferred sites, the user could listen to the MP3 file through the internet anywhere. Plaintiffs' sued for copyright infringement.)

The court entered partial summary judgment for the plaintiffs holding MP3.com liable for copyright infringement. In rejecting MP3.com's fair use defense, the court stated that even if the user owned the CD at the time of initial subscription, the user was listening to an unauthorized copy of the CD supplied by MP3.com. The court found that MP3.com's purpose and character of use of My.MP3.com was commercial in nature (attract large subscription base to draw advertising), the files supplied by MP3.com were exact copies of the entire copyrighted works, and MP3.com was simply retransmitting the copyrighted work in a different medium.

A & M Records v. Napster, Inc., 2001 U.S. App. Lexis 5446 (9th Cir. 2001) (Through a peer-to-peer file sharing process, Napster allows or facilitates its users to share, copy, and exchange MP3 files for free through the internet. Plaintiff brought charges of contributory and vicarious copyright infringement against Napster. In defending its case, Napster argued that as an internet service provider, its web site was within the safe harbor provisions of the

DMCA (see below). The district court ruled that Napster system did not fall within the safe harbor provision. Napster might assist users in sharing, but the MP3 files are actually transferred through the Internet and not Napster's web site. And if Napster met the service provider requirement of DCMA, it did not provide written notice that infringers would be terminated or take measures to prevent repeated infringement. The district court issued a preliminary injunction, finding that Napster users directly infringed the A & M copyrights and that downloading MP3 files to see whether one would like to purchase them does not constitute a "fair use." Napster appealed.)

With regard to Napster's defense of fair use, the court affirmed the district court's findings that users downloading MP3 files to "sample" the music and space-shifting do not constitute a fair use. In reviewing the plaintiff's claim for contributory infringement, the court found that Napster not only knew that its users committing copyright infringement, but also materially assisted them in such infringement because the users could not share the files without the Napster web site and software. Regarding the issue of vicarious liability, the court determined that Napster received financial benefits from an ever-increasing user base that was dependent on the availability of infringing material. Also, since Napster acted in a supervisory capacity by terminating users when it received complaints, the court determined that Napster met the requirements of vicarious liability. Finally, the court affirmed the district court's rejection of Napster's affirmative defenses under the Audio Home Recording Act and the Digital Millennium Copyright Act. Therefore, while the court affirmed the preliminary injunction, it slightly modified its scope.

3. New enforcement issues in copyright law

The Motorola, MP3.com, and Napster cases all have had enforcement of copyright protection as an underlying issue.

By its very nature, the Internet allows just about anyone to access copyrighted material, and then provides them with the opportunity to copy, manipulate, and distribute the underlying copyrighted material freely to the public. In enforcing the rights of the copyright holders, someone needs to be held accountable.

However, since most of the infringers are the invisible man (e.g., everyday individuals), there is little money or success in pursuing him. Therefore, the fear exists that in most cases, the copyright owners will go after the "deep pocket" service provider, and charge them with either direct, contributory, or vicarious copyright infringement since they provide the medium for sharing, copying, and posting of the unauthorized copyrighted material. However, if these providers are found liable for the copyright infringement of third parties, many worry that the Internet and ongoing technology would be stunted.

B. Digital Millennium Copyright Act of 1998

Congress in the Digital Millennium Copyright Act ("DMCA") addressed the tension between copyright protection and digital technology of 1998 (Public Law 105-304).

DMCA exchanges service provider liability protections for safeguards and other actions to protect copyrighted material and prevent ongoing infringement.

DMCA is divided into 5 Titles:

Title I. WIPO Treaties Implementation
Title II. Online Copyright Infringement Liability Limitation Act
Title III. Computer Maintenance or Repair Copyright Exemption
Title IV. Miscellaneous Provisions
Title V. Protection of Certain Original Designs

1. Title I. WIPO Treaties Implementation

Title I of DMCA is referred to as the "WIPO Copyright and Performances and Phonograms Treaties Implementation Act of 1998." This title implements the WIPO treaties by requiring the U.S. copyright law to:

(a) Extend US copyright law protections to works of individuals from other member nations that have not fallen into the public domain in the country of origin (foreign works are exempted from the formalities requirements of § 411(a).

(b) Adds a new *sui generis* Chapter 12 to Title 17, which requires member countries to provide effective protection against circumvention of copyright protection systems and maintaining the integrity of copyright management information.

   (i) Section 1201, however, still recognizes the affirmative defense of fair use and one may be justified in circumventing copy protection schemes in order to make fair use copies of a work.

   (ii) Section 1201(d)-(j) provides exemptions to the circumventing provisions for the following:

   - §1201(d) Nonprofit libraries, archives and educational institutions

- §1202(e) Law enforcement, intelligence, and other government activities
- §1202(f) Reverse engineering
- §1202(g) Encryption research
- §1202(h) Exceptions regarding minors
- §1202(i) Protection of personally identifying information (privacy)
- §1202(j) Security testing

(iii) Section 1202 prohibits anyone from knowingly providing or distributing false Copyright Management Information

(iv) Sections 1203 and 1204 outline the civil and criminal penalties for violating Sections 1201 or 1202.

2. **Title II: Online Copyright Infringement Liability Limitation Act**

Title II creates a new § 512 to the Copyright Act, which limits liability for service providers for:

(a) Transitory digital network communications (§512(a))
(b) System caching (§512(b))
(c) Information residing on systems or networks at direction of users (§512(c))
(d) Information Location Tools (§512(d))
(e) Nonprofit educational institutions (§512(e))

To qualify for any of these exemptions, under §512(i), the service provider must:

(1) Adopt and reasonably implement a policy of terminating the accounts of repeat infringers; and
(2) Accommodate and not obstruct "standard technical measures."

The eligibility requirements are:

(1) The provider cannot have actual knowledge of the infringement and must respond quickly to block or remove any infringing material as soon as the provider receives knowledge or notice;
(2) The provider cannot receive a financial benefit from the infringement; and
(3) The provider must quickly remove or block access to the infringing work as soon as the provider receives notice of the

claim of copyright infringement from its designated agent, which must be filed with the Copyright Office.

3. Title III. Computer Maintenance or Repair Copyright Exemption

Title III of DMCA is referred to as the "Computer Maintenance Competition Assurance Act." It amends 17 U.S.C. § 117 to allow the owners of computer program to make copies of a computer program for the purpose only of maintaining or repairing that a computer, provided the new copy is destroyed immediately after the maintenance or repair is completed.

4. Title IV. Miscellaneous Provisions

Below are a few of the topics covered by Title IV of DCMA:

Ephemeral Recordings

Section 402 of DMCA amends 17 U.S.C. § 112 to give a transmitting organization that is a broadcast radio or television station licensed by the FCC to make ephemeral recordings in order to digitally transmit a sound recording on a non subscription basis. Additionally, § 405 discusses the scope of exclusive rights in sound and ephemeral recordings.

Exemption for Libraries and Archives

Section 404 of DMCA amends 17 U.S.C. § 107 to exempt libraries and archives from placing copyright notices on copies the library or archive makes unless the original work bears a copyright notice. Also, libraries and archives are permitted to make up to 3 copies (instead of 1) of either digital or analog phonorecords, provided those copies are not distributed in that format or made available to the public outside the library or archive.

5. Title V. Protection of Certain Original Designs

Title V of DMCA is referred to as the "Vessel Hull Design Project Act," and is added to the Copyright Act as new chapter 13. It applies to any boat hull that is not longer than 200 feet that possesses "an original design of a useful article." The application of the boat hull design must be filed within 2 years of making the design public and the term of the copyright will be 10 years from the earlier of the date of registration or publication.

This provision represents the first statute that provides copyright protection for a design of a useful article with no mention of conceptual separability.

Chapter

11

APPLICATION FORMS

A. Original Registrations:

1. Form Group/Daily Newspapers: Registers complete month's issues of daily newspapers.
2. Form PA: Registers published and unpublished performing arts works.
3. Short Form/SE and Form SE/GROUP: Specialized SE forms
4. Form SE: Registers serial works that are issued in successive parts bearing numerical identification (volume 1, issue 1) and are meant to be continuous.
5. Form SR: Registers sound recording
6. Form TX: Registers published and unpublished non dramatic literary works.
7. Form VA: Registers published and unpublished visual arts.

B. Renewal Registrations

Form RE: Applies to claims to renewals under the laws effective through December 31, 1977 (1909 Copyright Act)

C. Corrections/Amplifications

Form CA.

D. Group of Contributions to Periodicals

1. Form GR/CP; and either
2: Form PA, TX, or VA.

Chapter

12

REGISTERING A COPYRIGHT

A. General

1. Most copyright registrations are easy and straightforward;
2. Proper computer software registration is much more difficult and an experienced attorney should always be consulted;
3. Prepare copyright application; and
4. Deposit the requisite number of copies with the U.S. Copyright Office.

EXCEPTION: Software, because of trade secrets, the applicant may be allowed to deposit something less than a copy.

B. Fees (effective July 1, 1999)

1. The fee for a basic registration is $30 per each application;
2. One can register a group of related claims (where appropriate) according to the following schedule:
   Serials (Form SE/Group) is $10/serial issue ($30 minimum)
   Daily newspapers and newsletters (Form G/DN) is $55
   Restored works (Form GATT/Grp) is $10/restored work ($30 minimum);
3. To correct or amplify a completed registration (Supplementary registration), there is a $65 fee; and
4. The U.S. Copyright Office can act on an expedited basis and the current fee is $500 per each application. (This is typically used if the work is going to be, or is currently involved in litigation.) This amount is in addition to the standard filing fee.*
   ($25 effective July 1, 1999).

C. Procedure for Registering

1. Completed application form;
2. Submit nonrefundable filing fee for each application; and
3. A non returnable copy (or copies) of work.

Send together to:
Register of Copyrights,

Copyright Office, Library of Congress,
Washington, D.C. 20559

* **Expedited applications** should be mailed to:

Special Handling
Library of Congress
Dept. 100
Washington, D.C. 20540

D. Procedure for Renewal

1. Property completed RE., Application; and
2. Nonrefundable $45 fee for each work effective July 1, 1999. The fee for an addendum to a renewal form is $15.

E. Incomplete Submissions

If the three elements under Procedure for Registering are not received together, the application will not be processed. Ordinarily, any incomplete submission is returned with notice of why it was not processed.

F. Effective Date of Registration

The effective date of registration is when the U.S. Copyright Office receives all of the required elements. It takes approximately 16 weeks to receive a certificate of registration if application is submitted for regular processing, or only 10 days if applicant submits application for special handling (expedited service).

Chapter 13

COPYRIGHT SECTIONS

I. General subject Matter of Copyright (§ 102)

A. Material Object Defined
1. Copies - all material objects which are not phonorecords.
2. Phonorecords - sound objects

B. Two Criteria
1. Originality
   a. Purposefully undefined;
   b. No requirement of novelty, ingenuity, or [a] esthetic merit;
   c. Others may use ideas or information revealed by the author.
2. Fixation in a Tangible Form
   a. Only writings may receive federal copyright protection.
   b. Any physical rendering of the fruits of the writing.
   c. Fixed Medium of Expression Necessary
      (1) Copy or phonorecord;
      (2) Sufficiently permanent or stable - now known or later developed;
      (3) Work is perceived, reproduced or otherwise communicated for longer than a temporary time.
         (i) May be aided by machine
         (ii) May be aided by other device.

***Unfixed works do not receive federal protection; however, they do receive protection under State common law or statute*.**

C. Illustrative Categories
1. Musical works
2. Dramatic works
3. Pantomimes and choreographic works
4. Literary works
5. Pictorial, graphic, and sculptural works

   a. No need for artistic taste or [a] esthetic value
   b. All original works intended to be useful articles regardless _of mass production, commercial exploration or potential patent protection (*Mazur v. Stein*). Useful article is one where the article has an intrinsic utilitarian function that does more than portray the article's information.
   c. Form but not mechanical aspects of work protected.
   d. Includes diagrams, models and technical drawing (architectural designs).
6. Motion pictures and audiovisual works
   a. A series of image;
   b. The capability of showing images in certain successive order;
   c. An impression of motion when the images are shown;
   d. Does not include the following:
      (i) Unauthorized fixation of live performances or telecasts;
      (ii) Live telecasts that are not fixed simultaneously with their transmission;
      (iii) Filmstrips and slide sets which, although consisting of a series of images intended to be shown in succession, are not capable of conveying and impression of motion.
7. Sound recording
   a. Original works that are musical, spoken or other sounds that have been fixed in a tangible form.
   b. Motion picture soundtracks are under the motion picture section.

D. Is a writing a Work of Authorship?
   1. Determine if the legislative history has expressly excluded it. Such as industrial or typeface design.
   2. Absent exclusion determine whether the writing has been historically excluded. Such as literary characters and title.

II. Compilations and Derivative Works (§ 102)

A. Compilations - process of selecting, bringing together, organizing and arranging previously existing material of all kinds, regardless whether the individual items are subject to copyright.

B. Derivative - process of recasting, transforming, or adapting one or more previous works. However, the preexisting work must be within § 102 General Subject Matter regardless whether it was actually copyrighted.

III. Exclusive Rights in Copyrighted Works (§ 106)

A. Five exclusive fundamental rights to copyright owners:
  1. Reproduction;
  2. Adaptation;
  3. Publication;
  4. Performance;
  5. Display.

B. Subject to §§ 107-20

IV. Ownership of Copyright (§ 201)

A. Initial Owner
  1. Author owns copyright
  2. Joint-authors
     (i) Collaboration;
     (ii) Each prepared their contribution with knowledge and intention that it be merged with the other;
     (iii) To make an inseparable work.

B. Works Made for Hire
  1. Employer is the author unless agreement.
  2. Agreement must be in writing and signed by the parties.

C. Contributions to Collective Works
  1. Collective work is a type of compilation.
  2. Each collective work must be a separate & independent work.
  3. Author's copyright in the individual piece is preserved, i.e., there is no transfer of rights.

D. Transfer
  1. Copyright may be transferred by any means.
  2. Copyright is considered personal property.
  3. Transfer must be voluntary for the rights to transfer

V. Distinction between Ownership of Copyright and Material Object (§ 202)

VI. Termination of Transfers and Licenses (§ 203)

A. Scope
  1. Advance notice within specified time limits.
  2. Includes any transfer of copyright ownership and any non-exclusive license.

B. Who May Terminate a Grant
  1. Two issues of dispute.
     a. The specific class of beneficiaries in the case of joint works.
     b. Whether anything less that unanimous consent can effectively terminate the grant.
  2. Majority of joint authors who signed the grant may terminate.
  3. Three situations in which the shares of joint authors (or their survivors) must divided under the statute:
     a. The right to effect a termination;
     b. The ownership of the terminated rights;
     c. The right to make further grants of reverted rights.
  4. Survivors who receive rights take them under a per stirpes share.

C. When Can a Grant be Terminated
  1. Five years following the expiration of a period of 35 years from the execution of the grant.

     Exception: If the grant includes right of publication the period is 35 years from the date of publication of work under grant or at the end of 40 years from date of execution of the grant, whichever term ends first.
  2. Advance notice must be provided before the 5 year window.

D. Effect of Termination
  1. Reverts ownership who owns termination interest on date termination was served regardless whether they signed the notice or not.
  2. If not effectively terminated within the 5 year window all rights will continue unchanged.

VII. Execution and Recordation of Transfers (§ 204, § 205)

A. Valid transfer
  1. Need writing
     a. Instrument of conveyance; or

   b. A note or memorandum of the transfer.
2. Signed by copyright owner or duly authorized agent.

B. Constructive notice of contents of writing:
   1. The document or attached material specifically identifies the work so that a reasonable search of title or registration number would reveal it; and
   2. Registration has been made for the work.

C. Non-exclusive license in writing and signed are valid against any later transfer regardless or recording.

VIII. Federal Preemption of Rights Equivalent to Copyright (§302)

A. Protected upon creation or when it is "fixed in a copy or phonorecord for the first time".

B. Arguments for the federal system:
   1. Promotes national uniformity;
   2. Helps give a clear interpretation of publication;
   3. § 301 will implant the limited times provisions of the Constitution;
   4. Need for effective international copyright relations.

IX. Duration of Copyright in Works Created After Effective Date (§302)

A. General
   1. Life of author and last 70 years after author's death.
   2. 1909 Act
      a. Begins date of publication.
      b. Continues 28 years from that date.
      c. May be renewed for a second 28 years (total of 56 years).
      d. Arguments for changing time based on author's life;
         (i) The present 56 year term is not long enough to insure author hand his dependents the fair economic benefits from his work.
         (ii) The tremendous growth in communications media as substantially lengthened the commercial life of a great many works.
         (iii) Although limitations on the term of copyright are obviously necessary, too short a term harms the author without giving any substantial benefit to the public.

(iv) A system based on the life of an author would go a long way toward clearing up the confusion and uncertainty involved in the vague concept of "publication," and would provide a much simpler, clearer method for computing the term.

(v) One of the worst features of the present copyright law is the provision for renewal of copyright. Under a life-plus 70 system the renewal device would be inappropriate and unnecessary.

(vi) Under the preemption provisions of § 301 and the single federal system they would establish that authors will be giving up perpetual, unlimited exclusive common law rights in their unpublished works, including works that have been widely disseminated by means other than publication.

(vii) A very large majority of countries have adapted a copyright term of the life of the author plus years after the author's death. Since American authors are frequently protected longer in foreign countries than in the United States, the disparity in the duration of copyright has provoked considerable resentment and some proposals for retaliatory legislation. A change in the basis of our copyright term would place the United States in the forefront of the international copyright community.

B. Under § 302, a work created after the death of the revise statute is protected for the life of the author plus 70 years.

C. Joint works are measured by the longest surviving author.

D. Anonymous Works, Pseudonymous and Works for Hire
   1. Protected for 95 years from publication or 120 years from creation, whichever is longer.
   2. Can be converted to life of author plus 70 years if the author is "revealed" in special records maintained by the Copyright Office.

E. Records and Presumption as to Author's Death
§ 302(d) and (e) furnish an answer to practical problems of how to discover the death dates of obscure or unknown authors.

X. Preexisting Works Under Common Law Protection (§ 303)

A. Copyrights will not expire before December 31, 2002 and attempts to encourage publication by providing 45 years more protection if the work were published before the end of 2002,
B. Protected as long as the work is not public domain in the United States.

XI. Duration of Subsisting copyrights (§ 304)

A. Increases present 56 years to 95 years in the case of copyrights subsisting in both their first and renewal term.

B. In the case of a renewal after the effective date but original copyright was prior maybe terminated under certain conditions and limitations. The 5 year window during which termination could be made effective would start 56 years after copyright was originally secured.

C. Copyrights in their First Term
   1. Preserves the renewal provision for all works in their first 28 year term.
   2. Renewal registration needed during the 28th year of copyright but length of renewal will be increased from 28 to 67 years.

D. Copyrights in their Renewal Term
   1. Copyrights in their 2nd term at any time during December 31, 1976 and December 31, 1977 (inclusively) would be extended to a total of 95 years.
   2. Adds another 39 years to any renewed copyright whose 2nd term stated during the 28 years immediately preceding January 1, 1978 (effective date).
   3. If renewal is to take place within the prior year of the effective date, the copyright is treated as in the second term and is automatically extended for 95 years.

XII. Year End Expirations of Terms (§ 305)

A. Copyright protection extend till December 31 of the year in which the term would have expired.
   Applies only to terms of copyright provided by §§ 302-04.

B. Renewal must be made within 1 year prior to the terminating December 31 date.

XIII. Notice on Visually-Perceptible Copies (§ 401)

A. Copyright Notice Functions:
   1. It has the effect of placing in the public domain a substantial body of published material that no one is interested in copyrighting;
   2. It informs the public as to whether a particular work is copyrighted;
   3. It identifies the copyright owner; and
   4. It shows the date of publication.

B. Notice on visually perceptible copies:
   1. "Copyright"; or
   2. "Copr."; or
   3. "©."

C. No need to list date of publication of preexisting compilation works.

D. Recognizable abbreviation of copyright owners are acceptable.

E. Fixed in a location and manner to give reasonable notice of claim to copyright.

XIV. Notice of Phonorecords of Sound Recordings (§ 402)

A. General
   1. Use the Symbol "P";
   2. Name of the sound recording; and
   3. Name of the copyright owner or an admissible variant.

B. Three reasons for using "P" instead of the "©":
   1. Avoid confusion between copyright in the sound recording an in the musical or literary work embodied in it;
   2. Distinguishes between copyright claims in the sound recording and in the printed test or art work appearing on the record label, album cover, etc.; and
   3. Symbol "P_" has been adopted as the international symbol for the protection of sound recordings.

XV. Notice for Publications Incorporating United States Works (§403)

Requires that when the copies or phonorecords consist "predominantly of 1 or more works of the United States

Government," the copyright notice (if any) identify those parts of the work in which the copyright is claimed.

XVI. Notice for Contributions to Collective Works (§404)

A. Basic Approach:
   1. To permit but not require a separate contribution to bear its own notice;
   2. To make a single notice, covering the collective work as a whole, sufficient to satisfy the notice requirement for the separate contributions it contains, even if they have been previously published or their ownership is different; and
   3. To protect the interests of an innocent infringer of copyright in a contribution that does not bear its own notice, who has dealt in good faith with the person named in the notice covering the collective work as a whole.

B. Separate contribution published with no notice of owner is treated as if it was published with the wrong name in the notice.

XVII. Omission of Copyright Notice (§405)

A. Protected 5 years even if omission was partial or total, unintentional or deliberate.

B. Omission of notice does not invalidate the copyright if either:
   1. If "no more than a relatively small number of copies or phonorecords have been publicly distributed without notice; or
   2. If registration for the work has already been made, or is made within 5 years after the publication without notice, and a reasonable effort is made to add notice to copies or phonorecords publicly distributed in the United States after the omission is discovered (unlike the 1909 Act).

C. Current notice requirements
   1. Unchanged for works first published before the effective date of the Act.
   2. Will be public domain if published without notice, and registration is not made before or within 5 years of publication.

XVIII. Prerequisite for Damages and Attorney's fees (§412)

Election of Statutory Damages and Attorney's fees not available if:

1. the copyright infringement of an unpublished work began before the effective date of its registration; or

2. the copyright infringement began after first publication of the work and before the effective date of its registration, unless the registration is made within 3 months of the first publication.

XIX. Infringement of copyright (§501)

A. Defined as someone "who violates any of the exclusive rights of the copyright owner as provided by §§ 106-20" of the bill, or who imports copies or phonorecords in violation of § 602.

B. Owner may sue for infringement while protecting rights of other possible owners whose rights might be protected.
   1. Allows original owner of collective or derivative works to be joined in the suit for infringement.
   2. Allows joinder of beneficial owner who is an author who had parted with legal title to the copyright in exchange for percentage of royalties based upon sales or license fees.

C. Related or Vicarious Infringer
   1. Actively operate or supervise the operation of the place wherein the performances occur; or
   2. Control the content of the infringing program, and expect commercial gain from the operation and either
      a. Direct; or
      b. Indirect benefit from the infringing performance

XX. Remedies for Infringement: (§502)

Court may grant temporary and permanent injunctions for copyright infringement.

XXI. Remedies for Infringement: Costs & Attorney's Fees (§505)

An infringer of copyright is liable for either-
1. the copyright owner's actual damages and any additional profits of the infringer; or
2. Statutory damages.

XXII. Remedies for infringement: Costs and attorney's fees (§505)

Courts have discretion to award the prevailing party of an action recovery of its full costs and/or attorney's fees.

COPYRIGHT STATUTE		
17 U.S.C. Section	**Title**	**Content**
§ 101	**Definitions**	Defines all the terms in the Copyright Act.
§ 102	**Subject Matter of Copyright in General**	Copyrights to works of authorships fixed in any tangible medium including (1) literary works, (2) musical works, (3) dramatic works, (4) pantomimes and choreography, (5) pictures, graphics and sculptures, (6) audiovisual and motion picture (7) sound recordings (8) architectural works. Protection does not extend to idea, procedure, process, system, method of operation, concept, principle, or discovery.
§ 106	**Exclusive Rights in Copyrighted Works**	Owner of © subject to §§107 to 121 can (1) reproduce material (2) prepare derivative work (3) distribute copies for sale, rental, lease, lending (4) perform the work (5) display the work and (6) for sound recordings perform means digital audio transmission.
§ 107	**Limitations on Exclusive Rights: Fair Use.**	Fair use is reproduction for the purpose such as criticism, comment, news, reporting, teaching (including multiple copies for classroom use), scholarship, or research. Reproduction for the purpose is not copyright infringement. **Test for Fair use**: (1) Purpose and character of use (2) copyrighted work's nature (3) amount and substantiality used compared to entire © work (4) effect of that use on a potential market. Fair use can be found for unpublished works as well
§ 109 (a)	**Limitations on Exclusive Rights: Effect of Transfer of Particular Copy or Phonorecord**	Can sell or dispose of possession, if subject to restored © can only do so for 12 months. Recall in patents: first sale doctrine – analog is *exhaustion of rights* (same term in Trademarks); **same proposition**: renting music, video, software is barred if there is no license.

§ 113	**Scope of exclusive rights in pictorial, graphic and sculptural works**	(a) exclusive right includes right to reproduce work in or on any kind of article. (b) no patent-like protection (c) criticism allowed (d) incorporation of artwork into building.
§ 117	**Limitations of exclusive rights: Computer programs**	Can make copy (a) if it is within use of program or for archival purposes (b) can sell or lease the program (c) can make copy for maintenance (d) definition of maintenance and repair.
§ 130	**Design protection for Boat hulls**	Design protection for Boat hulls (*Bonito Boats*) (b) definitions
§ 201	**Ownership of Copyright**	Works-for-hire employer owns the ©. For collective works, unless otherwise specified, the owner of the collective work only has the © for the contributions as part of the collective work. Ownership can be transferred
§ 202	**Ownership of copyright as distinct from ownership of material object**	Ownership of object does not mean ownership of the copyright.
§ 204 (a)	**Execution of transfers of copyright ownership**	Transfer of ownership needs to be in writing and signed by the ©'s owner.
§ 205	**Recordation of transfers and other documents**	Transfers may be recorded at the Copyright office: first come, first serve. Notice Statute.
§ 301	**Pre-emption with Respect of Other Laws**	(a) after January 1, 1978 all copyrighted works fixed in a tangible medium are only subject to the Copyright act not State Copyright law. (b) This statute does not limit State Common law before that date or in areas which the Copyright act does not protect. (c) State recording law shall not be pre-empted until 2067. (d) Statute does not pre-empt other

		Federal laws. (e) Statute has no effect on the Berne Convention. (f) Visual Artist Right's Act abolishes State common law for that area.
§ 302	**Duration of Copyright (works after 1978)**	(a) life of author plus 70 years; (b) for joint work life of last surviving author and 70 years beyond that authors death; (c) for anonymous works the © last 95 years after publication or 120 years after creation which ever comes first.
§ 408	**Copyright Registration in General**	Can register once published. For registration must deposit (b) one or more copies of the material depending on medium
§ 409	**Application for Copyright registration**	Has to include name, address, title, name of creator, year of publication etc.
§ 410	**Registration of Claim and Issuance of Certificate**	(a) Certificate is issued when the Registrar of © finds compliance with the article if there is no compliance (b) then no copyright will be issued. Can challenge that judicially under (c). Date of copyright is the date of deposit, application and fee.
§ 411	**Registration and Infringement Action**	Registration and Infringement: except for moral rights until action © registration made cannot sue. *Berne convention* full formalities at same time § 411 applies only in the U.S. to U.S. citizens
§ 412	**Registration prerequisite to certain remedies for infringement.**	Registration is required to receive statutory damages and attorney's fees.
§ 501	**Infringement of a Copyright**	Sets out definition of what infringement is.
§ 502	**Remedies for Infringement: Injunctions**	(a) can get temporary and permanent injunctions at a civil court's discretion subject to 28 U.S.C. § 1498. (b) injunction may be served anywhere.

§ 503	**Remedies for infringement: Impounding and Disposition of Infringing Articles**	(a) can impound while an action is pending. (b) Can order destruction of articles.
§ 504	**Remedies for infringement: Damages and Profits**	(a) get (1) actual damages and additional profits or (2) Statutory damages; (b) sets out *Actual Damages;* (c) *Statutory Damages* (1) no less than $ 750 up to $ 30,000 at Court's discretion and (2) up to $150,000 when © owner has the burden of proof (d) *Additional damages*
§ 505	**Remedies for infringement: Cost and Attorney Fees**	Can get attorney fees in certain © infringement actions.
§ 506	**Criminal Offenses**	(a) Criminal infringement is when a person willfully infringes a copyright (1) for commercial advantage or private financial gain or (2) distributes more than one copy of a record within 180 days with a value of more than $ 1000.
§ 507	**Limitations on Actions**	Statute of limitation for (a) criminal actions is 5 years and for (b) Civil Actions it is 3 years.

Chapter 14

TRADEMARKS

A. What Is a Trademark?

1. Generally

   a. **Definition.** A trademark is a word, logo, or package design, used by a manufacturer or merchant to identify its goods and services and distinguish them from others.

   b. **Types.** The different types of trademarks are:

      i. Brand names identify goods;

      ii. Service marks identify services;

      iii. Certification marks identify goods or services meeting certain qualifications; and

      iv. Collective marks identify goods, services or members of a collective organization.

2. How to Obtain Trademark Rights:
   To get common law trademark rights, you need not register. In order to obtain trademark rights, you should:

   a. Use the mark on or in connection with goods, or by displaying the mark in the sale or advertising of services to obtain automatic ® rights;

   b Apply to register the mark nationwide via intent to use (§ 1(b)-(d)) if you have a bona fide intent to use mark in commerce;

   c. Register with the U.S. Patent & Trademark Office (PTO).

3. Symbols Used to Give Notice of Trademark Registration

   a. Unregistered marks used to indicate that you claim common law trademark rights:

      i. TM (for trademark); or
      ii. SM (for service mark).

   b. Federal statutory trademark registration notice:

i. The symbol ®;
ii. "Registered U.S. Patent and Trademark Office"
iii. "Reg. U.S. Pat. & TM Off."

c. Federal statutory trademark registration notice is not mandatory, but you must use it to get damages from an infringer under some circumstances.

4. How Long Do Trademark Rights Last?
   a. Trademark rights may continue indefinitely as long as the owner does not abandon the mark or the mark does not become generic.
   b. Trademark must be renewed every 10 years.
   c. If the trademark is not used for 3 consecutive years, it is considered abandoned and someone else can claim an exclusive right to the mark. (*See* Lanham Act § 45, Abandonment).

5. What is Trademark infringement?
   It is an infringement for someone else to use:
   a. The same or a confusingly similar term,
   b. Within the same geographical area, or in some cases, within a natural area of expansion.

B. Purpose of Trademark Law

1. Generally:

   Policy reasons behind competition laws:
   a. Avoid monopolies: do not want one in control of the entire industry;
   b. Decrease prices for consumers;
   c. Promote fairness: if others copy a work, the product is cheapened. Therefore, competition lays out at minimum a fair playing ground; and
   d. Prevent free riding on the trademark owner's goodwill and reputation.

2. Congress, under the Copyright Clause (Art. I, § 8, cl. 8), has the power to enact laws and the court cannot abridge this power. Out of the entire world of goods Congress chose to protect the small group of patentable/copyrightable goods. The court cannot increase the scope of this on its own.

C. Two Theories of Trademark Protection

1. The Confusion Doctrine

a. The focus of early trademark law is for the prevention of deception in the market place, not the protection of intangible property rights.

b. The test of trademark infringement came to focus instead upon the ***likelihood of such confusion***.

c. The Lanham Act adopted the likelihood of confusion standard. Under both federal and state law, an unauthorized use of a trademark constitutes an infringement if it creates a likelihood of consumer confusion as to source or sponsorship.

2. The *likelihood of confusion* test serves three societal interests:
   a. Shields the public from misleading information in the marketplace.
   b. Prevents unjust enrichment of the infringer.
   c. Protects the trademark owner from the possibility that the infringer will pass off inferior products as those of the owner, thereby harming the owner's reputation among the consuming public.

3. Likelihood of Confusion Test ***(Polaroid Corp. v. Polaroid Electronics Corp.,*** 287 F2d 492 (2d Cir, *cert. denied,* 368 U.S. 820 (1961))
   a. Ability to identify goods from a particular source;
   b. Intent of the trademark owner seeks to enter the infringer's market;
   c. Good faith of the Infringer (junior) in using the mark;
   d. Quality of the infringer's product – whether it is an inferior product -- and the likelihood of confusion – whether it is less likely to cause confusion;
   e. Similarity of the marks;
   f. Similarity of the products, taking into account the following factors:
   i. style
   ii. price
   iii. appearance
   iv. function
   v. advertising
   g. Actual confusion; and
   h. Sophistication of consumers in distinguishing the products from the source.

4. <u>The Dilution Doctrine</u>

The owner's right to enjoin uses of its mark ceases at the point where consumer confusion as to source or sponsorship becomes unlikely.

The Lanham Act did not recognize the dilution theory of trademark protection until the Federal Dilution Act of 1995, but since the 1940's approximately half the states have enacted "anti-dilution" statutes. These states provide that the "likelihood of injury to business reputation or of dilution of the distinctive quality of a mark registered under this chapter or a mark valid at common law or a trade name valid at common law shall be a ground for injunctive relief notwithstanding the absence of competition between the parties or the absence of confusion as to the source of goods or services."

The law of trademark dilution aims to protect the distinctive quality of a trademark from deterioration caused by its use on dissimilar products or non-competing goods. The injury is the gradual whittling away or dispersion of the identity and hold upon the public mind of the mark or name by its use on non-competing goods.

The overriding purpose of the anti-dilution statutes is to prohibit a merchant of non-competitive goods from selling its products by trading on the goodwill and reputation of another's marks.

<u>Assuming that a mark is distinctive, dilution can occur in two ways:</u>

a. Unauthorized use may lessen the distinctiveness of the mark - such use may weaken the marks ability to bring to mind a particular product (i.e., Kodak bicycle); or

b. By undermining the positive image the owner built up for it (® tarnishment) - injury arises from the possibility that the appearance of the mark in a distasteful or inappropriate setting will lessen its commercial appeal (i.e., Tiffany Tavern).

D. An Economic Perspective behind Trademarks

1. Benefits of Trademarks

   a. Analogous to identifying individual by last, as well as first, name (Jeff Miller, not Jeff).
   b. Requires producer of ® goods to maintain a consistent quality over time and this gets across to consumers.

Self-enforcing feature - denote consistent quality and a firm has an incentive to develop a ® only if it is able to maintain consistent quality.

c. Saving in search costs made possible by the information or reputation that the ® conveys or embodies about the brand (or firm that produces the brand).
d. If the law does not prevent free riding, it will eventually destroy the information capital embodied in a ®, and the prospect of free riding may, therefore, eliminate the incentive to develop a valuable ® in the first place.

2. Costs of Legally Enforceable Trademarks

   a. A proper ® is not necessarily a public good. It has social value only when used to designate a single brand.
   b. Brand advertising presupposes trademarks. They are what enable a producer readily to identify his brand to the consumer.

3. Sources and Limitations for a Trademark
   a. Lanham Act
   b. Commerce Clause
   c. Copyright and Patent Clause
   d. First Amendment

E. Relationship between State and Federal Law

1. *Does federal action preempt state?*
   Is the product covered by federal law?

   a. If yes, then the company has a monopoly.
   b. If no, then it is either automatically free or covered by the state unfair competition law.

2. Constitution only grants patent/copyright monopoly for certain works and consumer interest is a separate issue. Unfair competition is only meant to prevent consumers from being deceived. Consequently:

   a. State can require warning label, but cannot protect copying.

   b. State can prevent manufacturers from confusing consumers through onerous schemes of fraud protection, but cannot expand upon federal patent protection.

3. Current law:

   Constitution says that in certain areas Congress can act. Therefore, in the world of products, some things are federally protected while others are not. States cannot redraw or expand this line. Thus, state unfair competition is only allowed to cover those areas not even contemplated by Congress - consumer protection. (***International New Services v. Associated Press***, 248 U.S. 215 (1918), is **overruled**). States can require stringent requirements that protect consumer confusion, but may not protect copying.

Chapter 15

TYPES OF TRADEMARKS

A. Trademark

1. Definition: "Trademarks" defined in Lanham Act § 45 as any word, name, symbol, or device, or any combination thereof used by a person or by a person who has a bona fide intention to use in commerce to identify and distinguish his or her goods, including a unique product, from those manufactured or sold by others and to indicate the source of the goods, even if that source is unknown.

2. Examples: Ferrari, Dodge.

B. Service Marks, § 3

"Service marks" defined in Lanham Act § 45 as any word, name, symbol, devices, or combinations thereof used by another to distinguish services of one person for those of another, and to indicate the source of that service even if the source is unknown (i.e., Greyhound Bus Service, Lexis, Westlaw). One must demonstrate that a service is sufficiently separate from the sale of goods. If it is only promoting, selling, or advertising one's own product, it cannot be registered as a service mark. If the service is normally expected and routinely rendered in furtherance of the sale of goods, it is insufficient to support registration of a service mark.

C. Collective Marks, § 4

"*Collective marks*" defined in Lanham Act § 45 as:

Collective membership marks are marks adopted for the purpose of indicating membership in an organization such as a union, professional society, or fraternity. It does not identify or distinguish goods or services, (i.e., ABA, Girl Scouts).

Collective trademarks and service marks are trademarks or service marks adopted by a collective organization (co-op) for use by its members in selling their individual goods or services and distinguishing those goods and service from those of non-members.

The organization cannot sell goods or services, but it may advertise or promote the goods or services under the mark (i.e., Diary Co-op; Florida Orange Growers). These marks, owned by a group, are very similar to certification marks (owned by an individual).

D. Certification Marks, § 4

1. ***Certification marks*"** defined in **Lanham Act § 45** as words, have names, symbols, devices, or combinations thereof used by one person other than its owner to certify that the goods or services of others have certain characteristics (i.e., Good Housekeeping).

    a. Owner of certification mark cannot use the mark in connection with his own goods or service.

    b. Owner must oversee other's use of the mark and prohibit others from using the mark for purposes other than certifying or from falsely certifying the existence of characteristics that their products or services lack (control the mark).

    c. Owner of certification mark may not discriminately refuse to certify goods or services that satisfy its stated objective standards for certification.

2. A geographic name can be registered as a certification mark even though it is primarily geographically descriptive. **§14(5)** - A certification mark may be canceled if the:

    a. Owner does not or is not able to control mark;

    b. Owner produces goods under the mark;

    c. Owner allows use of mark other than to certify; or

    d. Owner discriminately refuses to certify.

Chapter 16

TRADEMARK DISTINCTIVENESS

A. Four Categories of Mark Protection: In ascending order:

1. **Generic Marks are not protected**. Generic ® are the general name as to which something is called (identifies the product). Under § 14(3), at time a ® becomes generic, it is canceled. No amount of money or proof of secondary meaning can make it a valid trademark.

   a. Use of Nouns
   b. Phonetic
   c. Misspelling
   d. Adjectives
   e. Abbreviations
   f. Equivalent of Foreign Words, i.e., bank, soda, bread.

   Over time a higher "ranked" mark may descend to generic. Upon this happening, the trademark becomes unprotected.

   To stop a trademark name from becoming an unprotected generic, it is recommended that you place the generic term after the trademark (i.e., Xerox copier). Examples of common words that were once trademarks: escalator, yo-yo.

2. **Descriptive** - Under § 2(e), ® can be protected if secondary meaning is proved. Descriptive ® convey an immediate idea of the ingredients, qualities, or characteristics of the goods (describes the product). If the secondary meaning is distinctive then it may be protectable.

3. **Suggestive** - Entitled to registration with little to no proof of secondary meaning. Debate may exist as to whether ® is descriptive or arbitrary. Suggestive ® require imagination, thought, and perception to reach a conclusion. However, the title does not invoke the image of the product in the mind of the consumer, it still needs to be explained (i.e., Orange Crush, Playboy).

4. **Arbitrary or Fanciful** - Technical ®. Always protected without any proof of secondary meaning (i.e., "Kodak," "Pepsi"). There is no obvious connection between the trademark and the product/service.

   The plaintiff bears the burden of proof on the second meaning. A secondary meaning is acquired when the consuming public recognizes the mark as an identifiable good or service from a single source. One can have a different category in different markets. Today, it is very difficult to declare a ® descriptive, Therefore, a lower burden of proof to protect a ® needed.

B. Secondary Meaning

1. Definition. In order to establish secondary meaning for a term, one must show that the primary significance of the term in the minds of the consuming public is the source, not the product.

2. Factors relevant to the determination of secondary meaning include the amount and manner of advertising, the volume of sales, the length and manner of use, direct consumer testimony, and consumer surveys.

3. But the ultimate question is not the *extent* of the promotional efforts, but their ***effectiveness*** in altering the meaning of the word to the consuming public. The primary meaning is the trademark meaning

4. Secondary meaning must be the source not the product. Two ways to show secondary meaning:

   a. Exclusive and continuous use for 5 years

   b. Collect evidence (any way) of the public's perception.

Chapter 17

SUBJECT MATTER GRANTED TRADEMARK PROTECTION

A. Word Marks

Coca-Cola Co. V. Koke Co. Of America, 254 U.S. 143 (1920) Prevent the use of the name "Koke" for soda. Is Coca-Cola a generic name? At one point it was generic since it originally was made from cocaine (descriptive).However, today Coca-Cola has acquired secondary meaning (every time you see product, think of source). Although in this case we know that Coke is made by Coca-Cola, the requirement is that we all know that product comes from a single source, even though we may not who the source is.

B. Trade Dress

Test for Trade Dress Protection:

a. Acquired second meaning;
b. Feature is non-functional;
c. Consumers are likely to confuse the plaintiff's product with the defendant's product.

NOTE: If use was done in bad faith, then one will be prevented from using surname.

COLOR DEPLETION THEORY

There are a limited number of colors in the universe. To permit one, or a few, producers to use colors as ® would deplete the supply of usable colors to the point where competitors inability to find a suitable color will put that competitor at a significant disadvantage.

C. Slogans

§ 23(c) of the Lanham Act explicitly provides that slogans are registrable on the Supplemental Register.

Slogan or word series can be registered and protected if it functions to identify and distinguish the ® owner's goods or services from those of others. A slogans length is relevant to its ability to act as a

®. The longer it is, the harder it becomes to understand when read casually and without careful study, thereby diminishing the uniqueness and distinctiveness of the phrase which are essential to its function. Slogan must be distinctive. However, if it is merely descriptive but has acquired secondary meaning, it is protected.

D. Surnames

§ 23(c) of the Lanham Act explicitly provides that surnames are registrable on the Supplemental Register.

§ 2(e) (4) prohibits registration of ® which are ***primarily merely a surname***. However, this rule is not an absolute bar. A name that has a meaning other than as a surname (i.e., Bird, Miller, King) is not primarily merely a surname. One can register a surname if it has acquired, through usage, a secondary meaning. If a surname has acquired secondary meaning, and is registered, and a person with the same surname wishes to use that the ®, courts must balance:

1. Rights of the first user against the rights of a second user who wishes in good faith to use his true family name in a similar line of business. In order to prevent customer confusion, one may have to add initial or first name to surname or a disclaimer to ®. If court finds that second user has acted in bad faith (riding on coattails), then registration will be denied.
2. Personal property right for oneself to use his name in business against the public's right to be free from any confusion resulting from the concurrent use of similar names.

E. Sound

Sound can be granted trademark protection as long as it is distinctive, and not merely functional. For example, think of the 'Intel Inside' music, or the 'NBC' chimes.

F. Scent

A scent can also be granted trademark protection as long as it is distinctive, and not merely functional.

G. Composite Marks

A composite mark, which contains two or more different elements, can be registered even though not all of its elements could be granted protection individually. Thus, a composite mark is evaluated as a whole - protection is granted for the combination of the terms.

Chapter 18

ACQUIRING TRADEMARK RIGHTS

A. Generic Marks

A generic mark is the common descriptive name of the good or service it is used to identify. It cannot serve as a valid ® because it is the common name of all goods and does not distinguish origin. Often generic words originated as is. However, once the public took over the name, the original user lost all rights (i.e., thermos, aspirin).

B. Immoral or Scandalous Marks

1. **Definition**. § 2(a) of the Lanham Act prohibits registration of Immoral, Deceptive, Scandalous, or Disparaging Matter.
2. Example of Scandalous. Not many things are scandalous, but the following have been determined to be scandalous:
   a. Mark comprising of a photograph of a man and woman kissing in a manner appearing to expose the man's genitalia.
   b. "Bullshit" for attaché cases, handbags, purses, belts, and wallets.
   c. Silhouette of a defecating dog.
3. **What is scandalous?** Something that is vulgar or shocking to the sense of decency or propriety.
4. **TEST** for scandalous:
   a. Look at seriousness of purpose (message conveyed).
   b. No vulgarity, swear words, feces, or naked body parts.

C. Deceptive and Deceptively Misdescriptive

1. Difference between Deceptive and Deceptively Misdescriptive Terms:
   a. ***Deceptive*** (§ 2(a)) – It leads the consumer to think the product is what it is not and influences her buying decision. Complete bar: One cannot get registration on a deceptive mark under § 2(a).

b. ***Deceptively misdescriptive*** (§ 2(e)) – Manufacturer misdescribes product, or the product name appears to claim that it is what it is not, but does not influence the buying decision, does not hurt the market or undermine buying power. Not barred if can prove secondary meaning (distinctiveness).

2. Test for Deceptiveness:
   a. Is the term misdescriptive of the character, quality, function, composition, or use of the goods?
   b. If so, are prospective purchasers likely to believe that the misdescription actually describes the goods?
   c. If so, is the misdescription likely to affect the decision to purchase?

D. Geographic Terms: Primarily Geographically Descriptive or Deceptively Misdescriptive Marks

1. § 2(e) of the Lanham Act prohibits registration of Geographic Terms.

   a. ® shall be refused registration if ® is primarily geographically descriptive (except as indication of origin) § 2(e) (2)), or primarily geographically deceptively misdescriptive (§ 2(e) (3)).

   b. ® is primarily geographically descriptive or deceptively misdescriptive if it conveys to meaningful segment of the purchasing public primarily a geographic connotation and those persons are likely to think that the goods come from that place. This includes cities, states, countries, regions, mountains, rivers, nicknames of any of these (Rockies, Lone Star State), or map like configurations (shape of state).

2. If the goods actually come from that geographic location, it is geographically descriptive. Therefore it is registrable if secondary meaning is demonstrated.

3. If the goods do not come from the geographical location, you must determine if it is deceptive or geographically deceptively misdescriptive.

   a. If geographically deceptively misdescriptive, it is registrable if secondary meaning was obtained prior to December 8, 1993.
   b. If deceptive, it is never registrable.

E. Marks That Are Merely a Surname

§ 2(e) of the Lanham Act prohibits marks that are merely a surname ® shall be refused registration if ® is primarily merely a surname (§ 2(e) (4)).

F. Confusion

§ 2(d) of the Lanham Act prohibits registration of confusing mark ® shall be refused registration if it would cause confusion based on concurrent use of another ®. *See infra* Concurrent Use.

G. Prior Use

Lanham Act § 2(d) prohibits the registration of any ® that is confusingly similar to another ® that is in use and that has not been abandoned. However, if two ®s are concurrently being used, the PTO may grant both ®s registration based on certain limitations or conditions in order to prevent consumer confusion. *See infra* Priority and Concurrent Use

H. Functionality

1. Courts do not want to give ® monopolies where patent law protection is denied. However, the line between functional features (which cannot serve as ®) and nonfunctional features (which can serve as ®) reflect the courts judgment that competitor's legitimate need for the latter, outweighs the danger of consumer confusion while the need for functional features does not.

2. <u>Main Tests for Functionality</u>:

    a. Whether competitors need to copy the feature in order to compete effectively. They will need to copy if the feature in question will give them a competitive advantage (if it functions in manner superior to all alternatives; or if it is more economical to manufacture than the alternatives). Therefore, one can copy the feature if it is the best or cheapest way to do it. This test is used by majority of courts, including the Federal Courts.

    b. If the feature plays a part in the ultimate utilitarian function of the product, then it is functional. However, if the feature primarily only serves to identify the producer or is only ornamental, it will not be deemed functional. Availability of alternatives is not determinative.

c. Utility patent will usually make the feature functional, especially if it is dictated by the patented invention. But, a design patent usually helps in showing that a feature is not functional.

***de facto* functional** means that the design of a product has a function (i.e., a bottle of any design holds fluid).

***de jure* functional** means that the product is in its particular shape because it works better in this shape.

NOTE: The potential for merger problems gives rise to the requirement that the design element be nonfunctional or else one could prevent competition by trademarking all potential containers. The question is: Is the subject matter made in the form it must be made if it is to accomplish its purpose? Thus, the public policy objective is not the right to copy the article, but the need to copy the article, or the right to compete effectively.

Will enjoining others from using the design inhibit competition in any way? - Yes, **if** the design is the best or one of a few superior designs available.

3. Four categories of evidence which are useful to demonstrate that a particular design is superior, and hence *de jure* functional:
   a. A utility patent that discloses the utilitarian advantages of the design;
   b. Advertising materials touting the design's utilitarian advantages;
   c. Facts tending to establish the unavailability to competitors of alternative designs; and
   d. Facts indicating that the design results from a comparatively simple or cheap method of manufacturing the product or container.

4. To gain protection, form cannot be dictated by function ***and*** there must be secondary meaning.

   When one considers whether a color is functional, for example, one must consider whether alternative colors are available in order to avoid the fettering of competition. If competition will be hindered, the color in question is *de jure* functional.

I. Other Bars to Registration

§§ 2(b) and 2(c) of the Lanham Act.

No ® by which the goods of the applicant may be distinguished from the goods of others shall be refused registration on the principal register on account of its nature unless it:

a. **§ 2(b)** - Consists of the flags or code of arms of the United States, state, or foreign nation;

b. **§ 2(c)** - Consists of the name, portrait, or signature of living individual without individual's consent, or the name, signature, or portrait of a deceased President of the United States during the life of his widow, if any, except by the written consent of the widow.

Chapter

19

ACQUIRING TRADEMARK RIGHTS

A. Adoption and Use

"***Use in Commerce***" defined in **Lanham Act § 45** as the "bona fide intent use of the mark in the ordinary course of trade, and not merely to reserve a right in a mark."

"***Commerce***" defined in **Lanham Act § 45** as "all commerce which may lawfully be regulated by Congress." Thus, it only applies to interstate commerce, not intrastate commerce.

"***Trademark***" defined in **Lanham Act § 45** as "any word, name, symbol, or device, or any combination thereof- (1) used by a person, or (2) which a person has a bona fide intention to use in commerce and applies to register on the principal register established by this Act, to identify and distinguish his or her goods, including a unique product, from those manufactured or sold by others and to indicate the source of the goods, even if that source is unknown."

B. Ownership

1. **Ownership of a mark is established** by priority of appropriation. Priority is established not by conception but by bona fide usage. However no single factor is determinative. Aside from federal registration, determining ownership must take into account:
    a. Invented and first affixed the mark onto the product.
    b. Which party's name appeared with the trademark.
    c. Which party maintained the quality and uniformity of the product.
2. With which party did the public identify the product and make complaints. What does the public associate with the ®? Who controls the use?
    a. Marketing - producer usually owns the ®.
    b. Personality - performers own the ®.

3. **What Is Needed to Own a ®:**

Must be first person to have bona fide use in open trade on a particular product and continue control.

a. Timing (first to use)
b. Bona fide usage
c. Exhibit control over ®
d. Use has to be open (If not trying to enter market, then you do not get protection.)

A ® is distinct from a © where protection attaches from moment of creation. In ®, if you are not intending to use ®, you get no protection.

Purpose of © - want to promote creative process.
Purpose of ® - reward those who keep market distinguishable.

NOTE: Internet activity is interstate commerce. If there is no interstate commerce, then there can be no Lanham Act protection.

C. Priority and Concurrent Use

1. Priority

Rule: The first person to USE a ® in trade obtains ownership rights in it.

If two people begin to use a ® in ***Good Faith*** at the same time, courts may consider the equities of the case in determining who is the owner (i.e., money spent, advertising, how much work one has done, "token" use). If the court finds a way for ***Both*** users to continue using the ® without undue consumer confusion, it will do so (i.e., different labeling or colors). If priority is close, then it will boil down to race to establish a secondary meaning between the parties.

"**OPEN USE**" = To acquire ® rights, there must be "open" use. Internal shipment of goods which do not reach the relevant class of purchaser is not considered an open use, thus cannot give rise to ® rights. Must be open to the market in which you intend to sell to - actual use in trade.

Defining markets is a matter of art. Who wins depends on how attorneys present case. Stadium has the right to maintain control of its ®. Wants money from Becker for usage, thus, Becker should obtain a license from MSA. ® encourages overprotection. If the trademark holder does not protect her trademark, she loses all her rights.

Examples of use analogous to ® use to enable the user to tack on non-trademark usage to establish priority under § 2(d) include prior use of a term: in advertising brochures; in catalogues and newspaper ads; and in press releases and trade publications. Analogous use priority may be found even where the goods or services are not yet offered or available at the time the analogous use activities are undertaken.

2. ***The Evans Chemetics 2-Prong Test:***
   a. Whether use of a ® in advertising prior to the actual rendition of services under the ® is adequate to establish rights in the ® depends on the evidence: at least the character and amount of the advertising must have been sufficient to have created a public awareness of the ® and its connection with the services to be offered.
   b. Whether the services were actually rendered or available for performance soon enough after the initial advertising campaign to preclude a finding that the advertising was merely an attempt to preempt a ® for use at an indefinite future date.

3. Concurrent Use. Where there is concurrent use, there are two questions to ask:

   a. When was the mark applied for?
   b. Was there continuous prior use in the area?

      If a junior user occupies a remote geographic area in good faith, he will have a defense against the senior users attempt to stop him within that territory. This is true even if the marks are confusingly similar because the senior user had adequate notice of the situation.

4. **§ 22 Registration as Constructive Notice of Claim of Ownership** - *Registration* of a ® on the Principal Register is *constructive notice* (see § 7(c)) to the world of this registrant's use of the ®. Anyone who begins using a confusingly similar ® after the effective date of the constructive notice cannot claim to have begun his own use in good faith.

5. **§ 7(c) Constructive Notice** - Contingent on the registration of a ®, the *filing* of the application of ® shall constitute constructive use of the ®, conferring a right of priority,

nationwide in effect, on or in connection with the goods or services against any person except for a person whose ® has not been abandoned and who, prior to such filing:

a. Has used the mark (see § 33);
b. Has filed an application to register the ® which is pending (both still in PTO) or has resulted in registration of the ®; or
c. Has filed a foreign application to register the ® on the basis of which he or she has acquired a right of priority, and timely files and application under § 44(d) to register the ® which is pending or has resulted in registration of the ®.

6. **§ 33(b)(5) Limited Area Defense to Registrant's Exclusive Use** - Confers upon a junior user, such as Thrift Cars, the right to continued use of an otherwise infringing ® in a remote geographical area if that use was established prior to the other party's federal registration.

   Even if a ® owner has superior rights in a particular area due to federal registration, he will not be entitled to enjoin another's use in that area unless:

   i. The registrant is also using the ® in the area that the defendant is occupying;
   ii. Has presence in that area;
   iii. Has concrete plans to begin use there in the immediate future; or
   iv. Likely to cause consumer confusion.

D. Intent to Use

1. 15 U.S.C. § 1051(b) [Lanham Act § 1(b)] (enacted in 1988)

   A person who has a bona fide intention, under circumstances showing the good faith of such person, to use a trademark in commerce may apply to register the trademark on the principal register hereby established:

   a. By filing in the PTO -
      - a written application; and
      - a drawing of the mark.

   b. By paying in the PTO the prescribed fee.

   c. By complying with such rules or regulations, not inconsistent with law, as may be prescribed by the Commissioner.

2. Process for Obtaining a Mark through an Intent-to-Use Application:

a. File an application with the PTO claiming a bona fide intent to use a ® in connection with a particular product or good in interstate trade or commerce (§ 1(b) (1) (A)).
b. Application must identify the goods or service on which the ® will be used and the manner of intended use (§ 1(b) (1)).
c. Application must state that to the best of applicant's knowledge, no other person has the right to use the ® (§ 1(b) (1)).
d. PTO makes an initial examination (looks for descriptiveness or other reasons for lack of trademarkability) and publishes for opposition (§ 12(a)).
e. If no successful opposition, then PTO will issue notice of allowance (§ 13(b) (2)). (Opposition under § 13(a)-Anyone who feels they will be harmed by ® can oppose ® within 30 days of publication (can get extensions)).
f. Applicant has 6 months to begin actual use of ® (§ 1(d) (1)).
g. One 6-month extension is available automatically upon applicant's request (need to show bona fide intent to use (§ 1(d) (2)).
h. Up to four additional extensions are granted upon a showing both a bona fide intent to use and good cause (§ 1(d) (2)).
i. Therefore, applicant has a maximum of 3 years to begin actual use of its ®.
j. When applicant actually uses the ® in trade or commerce, he must file a statement of use (§ 1(d) (1)).
k. PTO then conducts a second examination (§ 1(d) (1)).
l. If accepted, then the ® is registered (§ 1(d) (1)).
m. Under § 7(c), constructive use will allow a registrant to prevail over any other person who actually used the ® before registration, but after time of filing intent-to-use application.

3. Registration Problems

a. Opposition to mark.
b. Examiners consider mark unregistrable.
c. More than one person is applying to use same mark at the same time.

NOTE: Under § 1(c), any time during examination of an application, an applicant may amend his application to fit the requirements of § 1(a) if he has used the ® in commerce.

Under § 1(d) (4), failure to file a timely statement of use (i.e., within 3 years) results in abandonment of the application. Under § 44, foreign applicants may, relying upon a home country registration, register in the United States, notwithstanding their lack of use of the ® anywhere in the world.

Chapter 20

FEDERAL REGISTRATION OF TRADEMARKS

A. The Process of Obtaining a Registered Trademark ®

1. Must have already used the ® in trade or interstate commerce.
2. File an application with PTO that contains:
    a. Identification of the ® with particular features;
    b. Specify the official class in which the goods or services fall;
    c. Applicant's name and address;
    d. Identify in specific ordinary terms the goods or services for which the ® has been used;
    e. Date of first use of ® (can be anywhere, i.e., intrastate commerce);
    f. Date of first interstate commerce or international use of ®;
    g. Manner of use (i.e., labels, hang tags, brochures, stationery, advertisements);
    h. 3 specimens showing how ® actually used;
    i. Color features of ®;
    j. Declaration (all statements are true and no other person has a right to the ®);
    k. Drawings to accompany the certificate of registration.
3. Filing fee - currently $245 per class.
4. Examination by the PTO to verify that ® complies with statutory requirements and determine if any grounds for rejecting the ®: generic;
    a. § 2(a) - scandalous, immoral, or deceptive;
    b. § 2(b) - flags or code of arms of the United States, state, or foreign nation;

c. § 2(c) - name, portrait, or signature of living individual without individual's consent, or the name, signature, or portrait of a deceased President of the United States during the life of his widow, if any, except by the written consent of the widow;

d. § 2(d) - any ® that would cause confusion based on concurrent use;

e. § 2(e)

(1) merely descriptive or deceptively misdescriptive,
(2) primarily geographically descriptive (except as an indication of origin),
(3) primarily geographically deceptively misdescriptive, or
(4) primarily merely a surname;

f. § 2(f) - merely descriptive, deceptively misdescriptive, primarily geographically descriptive (except as indication of origin), and primarily merely a surname can be overcome by secondary meaning (proof of substantially exclusive and continuous use of ® in commerce for 5 years before the date on which the claim of distinctiveness is made).

5. If application is approved, it is then published in the "Official Gazette."

6. Time for opposition (challenge the registration as inappropriate under the Lanham Act) or concurrent use proceeding (§ 2(d)).

7. If no opposition, they will issue certificate of registration within 3 months.

8. If examiner rejects application, one can appeal to the Trademark Trial and Appeal Board (T.T.A.B.). Later appeals are taken to a federal circuit court. However, federal courts do not hold exclusive jurisdictions over trademark claims. Burden is on PTO.

B. Principal Register

1. Shows ownership and validity thereof;
2. National protection;
3. Protection against counterfeiting;
4. Publication to others;
5. Bars infringing imports;
6. Incontestability after 5 years;
7. Treble damages;

8. Promotes settlement; and
9. Evidence in Court

C. How to Maintain Trademark Rights

1. **§ 8** - During the 6th year of registration, the owner must file an affidavit stating that the ® is still in use (together with specimens which evidence such use). Failure to do so is automatic cancellation of the registration.

2. **§ 9** - Every 10 years after registration, the owner must renew the registration by filing a similar affidavit of use and specimens. Failure to do so is automatic cancellation of the registration.

D. Cancellation of Registration - § 14

1. During the first five years of a ®'s registration a person who believes himself injured by the registration may file a petition with the PTO to cancel the registration on any ground that would have precluded registration in the first place.

2. After five years of registration, the Lanham Act narrows the available grounds for cancellation. After five years, available grounds for cancellation are narrowed irrespective of ® incontestability status.

3. Available Grounds for cancellation after 5 years of registration:
   a. generic;
   b. abandonment;
   c. obtained through fraud;
   d. deceptive, scandalous, disparages a person, institution, belief, or national symbol or brings him or it into disrepute; constitutes a geographical indication which, when used on or in connection wines or spirits, identifies a place other than the origin of the goods;
   e. includes the insignia of a government, or includes the name, likeness or signature of a living person without his written consent or of a deceased U.S. President without the written consent of his or her surviving spouse; or
   f. in the case of certification mark, the owner has made improper use of the mark or has failed adequately to police others' use of it.

4. **Unavailable Grounds for cancellation after 5 years of registration:**

   a. Not inherently distinctive and lacks secondary meaning;

b. ® is confusingly similar to a ® or trade name that someone else used prior to the registration and continues to use; or
c. ® is functional.

E. Supplemental Register

1. Marks "not registrable on the Principal Register" may be registered on the Supplemental Register if they are "capable of distinguishing the applicant's goods or services."

2. Advantages of the Supplemental Register:
   a. Use of federal courts in regards to state rights.
   b. Limited benefits under trademark treaties.
   c. Publication to others.
   d. After 5 years use the mark may be transferred to the Principal registry.
   e. Evidentiary purpose.

3. <u>Disadvantage</u>. However, a huge disadvantage is that the mark is not fully protected as it could be under the Principal Registry and federal laws.

Chapter 21

TRADEMARK INFRINGEMENT

Lanham Act § 32 - Infringement

To win an infringement suit under § 32 must show:
Use in commerce, or a reproduction, counterfeit, copy or colorable imitation of a ***registered*** mark, that is likely to cause confusion, or to cause mistake or to deceive.

At one time it was that only the same ® on directly competing goods was an infringement. Thus, in the 1912 case of *Borden Ice Cream v. Borden Condensed Milk*, the court found no infringement because ice cream and milk do not directly compete. Five years later however, the Second Circuit found that Aunt Jemima's pancake syrup infringed Aunt Jemima's pancake batter.

A. Likelihood of Confusion

1. Factors

Legal Likelihood of Confusion vs. Actual Confusion

Polaroid Corp. V. Polarad Electronics Corp., 287 F.2d 492 (2d Cir.), *cert. denied*, 368 U.S. 820 (1961). Eight factors for evaluating likelihood of confusion between non-identical goods or services:

i. Strength of plaintiff's ®;
ii. Degree of similarity between P's and D's ®s;
iii. Proximity of the products or services;
iv. Likelihood that plaintiff will bridge the gap;
v. Evidence of actual confusion;
vi. Defendant's good faith in adopting the ®;
vii. Quality of defendant's product or service;
viii Sophistication of the buyers.

> "Even this extensive catalogue does not exhaust the possibilities - the court may have to take still other variables into account."

2. **Analysis for evaluating likelihood of confusion factors:**

   a. **Strength of plaintiff's ®** - The stronger the plaintiff's ®, the more likely it is that consumers seeing the defendant's allegedly similar ® will be confused about its source.

   b. **Degree of similarity between plaintiff's and defendant's ®s**

      i. *Similarity of Appearance* - This is usually dealing with picture or design ®s. A court will look at the *overall impression* created by each ®.

      ii. *Similarity of Sound* - This focuses on how the ® sounds phonetically. It is important because very often consumers never actually see the ®, but only hear it (i.e., S.O. & ESSO do not look alike, but sound confusingly similar when heard; DRAMAMINE & BONAMINE are also confusingly similar based on a linguistic test).

      iii. *Similarity of Meaning* - The mental image evoked by ®s may overpower any differences between them in sound or appearance, leading to a finding of likelihood of confusion (i.e., CYCLONE & TORNADO or PLEDGE & PROMISE for similar products are confusingly similar because they evoke similar images in the consumers' minds; *Pegasus* case is also an example of this; CHATNOIR & BLACK CAT are confusingly similar because to people who speak French, they mean the same thing).

      If the ® looks or sounds similar, but presented in a way that is distinctive, courts will not find confusion even if they are for similar goods. If you have the brand name in addition to the product name very obviously displayed on the label, likelihood of confusion will be reduced.

   c. **Proximity of the products or services** - Are the plaintiff's and defendant's goods likely to be sold in the same or same kind or same area of stores?

   d. **Likelihood that plaintiff will bridge the gap** How likely the plaintiff is to begin selling the products or services which the defendant is trying to sell with a similar ®. Even if the plaintiff has no immediate plan to sell the same kind of goods or services through use of the ®, the court may still consider the plaintiff's interest in reserving the option to use the ® on such goods or services in the more distant future.

e. **Evidence of actual confusion** - Not necessary to prove that the defendant's use causes a likelihood of confusion. If available, however, such evidence could be highly persuasive. Such evidence is highly persuasive. This is proven by survey evidence.

f. **Defendant's good faith in adopting the ®** - Usually when the goods are not directly competitive, court will weigh the equities of each parties use. If the defendant did not intentionally copy to "cash in" on the plaintiff's goodwill and has expanded significant amounts of money in promoting its ®, a court will be more hesitant to provide relief to the plaintiff.

If have bad faith, there is a presumption of actual confusion...

g. **Quality of defendant's product or service** - If both parties use their ®s on the same or related types of services, then there is a *greater* likelihood of confusion.

h. **Sophistication of the buyers** - What is the market of consumers? The more sophisticated the potential purchasers and the more costly the goods or services, the more careful and discriminating the purchasers will be and the less likely the chance they will be mislead or confused.

3. Infringement occurs in 2 ways:

a. Prevents a defendant's use of a confusingly similar ® that may cause consumers to buy defendant's goods when they meant to buy the plaintiff's (diversion of sales).

b. Damage to goodwill: non-competing goods, but defendant has a confusingly similar ® that suggests affiliations with the plaintiff that does not exists and leads consumers into assigning blame on the plaintiff for the poor quality.

A **test for ® infringement** is whether the defendant's use of the ® is likely to cause an appreciable number of consumers to be confused about the source affiliation or sponsorship of goods. Does the use create a likelihood that consumers will associate the defendant's goods with the plaintiff?

One cannot assume a side-by-side comparison by the consumer of plaintiff and defendant's goods. A defendant's intent to cause confusion is strong evidence that confusion is likely.

- When looking at ® infringement cases, what matters is the evidence that the parties set forth and how they make their case (fact determinative).
- Where an infringer adopts a particular name with knowledge of plaintiff's ®, courts presume that there was an intent to copy the ®.
- Today, court's have found that placing a brand name in connection with a ® is starting to have great weight in likelihood of confusion cases (if you have a house name, less likelihood of confusion will be found).
- Looking at *Mobil*, *Gallo*, and *CBS*, the strength of the ® is extremely important. If you invest in a ® and build it up, you will have an easier chance in keeping others out.

c. Determinative Factors (in general):

i. Strength of plaintiff's ®; and
ii. Intent to deceive – See ***Banfi Products v. Kendall-Jackson Winery Ltd.***, 74 F. Supp.2d 188 (E.D.N.Y. 1999)

4. Secondary Confusion/Post-Sale

Secondary Confusion: Post-sale confusion is when the purchaser is not confused about what he is buying (i.e., knows that it is an imitation), but other people (potential purchasers) seeing the goods in the purchasers possession after the sale may be confused about their source. This could lead to injury of the producer's goodwill (i.e., *Rolex* watches).

Even if a consumer is not "actually" confused at the point of sale, this will not change the likelihood that others will associate the copy with the original, whether at the point of sale or post-sale. We care about both the purchaser and ***subsequent viewers*** of the product (potential purchasers).

5. *The Court went through factors similar to Polaroid:*

a. **Similarity**: Pre-sale packages are not similar and each has the brand name on the package.

b. **Proximity**: Irrelevant because there are few brands in the market. Therefore, it is nature that they would be sold in close proximity.

c. **Intent to Pass-off**: Jockey is not trying to pass-off because they prominently indicate their name and spent a lot of money in advertising.

d. **Actual Confusion**: No evidence probative of actual confusion.

e. **Survey Evidence:** No surveys were submitted.

f. **Costs and Conditions of Purchase**: Both same level of quality, cost the same, and are both inexpensive. Inexpensive products lead to unsophisticated consumers.

g. **CONCLUSION:** The Court found that Jockey established that no likelihood of confusion exists between the two products.

6. Reverse Confusion:
The public comes to assume that the senior user's products are really the junior user's products or that the former has become somehow connected to the latter. The result is that the senior user loses the value of the ® in its product identity, corporate identity, control over its goodwill and reputation, and ability to move into new markets. Even after you find that the theory of reverse confusion applies, you still need to find if there exists legal likelihood of confusion.

B. Contributory Infringement

Contributory Infringement - A person may be found to be vicariously liable for another's ® infringement if he has assisted in the infringement by:

1. Inducing infringement - Intentionally suggesting either directly or impliedly that the other person infringed the plaintiff's ® and the other does infringe (*i.e.*, Manufacturer suggests to retailer substitute his goods for another's similar goods to customers who ask for the others by name - If the retailer does this, he is an infringer and by the manufacturer asking to do this, he is a contributory infringer); or

2. Knowingly aiding infringement - When a defendant sells goods to another knowing or having reason to know that the buyer will use the goods in direct infringement of the plaintiff's ®.

RULE ABOUT CONTRIBUTORY INFRINGEMENT:

One has no duty to actively discover infringing activities, but once you have actual knowledge of infringement, if you fail to prevent it, you will be liable for contributory infringement.

Chapter

22

TRADEMARK MECHANICS

A. Genericism

1. Definition. A generic mark is the common descriptive name of the good or service it is used to identify. It cannot serve a valid ® because it is the common name of all goods and does not distinguish origin. Often generic words originated as ®s. However, once the public took over the name, the original user lost all rights (i.e., thermos, aspirin).

2. ***Standard for Determining Whether a ® Is Generic:*** Look to see if the primary significance of the ® to the public is:

   a. The common name of the product or service; or
   b. An indication of origin.

   The fact that there are alternative common names is irrelevant as is evidence regarding measures the person claiming the term as a ® has taken trying to prevent the public from using the term as a common name.

   A descriptive term, such as "tasty," "delicious," or "light" is not absolutely generic - one must look at the specific use.

3. Finding of Genericism. A finding of genericism is not the end of the story. You may still have a claim of passing off. Therefore, maybe be subject to labeling remedies to avoid confusion.

4. Evolution of Genericism. One can turn a competitor's ® into a generic ®. However, if act prematurely, this will be ® infringement. One needs public to come along with you.

5. **Using Survey Evidence to Prove Genericism.** Survey evidence usually is the strongest evidence you can get.

   a. **Two Questions you must ask:**
      i. How many people identify the ®?
      ii. How many people identify the ® as a particular source?

If you put these two questions together, can determine how many people use the term generically.

b. **How can one negate survey evidence?**
   i. What manner were questions asked? (If one asks a leading question or subjective question, evidence is weaker).
   ii. How many people did you ask?
   iii. Who did you ask? (A particular market, random sample, actual purchasers).
   iv. If the case deals with a trademarked color, the survey could possibly be thrown out if the questions on the survey failed to take color blindness into account.

NOTE: The survey evidence used here is as good as one can get. Found out number of people who use the subject term, number of people who knew that the term represented a particular source, and the number of people who used a different term.

B. THE TRADEMARK CLARIFICATION ACT OF 1984

Congress overruled the *Anti-monopoly* decision by amending the Lanham Act:

i. Trademarks can apply to unique products.
ii. The single source (producers) of the goods may be unknown (name). No need to know the name of the source as long as you know that it is one source.
iii. Purchaser motivation shall not be a test for loss of ® significance.
iv. Trademark may be used for a dual purpose (identifying source and goods).

C. Abandonment

1. Statutory Language. ***Abandonment*** [§ 45] - A mark shall be deemed to be "abandoned" when either of the following occurs:

   a. When its use has been discontinued with intent not to resume such use. Nonuse for 3 consecutive years shall be *prima facie* evidence of abandonment.
   b. When any course of conduct of the owner, including acts of omission as well as commission, causes the mark to become the generic name.

2. Discontinued Use. A ® will be deemed abandoned when the registrant has discontinued use of the ® through the country in connection with the particular good or service and manifests no intent to resume use within the reasonably foreseeable future.

3. Loss of Significance. A ® is also considered abandoned when the registrant through acts or omissions cause the ® to lose significance as a ®.

   a. Assignment of a ® in gross (without goodwill attached): If this is done, there is no way to insure that the ® will continue accurately to inform perspective customers about the nature and characteristics of the product or service the ® identifies (i.e., mislead consumers).

   b. If you license a ® without adequate supervision, it will lose its significance as a ® because there will be no assurance that the licensees product or services will retain the characteristics and level of quality that the public has come to associate with the ® (i.e., may deceive the public). ® no longer has an informative function, therefore loses significance as a ®. To protect oneself against this, assignor must make routine inspections of the licensees' operation. Trivial or token interim use is insufficient to avoid a finding of abandonment.

4. **Non - Use**

5. **Assignment in Gross**

   Prior to the Lanham Act, some courts held that licensing of a ® worked as an abandonment. Others allowed it so long as the licensor retained control over the quality of the goods produced by the licensee. The Lanham Act adopts the latter view.

   § 5 provides that use of the mark by related companies does not affect the validity of the mark and its registration.

   § 45 then defines a related company as one over which the registrant controls the nature and quality of the goods or services in connection with which the mark is used. This is to prevent the public from the danger that products bearing the same ® might be of diverse qualities.

   An owner is not required to act immediately against every possible infringing use to avoid a holding of abandonment. (*See University Bookstore v. Board of Regents* (T.T.A.B. 1994)).

In cases in which courts have found that a licensor justifiably relied on a licensee for quality control, some special relationship existed between the parties. (*See Stanfield v. Osborne Industries* (10th Cir. 1995)).

NOTE: Crucial Question: Is the licensor still exercising a degree of control over the licensee?

D. Incontestability

1. **§ 15 of the Lanham Act - *Incontestability***
   A ® that has been in continuous use for five consecutive years will obtain "incontestability" status upon the registrant's filing of an affidavit to that effect that truthfully states that there has been no final decision adverse to the registrant's claim of ownership of ® and that there is no proceeding presently pending involving the registrant's rights in the ®. Incontestability gives the registrant an advantage in an infringement action (regardless of whether the registrant is the plaintiff or the defendant), though not as great an advantage as the name might suggest. For the most part, the incontestable ® is subject to all the same challenges and defenses as a ® that had not attained incontestability status would be.

2. Challenging a Trademark. **However, the following arguments can always be raised challenging a ®.**

   a. The trademark is generic.
   b. The mark has been abandoned.
   c. There was a fraudulent registration. OR
   d. There was an improper use of a certification ®. (Also disparaging ® - "Bullshit" for purses or a defecating dog).

   NOTE: Fact that a ® is incontestable does not mean that it will have exclusive rights to a descriptive term. Parents Magazine has an incontestable ® over logo and distinctive style but not over word "Parents," even as applied to another magazine. Parents Digest does not infringe upon its ®.

3. Defenses to Inconstestability:

   a. ***§ 33(b): Defenses to Incontestably Registered Marks:***
   § 33(b) says that if someone alleges infringement of an incontestable ®, the following defenses are allowed:
   (1) Fraudulent acquisition of ® registration;
   (2) Abandonment;

(3) Use of the ® to misrepresent source;
(4) Fair use defense;
(5) Limited territory defense;
(6) Prior registration by defendant;
(7) Use of ® to violate antitrust laws; or
(8) Equity.

b. Incontestability is not the same as "invincibility"
   (1) Doesn't protect generic parts of names
   (2) Procedure
      a) First file § 8 Affidavit (registration) – still using mark in conjunction with listed goods or it is abandoned.
      b) Then file § 15 Affidavit

c. Requirements for § 8 Affidavit
   (1) Affidavit declaring mark that has been registered is in *current use* and state specific goods and services with which it is still in current use.
   (2) Without this being done between the 5th and 6th year, the PTO will consider the mark abandoned.
   (3) No continuous use requirement as in § 15
   (4) Merely current use
   (5) MUST FILE THIS, or you will lose your registration
   (6) MOST REGISTRANTS file § 8 and § 15 affidavits together

d. Requirements for § 15 Affidavit
   (1) Signed by owner or federal registration
   (2) Must identify by number and date
   (3) Recite goods or services stated in registration in connection with which mark has been in continuous use in commerce for 5 consecutive years anytime after the registration issues
   (4) State that the mark is still in use in commerce and specify the type of commerce
   (5) Specify that no final decision adverse to registrant's claim of ownership and no pending non-final proceeding in PTO
   (6) File in a timely manner
   (7) "Continuous use of marks" – Must show *continuous use* for the last five years
   (8) Can this be said even if the product hasn't been on the market continuously for 5 years because of some unusual circumstance? No. It's not 5 years of continuous trademark use

(9) What about advertising? If marketing services, 5 years of advertising is ok. If marketing products, 5 years of trademark use (affixing on goods, use in commerce)

e. Timing - § 8 vs. § 15 Affidavits
   (1) §15 Incontestability doesn't have to be filed within a specific time period – the only requirement is that you must wait until you have used the mark in commerce for at least 5 consecutive years before filing
   (2) § 8 Registration must be filed within grace time (until 6 years after registration) or trademark is deemed to be abandoned

f. Benefits of Incontestability § 15 Affidavit filing
   (1) Evidentiary status: Incontestable registration is conclusive evidence of:
      a) registration of the mark;
      b) validity of the mark;
      c) registrant's ownership of the mark;
      d) registrant's exclusive right to use the mark in commerce

   (2) Procedural advantages (in an infringement action):
      a) Burden of proof is on plaintiff to prove "generic-ness"
      b) Registered owner has presumptive validity (cannot be attacked as descriptive mark) (***Park 'N Fly***)
      c) Incontestable status of a trademark is not dispositive regarding whether the Defendant is infringing or diluting the registered owner's mark – there must be a showing of infringement or dilution
      d) Arguments against an incontestable mark include: genericness, fraudulent registration, improper use of certification, abandonment, disparaging mark, etc.

E. Fair Use

Fair Use - Owners of a descriptive ® may prohibit others from using the descriptive ® as a ® if it causes a likelihood of confusion. However, they may not assert monopoly rights in the descriptive meaning of their ®. A defendant is free to use the descriptive ® in a strictly descriptive capacity to describe their own product or its geographical origin or to identify its producer.

§ 33(b) (4) - Courts will usually consider 3 factors:

1. *The manner in which the defendant uses the ®*
    - Is it meant as a ® or does it merely describe the product of service?
    - Is the word or symbol prominently featured or secondary to the other words? (i.e., "CRUNCHY COOKIES" will not be infringed by DELECTO COOKIES merely because the Delecto box states "They are quite crunchy.")
2. *Whether the defendant is using the ® in good faith.*
3. *Whether the defendant's use is likely to cause confusion.*

   If factors 1 & 2 indicate a fair use, the court may tolerate a greater chance of consumer confusion.

United States Shoe Corp. V. Brown Group Inc., 740 F. Supp. 196 (S.D.N.Y.), *aff'd,* 923 F.2d 844 (2d Cir. 1990)

FACTS: USSC has slogan "Looks like a pump, feels like a sneaker." BG has slogan "Think of it as a sneaker with no strings attached;" USSC (Easy Spirits) alleges that BG (Naturalizer) sneaker logo infringes on their ® slogan and wants them to stop making comparison to sneaker.)

HOLDING: Court held for BG (Naturalizer) finding that the use was a fair use. Under § 33(b)(4) competitors have the right to use in good faith terms that fairly describe but do not designate goods or services.

> **NOTE:** Descriptive word cannot be arbitrary. Looking in the dictionary is a good place to start. However, language often out paces dictionaries.

Chapter 23

REMEDIES - TRADEMARKS

A. *See* § 43(c)(2) Successful plaintiffs are entitled to a wide range of remedies under federal law. Such plaintiffs are routinely awarded injunctions against further infringing or diluting use of the trademark. 15 U.S.C. § 1116(a).

B. In infringement suits, the types of damages that can be awarded include (15 U.S.C. § 1117(a)):
   1. defendant's profits
   2. damages sustained by the plaintiff
   3. costs of the action
   4. treble damages upon showing of bad faith

C. In dilution suits, damages are available only if the defendant <u>willfully</u> traded on the plaintiff's goodwill in using the mark. Otherwise, plaintiffs in a dilution action are limited to injunctive relief. *See* 15 U.S.C. § 1125(c).

D. Civil remedies available under the federal law and most state laws:
   1. an injunction against future infringement
   2. infringer's profits
   3. damages for past infringement suffered by the owner of the mark (which may be trebled under the federal law)
   4. destruction of all material bearing the infringing mark
   5. costs of the action and, in exceptional cases, reasonable attorney's fees
   6. punitive damages
   7. prejudgment interest.

E. Preliminary Injunction
   1. Criteria for Burden of Proof
      a. Plaintiff's probability of success on the merits
      b. Plaintiff showing irreparable harm
      c. Will by granting the injunction preserve the status quo
      d. Equity: a balancing of hardships of defendant and plaintiff

2. Purpose
    a. Necessary to preserve the status quo
    b. Necessary to protect third parties (namely consumers) and prevent confusion

3. Defenses
    a. Laches
        (1) Elements:
            - Plaintiff had knowledge of defendant's use of the mark;
            - Unreasonably delay by plaintiff in taking action against defendant;
            - Justified detrimental reliance on part of defendant

        (2) Additional key points to remember:
            - Despite showing the above 3 elements, whether the court will grant the claim will depend on "consideration of the circumstance of each particular case and a balancing of the interests and equities of the parties." *See Saratoga Vichy v. Lehman*, 433 F.2d 686 (2d. Cir. 1980)
            - Legitimate engagement in settlement negotiations does NOT "toll the clock."
    b. Abandonment
        (1) When use has been discontinued with the intent not to resume (intent may be inferred from the circumstances)
        (2) Nonuse for 3 consecutive years is prima facie evidence of abandonment

    c. Unclean hands – deceptive use or misuse by the registered owner

F. Mandatory Injunction

1. Order by the court to do something
    a. Place disclaimer on goods
    b. Surrender goods to the Court
    c. Recall order
    d. Destruction of goods
    e. Corrective advertising – say that Y is not affiliated with X

2. This remedy is only available after a full trial on the merits

G. Monetary Damages – *See* § 35(a)

1. Burden of Proof: Must show willful intent to trade on owner's reputation or to cause dilution of trademark

2. Defendant's profits
    a. Must prove wrongful intent, willful infringement and/or unjust enrichment
    b. Plaintiff need only prove defendant's sales
    c. Burden on the defendant to prove costs or deductions
    d. Court has discretion to adjust award based on profits either up or down depending upon the circumstances
    e. No double recovery is allowed – Plaintiff cannot get both defendant's profits and plaintiff's loss of profits

3. Plaintiff's damages
    a. Must prove actual confusion
    b. Loss of profits, corrective advertising, investigation of product liability claims (only of products that are mistakenly believed to be your product, when in fact they are not)
    c. Court can treble damages if the act is egregious
    d. Profits lost from licensing
    e. Product liability cases (your product or other product)
    f. Loss of business goodwill
    g. Must show actual confusion in the marketplace
    h. § 35 is usually used when plaintiff has to rely on a reasonable royalty award

4. Attorneys' fees
    a. Only in exceptional cases
    b. Plaintiff must prove bad faith (such as intentional or willful infringement by defendant)
    c. For defendant to get attorney fees, they must prove a lack of merit in the case or an intent to harass by plaintiff's in bringing the action
    d. Mandatory if a counterfeiting case
    e. Only get this in exceptional cases under Lanham Act. To be exceptional, must show willful infringement (if plaintiff) or frivolous claim (if defendant)

H. Alternatives to litigation to resolve TM dispute:

1. <u>Arbitration</u> (binding or non-binding): judicial proceedings are incorporated – opportunity to answer, discovery opportunity and maybe not. Mini-litigation and is usually less expensive. Arbitrator is both the judge and the fact-finder. This alternative may be better for transnational dispute resolution.

2. <u>Mediation</u>: More informal approach and doesn't have judicial tone – mediator may act as a judge but acts within the

framework agreed upon. It's more considered as reconciliation. Mediator facilitates the solution but both sides are the ones who come up with it. Mediator does not serve as a judge.

Chapter 24

15 U.S.C – THE LATHAM ACT

A. False Representations

1. **15 U.S.C. § 1125(a)(1)(A) - [Lanham Act § 43(a) (1) (A)]** Any person who, on or in connection with any goods or services, or any container for goods, uses in commerce any word, term, name, symbol, or device, or any combination thereof, or any false designation or origin, false, or misleading description of fact, or false or misleading representation of fact, which

   (A) is likely to cause confusion, or to cause mistake, or to deceive as to the affiliation, connection, or association of such person with another person, or as to the origin, sponsorship, or approval of his or her goods, services, or commercial activities by another person . . . . shall be liable in a civil action by any person who believes that he or she is or is likely to be damaged by such act.

2. **15 U.S.C. § 1125(a) (1) (B) - [Lanham Act § 43(a) (1) (B)]** Any person who, on or in connection with any goods or services, or any container for goods, uses in commerce any word, term, name, symbol, or device, or any combination thereof, or any false designation or origin, false, or misleading description of fact, or false or misleading representation of fact, which -

   (B) in commercial advertising or promotion, misrepresents the nature, characteristics, qualities, or geographic origin of his or her or another person's goods, services, or commercial activities, shall be liable in a civil action by any person who believes that he or she is or is likely to be damaged by such act.

§ 43(a)(1)(B) prohibits the use of false or misleading description or description of fact in commercial advertising or promotion, misrepresents the nature, characteristics, qualities, or geographic origin of his or her (false advertising) or another person's disparagement) goods, services, or commercial activities.

3. **Elements for a §43(a)(1)(B) cause of action (injunctive relief):**
   a. Defendant uses false or misleading statement of fact in advertising about its own product;
   b. Statement actually deceived or had the capacity to deceive a substantial segment of the audience;
   c. Deception was material in that it was likely to influence the purchasing decision;
   d. Defendant caused its goods to enter interstate commerce; and
   e. Plaintiff has been or is likely to be injured as a result.

3. ***Standing to Sue under § 43(a)***
   While § 43(a) protects both consumers and competitors, most courts thus far have ruled that ***only competitors*** have standing to assert a § 43(a) claim of false representation.

4. **Falsity and Materiality**

   a. To prove falsity, plaintiff must demonstrate either:
      i. *That an advertisement is literally false; or*
      ii. *That the advertisement, though literally true, is likely to mislead and confuse customers.*

   b. When a ***merchandising statement or representation is literally or explicitly false***, the court may grant relief without reference to the advertiser's impact on the buying public.

   c. When the ***challenged advertisement implicitly false*** rather than explicitly, its tendency to violate the Lanham Act by misleading, confusing or deceiving should be tested by public reaction.

   d. <u>Burden of Proof</u>. It must be shown that it would be likely to affect an ordinary consumer's purchasing decision.

   e. Representations that are literally true but misleading, may be deemed "implicitly false" and give rise to liability. Plaintiff must prove that consumers in fact understood the advertisement to convey the alleged false message.

   f. **Intent**
      It is unnecessary for the plaintiff to demonstrate that the defendant acted with the intent to deceive consumers. However, if the plaintiff does prove deceptive intent, the court may presume that consumers are in fact deceived (burden will shift to the defendant to prove an absence of consumer deception).

15 U.S.C. §1051 ET. SEQ. (LANHAM ACT)

15 U.S.C. §1051 § 1	(a) How to Apply to Register a (b) Applications based on Intent to Use. (c) Examiner may examine the factors set forth in 15 U.S.C. §1052(a) - (e).
15 U.S.C. §1052 § 2	No trademark used to distinguish goods shall be refused registration unless: (a) Immoral, deceptive, scandalous, etc.; (b) Flag, coat of arms; (c) Name, portrait, signature; (d) So resembles an existing registered mark that it will be likely to cause confusion, although concurrent registrations may be issued if confusion, mistake, and deception are not likely; (e) Merely descriptive, deceptively misdescriptive, primarily geographically descriptive, geographically misdescriptive, or primarily a surname; (f) Nothing shall prevent registration of a mark that has attained secondary meaning except (15 U.S.C. §1052 2(a)-(d). Commissioner may except as prima facie evidence of secondary meaning proof of substantially exclusive and continuous use in commerce for 5 years.
15 U.S.C. §1054 § 3	Service Marks.
15 U.S.C. §1054 § 4	COLLECTIVE AND CERTIFICATION MARKS.
15 U.S.C. §1056 § 6	Disclaimers.
15 U.S.C. §1057(b) § (b)	Certificate of registration is prima facie evidence of validity of registration.
15 U.S.C. §1057(c) § 7(c)	Filing of application on principal .register §7(c) constitutes constructive notice. Constitutes constructive notice.
15 U.S.C. §1058 § 8	Duration--registration good for 10 years, must renew after 5 years.
15 U.S.C. §1059 § 9	Renewal--may renew for periods of 10 years.

15 U.S.C. §1063 § 13	30 days to file opposition, may extend for additional 30 day periods.
15 U.S.C. §1064 § 14	Cancellation within 5 years or at any time if generic, abandoned, obtained fraudulently, contrary to (15 U.S.C. §1052(a)-(c). In the case of a certification mark, at any time, if registrant does not control, markets goods to which mark is applied, or permits use for purposes other than to certify, or indiscriminately refuses to certify.
15 U.S.C. §1065 § 15	Becoming Incontestable.
15 U.S.C. §1072 § 22	Registration is constructive notice, but see 15 U.S.C. §1057(c)).
15 U.S.C. §1091(c) § 23(c)	Explicitly provides that surnames and slogans are registrable on the Supplemental Register.
15 U.S.C. §1114 § 32	Remedies for Infringement of ® in use in commerce or any reproduction, counterfeit, copy, or colorable limitation of a registered mark which is likely to cause confusion.
15 U.S.C. §1115(a) § 33(a)	Registration is prima facie evidence of validity.
15 U.S.C. §1115(b) § 33(b)	Defenses to incontestability (obtained fraudulently, abandoned, used by registrant to misrepresent source, fair use, local prior use, equitable principles).
15 U.S.C. §1116 §32	Injunction.
15 U.S.C. §1116(d) § 34(d)	Counterfeit marks.
15 U.S.C. §1117 §35	Monetary relief.
15 U.S.C. §1118 § 36	Destruction Orders.
15 U.S.C. §1125 §43	False designations of origins and false descriptions.
15 U.S.C. §1127 §35	Definitions (see Glossary).

Chapter 25

INTERNATIONAL PROTECTION OF TRADEMARKS

A. Paris Convention

1. Article II: Universal treatment of producers who are in a country signing the Paris Convention - extends the national trademark protection.
2. Article IV: Priority Rule.
   A filing applicant in a Paris Convention country:
   May use same date when filing in another Paris Convention country as long as second filing occurs within 6 months at the first filing; and the first filing matures to registration.
3. Article VI
   a. International goodwill.
   b. Protects against pirating and infringement.
4. Articles IX & X
   a. Protects from unauthorized trademarks.
   b. Protects from false designations of origins and source.

B. Madrid Agreement

1. United States is not a signing member.
2. International Registry of any mark registered in the member country.
3. Way of converting domestic application to international scene.

C. GATT (1994)

1. Minimum trademark standards.
2. Priority system like Article IV of Paris Convention.
3. All member countries enjoy benefit of treaties - Entered into by all the other member countries.
4. Protection of trademarks through all member countries.

Chapter 26

DILUTION

A. State Law Dilution

1. ***Blurring***

   a. Plaintiff has a very strong ® or trade name which the public closely associates with the plaintiff (i.e., McDonalds) in association with a particular type of good or service. Defendant uses the same or highly similar ® on different goods or services.

   b. Dilution. This does not cause a likelihood of confusion about source, however, the defendant's use "***whittles away or dilutes the strong association consumers have between the ® and the plaintiff.***"

   c. Property Rights. Because the strong association has commercial value, dilution law recognizes it as a property right. Thus, the plaintiff can enjoin the defendant's use even though there is no deception to consumers because of the diminution of the uniqueness and commercial effectiveness of the plaintiff's ®.

   d. Limitation. Due to anti-competitive results of dilution, it only works for very strong, distinct, well-known ®s.

   e. Six Factors to Consider for Blurring:
      i. Similarity of the ®s,
      ii. Similarity of the products covered by the ®s,
      iii. Sophistication of consumers,
      iv. Predatory intent,
      v. Renown of the senior ®, and
      vi. Renown of the junior ®.

2. ***Tarnishment*** (Disparagement)
   This occurs when the defendant's use of a similar ® or trade name casts the plaintiff's distinctive, well-known ® or trade name in a bad light and thus tarnishes the lust of the plaintiff's commercial image or reputation. This may occur when the defendant uses the ® or trade name in a context which is

unwholesome or at least out of keeping with the plaintiff's high quality image. No need to show a likelihood of confusion about source. Tarnishment may enable ® owners to prevent parodies of their ®s. ***Examples:*** "Debbie Does Dallas" in Dallas Cowboy's cheerleading uniform and "Enjoy Cocaine" which looks like Coke's symbol.

3. ***Dilution v. Tarnishment***

   Dilution - Blurs the distinctiveness of a ® by trying to disconnect association between product and source.

   Tarnishment (Disparagement) - Creates negative image of ® in public's mind through an association with unsavory, unrelated goods or services (does not need to be sex or drugs).

   Dilution is an add-on to ® law. ® allows a company to build up goodwill for a symbol, etc. and seriously penalizes those who do not police. Dilution says that all the work you put in to make your ® must be protected. Thus, others cannot make it less valuable for an inappropriate reason. Dilution protects fairness.

B. Federal Trademark Dilution Act of 1995

1. ***Lanham Act Dilution - § 43(c): Federal Trademark Dilution Act of 1995.*** The owner of a famous ® (not trade name) shall be entitled to an injunction against another person's commercial use in commerce of a ® or trade name if such use begins after the ® has become famous and causes dilution to its distinctive quality.

2. ***Definition of a "famous ®"*** (§ 43(c) (1)) - There are 8 factors to be considered in determining whether a ® is famous:

   a. The degree of inherent or acquired distinctiveness of the ® (§ 43(c) (1) (A));
   b. The duration and extent of use of the ® in connection with the goods or services with which the ® is used (§ 43(c) (1) (B));
   c. The duration and extent of advertising and publicity of the ® (§ 43(c) (1) (C));
   d. The geographical extent of the trading area in which the ® is used (§ 43(c) (1) (D));
   e. The channels of trade for the goods or services with which the ® is used (§ 43(c) (1) (E));

f. The degree of recognition of the ® in the trading areas and channels of trade the ®'s owners and the person against whom the injunction is sought (§ 43(c) (1) (F));
g. The nature and extent of use of the same or similar ®s by third parties (§ 43(c) (1) (G)); and
h. Whether the ® was federally registered (§ 43(c) (1) (H)).

2. ***Other limitations*** (§43(c)(4)) - The following acts will not constitute actionable dilution:

   a. Fair use of a famous ® (§ 43(c) (4) (A));
   b. A non-commercial use of a ® (§ 43(c)(4)(B));
   c. All forms of news reporting and news commentary (§ 43(c)(4)(C)). If federally register ®, cannot bring state dilution action (§ 43(c)(3)). Can bring state dilution action against non-federally registered ®.

Chapter 27

THE INTERNET AND TRADEMARK LAW

A. Introduction

With the emerging popularity of the Internet, intellectual property owners are provided with an unlimited market for their work. Along with this, though, come many challenging trademark issues. Before proceeding, although the Internet is a new medium, the most important rules to remember to apply are the basic principles of trademark law.

In registering a domain name, the following different domains are available (to name a few):

.com
.org
.net
.info
.eu
.us
.biz

B. Cybersquatting

Cybersquatters register famous trademarks as domain names and then attempt to license or sell them to the companies or individuals that own the trademark and that have invested large amounts of money in developing the goodwill for such mark.

C. Different Procedures for Enforcing Trademark Infringement on the internet

1. Anti-Cybersquatting Consumer Protection Act (ACPA)

   The ACPA, which was enacted November 29, 1999, protects ® owners against infringement of their ®s. The owner of a ® (including a famous ®) can sue for infringement if, without regard to the goods or services, it can prove that:

a. The infringer had bad faith intent in using the ®, with the hope to benefit; and

b. The infringer registers, traffics, or uses a domain name that:
   i. Is identical or similar to ®;
   ii. Dilutes the ®; or
   iii. Is a ®, word, or name protected by 18 U.S.C. § 703 or 36 U.S.C. §2205-06.

2. The statute outlines the following factors to determine whether an infringer acted in bad faith:

   a. Intellectual property rights of the domain name registrant;
   b. Whether the domain name is the legal name of the registrant;
   c. Whether the domain name had prior lawful uses with bona fide offering of goods/services;
   d. Registrant's intent to divert consumers from the lawful ® owner's site;
   e. Registration of multiple and identical or confusingly similar domain names;
   f. Offer to sell, transfer or assign domain name for money without a bona fide prior use or intent to use the ® for goods/services; or
   g. When applying for registration of the domain, submitting material or misleading information.

3. Available remedies are:
   a. Injunctive relief;
   b. Actual damages; or
   c. Statutory damages ranging from $1,000 to $100,000 per infringed domain name (within the court's discretion.

4. Some of the benefits of enforcing one's ® under ACPA include:

   a. Determination by a court;
   b. Many different jurisdictional options;
   c. Availability of damages;
   d. Availability of an injunction; and
   e. Protects personal name, whether or not a ®.

5. <u>Internet Corporation for Assigned Names and Numbers (ICANN)</u>
   ICANN is currently in charge of administrating the Internet domain name system. As an alternative to litigation, ICANN developed the Uniform Domain Name Dispute Resolution Policy (UDRP) to resolve domain name disputes. If one elects to follow UDRP, the claimant must abide by the following procedure:

a. Commence proceedings by filing a complaint with one of the following service providers:
    i. World Intellectual Property Organization (WIPO);
    ii. The National Arbitration Forum (NAF);
    iii. Disputes.org/ e Resolution Consortium (DeC); or
    iv. CPR Institute for Dispute Resolution.

b. The claimant selects whether to submit the dispute to one or three panelists. The ICANN proceeding is determined on the complaint and response submissions. No additional disclosure is permitted, unless the ICANN panel specifically requests additional information.

    <u>The claimant must prove</u>:

    i. The domain name at issue is identical or confusingly similar to its ®;
    ii. The registrant has no legitimate rights or interest in the domain name (i.e., surname); and
    iii. The registrant had bad faith in its registration and use of the domain name.

    <u>To establish bad faith:</u>
    i. Acquired the domain name for the purpose of sale or transfer;
    ii. Registered domain name to prevent owner of ® from using it;
    iii. Registered domain name to primarily disrupt competitor's business; or
    iv. Used domain name to intentionally cause likelihood of confusion.

    <u>Defenses to bad faith include:</u>
    i. Show bona fide use in connection with offering goods/service prior to notice of dispute;
    ii. Registrant shows that it is known by domain name, even though does not own ®; or
    iii. Legitimate fair use or non-commercial use.

c. The only remedies available are:
    i. Canceling domain name; or
    ii. Transferring the domain name to claimant.

NOTE: Either party can appeal the decision of the UDRP panel. To allow for the filing of a lawsuit, UDRP requires ICANN to wait 10-business days before enforcing the panel's decision.

Chapter

28

LICENSING TRADEMARKS

A. **No licensing of trademarks existed before the Lanham Act**

B. **There is no naked licensing or transfer -** So what is required?

1. Goodwill of the business for assignment.
2. Control of the quality. Quality control provision is the most important in a Trademark. Quality control – *sine qua non:*
    i. Goods have to be identical to the licensor's but there might be variations due to the local customs.
    ii. Only trademark licenses have quality control. Absolutely mandatory, need two parts:
        - maintenance of quality by the licensee under approval by the licensor; and
        - licensor has rights to inspect the premises and receive samples at reasonable intervals as the quality has to be consistent; or else the trademark is invalid
3. No sublicensing. For the quality control reason sub-licensing is out and because of consumer confusion.

C. **Estoppel**

1. A Trademark presumed to be valid if the licensee takes out a license. A licensee cannot contest the validity of a Trademark for which he/she obtained a license.
2. One needs to register a trademark ***Quickly***. The old process of interstate commerce is no longer used as the Patent and Trademark law has changed – i.e., the *intent to use application*.

D. **Assignment**

1. A sells, conveys and assigns to B all its title and interest.
2. In and to certain Trademarks together with the good will of the business symbolized by said Trademarks and the registration thereof.

3. **NOTE:** You have to have the *goodwill* in the assignment to have a valid trademark. This concept goes hand in hand with the fact that there has to be use.

E. **Royalties**

1. The general scheme as for patent licenses applies
2. In trademarks much more than patent licenses there is an initial lump sum payment.
3. Franchising has a trademark license at the core. For franchises there is usually a supply of goods to be purchased to ensure *quality control.*
4. Can have scaled up royalty payments.
5. Percentage of sales or fixed per good.
6. Royalty for a servicemark is based on the total business.
7. Often have minimum sales and royalties.
8. Advertising fees are very common - share of national advertising or separate share for local advertising.

F. **Product Liability**

1. General rule is that the trademark licensor is liable for defective products by the licensee.

2. The theory is that the licensor benefited from the license and retained rights to inspect the quality. Also licensor is involved in the manufacturing.

3. *Catch-22 Problem*: if there is no control the trademark is lost, but if you exercise control where will be liability. For the licensor to protect himself, a trademark license will usually have a provision for the licensee to get insurance and co-insure licensor. But, if you exercise too much control, you have an antitrust problem because of a tie-ins. Licensee cannot be forced to buy goods at the a price higher with the license if they are staple products of commerce. Can't have a tie-in situation unless you have a tied product and a tied-in licensee. Goes back to *Morton Salt*: illegal extension of the monopoly is improper. Even in an antitrust context cannot talk about intellectual property like a monopoly unless there is *market power.* Small companies usually have no market power but may still be accused of antitrust violations because of *price fixing.*

G. **Estoppel**

1. Licensee should not be able to question the validity of the intellectual property. The Doctrine of estoppel

prohibits the licensee to the question the validity of the intellectual property.

2. An assignor cannot renege the assignment as well on the basis that the intellectual property right is invalid = *Assignor estoppel.* **NOTE**: Patents are the exception to that general rule.

3. In trademarks there is question about things that invalidate trademarks that come out during the trademark. Licensor can also guard against trademark validity when the term of the agreement is up by putting in a simple contract clause for that. Because of *Lear v. Atkins*, the same cannot be said for patent licenses.

Chapter 29

LICENSING TRADE SECRETS

A. **Introduction**

1. The intellectual property is *know-how* but the intellectual property right is a *trade secret*.
2. It is possible to protect an invention by patents as well as a trade secret (*Kewanee Oil*).
3. There may be a trade secret in even a product that on its face does not have a trade secret. Usually, one can combine patents and trade secrets. For instance, a manufacturing process can be protected by a patent if new and non-obvious but can also protect it via a trade secret
4. For technical information and business information can have trade secrets and patents.

B. **Historical background**

1. Trade Secrets are the oldest form of Intellectual Property, dating back to Roman times and the middle ages.
2. Modern law evolved in England but was adopted in the US in *Peabody v. Norfolk*.
    a. Trade Secrets are property under that case. People have common law rights to an invention which implies property rights.
    b. Protected against misappropriation and lasts beyond the term of the employment.
    c. Recipient can be enjoined from using a misappropriated trade secret
    d. One time disclosure does not void the Trade Secret.
3. A trade secret may consist of any formula, pattern, device or compilation of information which is se in one's business and which gives him an opportunity to obtain an advantage over competitors who do not know or use it. It may be a formula for a chemical

compound, a process of manufacturing, treating or preserving materials, a pattern for a machine or other device, or a list of customers. Restatement of Torts § 757 comment b (1939)

4. A trade secret is any information that:
    a. Derives independent economic value (actual or potential) from not being generally know to, and not being readily ascertainable by roper means by, other persons who can obtain economic value from its disclosure or use; and
    b. Is the subject of efforts that are reasonable under the circumstances to maintain its secrecy. (Uniform Trade Secret Act § 1 (4) (1985 Supp 1989)
    c. Can be used in the operation of a business or other enterprise and that is sufficiently valuable and secret to afford an actual or potential economic advantage over other (Restatement of Unfair Competition § (1995))

5. The term "trade secret" means all forms and types of financial, business, scientific, technical, economic, or engineering information, including patterns, plans, compilations, program devices, formulas, designs, prototypes methods, and techniques. Processes, procedures, programs, or codes, whether tangible or intangible, and whether or owned stored complied, memorialized physically, electronically, graphically, photographically or in writing if the owner thereof has taken reasonable measure to protect the secret

C. **Scope and Characteristics of Trade Secrets**
    1. No registration requirement
    2. No subject matter or term limitations
    3. No tangibility requirements
    4. No novelty requirements
    5. But, secrecy is the most important criterion – a *sine qua non.* There are no exceptions
    6. Affirmative measures must be taken to safeguard a trade secret
    7. Sufficient economic value or competitive advantage is also a prerequisite.

8. Proper criterion is not "*actual use*" but "*value to the owner*", i.e. negative results can also give a competitive advantage

D. **Safeguarding Trade Secrets**
1. Memorialize the trade secret policy in writing
2. Inform employees of trade secrets
3. Have employees sign confidentiality agreements
4. Conduct exit interviews
5. Restrict access to the documents
6. Lock gates and cabinets
7. Label trade secret documents
8. Restrict public accessibility
9. Screen speeches and publication
10. Use contracts in dealing with third parties.

E. **Misappropriation of Trade Secrets**
1. Acquisition by *improper means*
2. Acquisition by *accident or mistake*
3. *Use of* or disclosure of a *trade secret*:
    a. Acquired improperly in violation of a duty to maintain confidentiality.
    b. *Improper means* include: theft, bribery, misrepresentation, breach of inducement, breach of duty to maintain secrecy
    c. *Proper means* do not support a claim for misappropriation, and include: independent discovery, reverse engineering, or discovery from observing what has been allowed to enter the public domain.
4. *Trade Secrets* are not prior art for patentability.

F. **Complementariness of Patents and Trade Secrets**
1. In R&D state before any patents issue, *trade secrets law "dovetails" with patent law*
2. Assuming that a development has been enabled and the best mode described, all associated know-how not disclose, whether or not inventive, can be retained as a trade secret.
3. All R&D data, including data pertaining to better modes, developed after filing, again whether or not inventive, can also be protected as a trade secret (99 % of R&D data is generated after the patent application).

4. With respect to technologically complex developments consisting of many patentable inventions and volumes of associated know-how, complementary patenting and secreting is tantamount to having the best of both worlds. E.g. GE's industrial diamond process technology.
5. The question then is not whether or not to patent or to padlock but rather what to patent and what to keep a trade secret and whether it is best to patent as well as to padlock

G. **Supreme Court on Trade Secrets**
   1. Patents & trade secrets are not exclusive (*Kewanee Oil).*
   2. Patents and trade secrets dovetail. (*Bonito Boats).*
   3. Need to exploit the overlaps. But, consider abandonment if a patent application is not filed.

H. **The Black Box dilemma**
   1. The dilemma comes in that the other parties will not buy something when they don't know what they are buying.
   2. The owner of a potentially value trade secret *cannot* let the cat out of the bag, or the trade secret rights will be lost even if the disclosure was accidental.
      a. The loss of rights upon uncontrolled disclosure is the downside of trade secrets.
      b. On the other hand, a potential trade secret licensee will not buy a license without knowing what the secret is.
      c. Resolution of this dilemma is a pre-negation agreement/a secrecy agreement/ a confidentiality agreement.
      d. The owner needs safeguards before trade secret disclosure to preserve the trade secret. In addition, the owner needs to consider what restrictions apply if the recipient has no interest in the information or how the information will be used if there is interest in the use of the trade secret, and for how long will the use be. Furthermore, should the owner charge and if so how much for peeking into the trade secret. Initial payments in pre-negotiation agreements are common.
      e. Recipient has reverse question: what restrictions, what to pay, what if the recipient

already has the trade secret or is developing it; what if the trade secret is part of the public domain.

f. All these concerns need to be incorporated into the terms of the agreement.

g. Rationale to have the potential licensee pay to look at the trade secret is that during the time the potential licensee evaluates the trade secret no one else can evaluate it.

I. All of Trade Secret licensing agreements have an "Obligation of the Recipient to Confidentiality": if there is no duty on the side of the recipient, the trade secret is lost and gone. The obligation gives a legally protected status and hence can sue if there is a breach.

1. *Written Agreement:* Is best for licensing in general. Written agreement makes for a contract. Oral agreements can sometimes be enforced but trade secret rights under Trade Secret statutes cannot be used. One may be relegated to *implied contract*. Breach of confidence and unjust enrichment could also be argued.

2. *Definition of the Technology*: so one knows what one has. Important to precisely define the technology. Don't want to define the technology too much. *Vito* case: Trade secret defined specifically in the contract and negotiations broke off and then the breaching party used the Trade Secret that was given in the agreement.

3. *Mechanisms of disclosure:* must mimic the confidential nature. There has to be provision for the return of the documents including licensee's papers on the trade secret. Needs to be in writing. Any disclosure should say it is confidential and forbid reproduction.

4. Establishment of a Legal Relationship

5. Statement of Purpose of relationship

6. **Exceptions:** Covers situations like when the Trade Secret is known. There are three basic exceptions:

   a. Recipient is a Potential Licensee has no obligations if it is already known without fault of the recipient.

b. If recipient later gets the trade secret from a third party that independently created the agreement.

c. Termination clause is required unless you want to pay for eternity. *Listerine mouthwash*: got to pay for eternity because of freedom of contract. The Termination clause is typically limited to three years.

OVERVIEW OF TRADEMARK STATUTES

15 U.S.C. Section	Applicability of Section
§ 1051 (b)	(1) May request registration in good faith for trademark used in good faith. (2) Application must include applicant's domicile and citizenship, specify the goods with which the Tm is to be used and a drawing of the mark. (3) A verified statement by the applicant specifying (A) that they are entitled to use the mark in commerce (B) the bona fide intention to use the mark in commerce (C) that the facts are to the best knowledge accurate (D) that to the best knowledge and belief there is no identical mark or a similar mark that the applicant's mark can cause confusion, mistake or deceit. No mark shall be filed until § 1051 (c) and (d) are satisfied. (4) The applicant has to comply with the rules.
§ 1052	No trademark distinguishing goods shall be refused unless: (a) it is immoral, deceptive or scandalous; or (b) it consists of or simulates the flag of any State or Nation; or (c) it portrays a living individual without consent; or (d) consists of a Mark that is previously registered; or (e) it is only descriptive.
§ 1057	(a) Issuances and Form: signed and with seal by PTO/Director. (b) Certificate as Prima Facie Evidence: certificates are prima facie evidence of the mark's existence (c) Application to Register Mark Considered Constructive Use must prove (1) use of mark (2) application has been filed, pending or resulted in mark (3) has filed foreign application on the basis of which there is priority. (d) Issuance to Assignee must be recorded in the PTO (e) Surrender, Cancellation, or Amendment by Registrant: Amendment permissible upon fee payment as long as the material character of

	mark is not altered. (f) Copies of Patent and Trademark Office Records as Evidence all are evidence in cases. (g) Correction of Patent and Trademark Office Mistake attach copy with mistakes. (h) Correction of Applicant's Mistake - Director can issue new certificate as long as changes do.
§ 1114	Defines infringement; limits action.
§ 1115 (Lanham Act § 33)	(b)(5) Use was without knowledge of misuse. (b)(4) defense to trademark infringement is that the trademark charged for infringing use has only been used to describe the goods or services of such a party.
§ 1125 (a) (43 (a))	Provides for liability in civil actions for misleading description or misrepresentation that (1) causes confusion of the origin/approval of good (2) by commercial misrepresentation. Under § 44 the act is extended to any foreign country with reciprocal rights. Liability for false or misleading representation of fact, false designation of origin and false and misleading representation of fact which (A) confuses/deceives the consumer (B) misrepresents the nature etc. in advertisement and the burden is on the person asserting trade dress protection. The Source of a federal cause of action for false advertising, disparagement and "common-law" confusion.
§ 1125 (c)	(1) owners of famous marks are entitled to an injunction against someone else using a mark as long as the first mark is famous and the other causes dilution of the distinctive quality of the mark. To determine distinctiveness or famousness of mark a court may look at: (A) degree of inherent or acquired distinctiveness of the mark (B) duration and extent of use of the mark in connection with the goods or services with which the mark is used (C) duration and extent of advertising and publicity of the mark (D) geographical extent of the mark's trading area (E) channels of trade for the mark's goods or

	services (F) degree of recognition of the mark in the mark's trading areas and channels of trade of both parties' mark (G) nature and extent of use of the same or similar marks by third parties (H) registered under the 1881 Act or 1905 Act. (2) under this section the injunctive remedy is specified by §1116. If there willful intent to dilute the mark the remedy is specified under § § 1117 (a) and 1118 at the Court's discretion. (3) Ownership under Federal Acts bars action under common law. (4) (A) fair use in advertising, (B) noncommercial use and (C) all forms of news and commentary are not actionable under this section. *Comparative advertising is allowed under this section.*
§ 1125 (c) (4)	Not actionable under § 43 (a): is (a) fair use in comparative use of advertising (b) noncommercial use of mark (c) news reporting and commentary.
§ 1127	Commerce is interstate commerce. Principal register is laid out in section 1051 to 1072 of this Chapter. Gives all the definitions of the Act.

Glossary

Abandonment - If Trademark is not used for 3 consecutive years, it is considered abandoned.

Acquiring Mark Rights - To get common law trademark rights, you do not need to register. In order to obtain trademark rights, you should:

1. Use mark on or in connecting with goods, or by displaying the mark in the sale or advertising of services to obtain automatic ® rights.
2. If you have a bona fide intent to use mark in commerce, you can apply to register the nationwide via intent to use (§ 1(b)-(d)).
3. Register with the U.S. Patent & Trademark Office (PTO).

Arbitrary or Fanciful - Technical ®. Always protected without any proof of secondary meaning.

Assignment in Gross - In licensing, to keep validity of the Trademark, the registrant controls the nature and quality of the goods or services in connection with which the mark is used.

Blurring - Defendant using the same ® dilutes the strong association consumers have between the ® and the plaintiff.

Bona Fide Intent to Use - You can register a particular ® attached to a specific product or good used in interstate commerce with a bona fide intent-to-use the ®.

Brand Names - Identify goods.

Cancellation of Registration - A cancellation of registration can be brought at anytime if it is scandalous, immoral, or disparages a person.

Coat of Arms - Used to distinguish goods shall be refused registration.

Collective Marks - Identifies goods, services or members of a collective organization.

Color Depletion Theory - Because of the limited amount of colors the ® of the color only exists for the product's market.

Color Pattern - ® may consist of a color pattern if the pattern is distinctive, rather than functional or merely ornamental.

Composite Marks - A composite mark, which contains two or more different elements, can be registered even though not all of its elements could be granted protection individually

Concurrent Use - ® shall be refused registration if it would cause confusion based on concurrent use of another ®.

Confusion Doctrine - The likelihood of confusion standard.

Confusion Test - (*Polaroid*) distinguishing the products from the source.

Contributory Infringement - One has no duty to actively discover infringing activities, but once you have actual knowledge of infringement, if you fail to prevent it, you will be liable for contributory infringement.

Constructive Notice, Registration - Registration of a ® on the Principal Register is *constructive notice* to the world of this registrant's use of the ®.

Convention Madrid Agreements - Provide a way of converting a domestic application to the international scene.

Copyright - © protects "original works of authorship."

Counterfeit Marks - Identifies goods or services by use of a false mark.

***de facto* functional -** Means that the design of a product has a function (i.e., a bottle of any design holds fluid).

***de jure* functional** - Means that the product is in its particular shape because it works better in this shape.

Deceptive - You think product is what it is not and influences your buying decision.

Deceptively Misdeceptive – the name appears to claim that it is what it is not, but does not influence a buying decision, does not hurt the market, or undermine buying power. Not barred if can prove secondary meaning (distinctiveness).

Deceptiveness Test -

1. Is the term misdescriptive of the character, quality, function, composition, or use of the goods?
2. If so, are prospective purchasers likely to believe that the misdescription actually describes the goods?
3. If so, is the misdescription likely to affect the decision to purchase?

***defacto* Secondary Meaning** - Reflects the legal conclusion that even if the public is aware that there has been only one source for the goods whose term is at issue, or even if the public further perceives the term as a brand name, that term must be held free for competitive use if it is in fact the commonly recognized name of the goods.

Definition of a Famous Trademark - The owner of a famous ® (not trade name) shall be entitled to an injunction against another person's commercial use in commerce of a ® or trade name if such use begins after the ® has become famous and causes dilution to its distinctive quality.

Dilution Doctrine - The law of trademark dilution aims to protect the distinctive quality of a trademark from deterioration caused by its use on dissimilar products or non-competing goods.

Disclaimer - In order to prevent customer confusion, one may have to add initial or first name to surname or a disclaimer to ®.

Distinctive Trade Dress - "Total image of a product, the overall impression created, not the individual features." - need not prove that the design has in fact secondary meaning.

Duration - Registration good for 10 years, must renew after 5 years.

Fair use - A defendant is free to use the descriptive ® in a strictly descriptive capacity to describe her own product or its geographical origin or to identify its producer.

Federal Registration of Marks Notice - Federal statutory trademark registration notice:

a. The symbol ®;
b. "Registered U.S. Patent and Trademark Office"
c. "Reg. U.S. Pat. & Tm. Off."

Flag - If ® is not scandalous and does not disparage the American flag then OK.

Functionality - Courts do not want to give ® monopolies where patent law protection is denied.

Functionality Tests - One can copy the feature if it is the best or cheapest way to make the product.

GATT - Protection of trademarks through all member countries.

Generic - ® is the general name as to which something is called. It cannot serve a valid ® because it is the common name of all goods and does not distinguish origin.

Goods-Place link - The public associates the geographic area with the goods

Immoral - The Lanham Act prohibits registration of Immoral, Deceptive, Scandalous, or Disparaging Matter.

Incontestability Defenses - Obtained fraudulently, abandoned, used by registrant to misrepresent source, fair use, local prior use, equitable principles.

Infringement - If it creates a likelihood of consumer confusion as to source or sponsorship.

Injunction - No need to show actual economic loss in order to obtain an injunction. It is likelihood of deception which this remedy may be invoked to prevent.

Intent to Use - Only applies to a bona fide intent-to-use.

International Protection of Trademarks:

Paris - Extends national trademark protection.

Convention Madrid Agreements - Provides a way of converting a domestic application to the international scene.

GATT - Protection of trademarks through all member countries.

Lanham Act - In 1947, Congress enacted the Lanham Act as a source of federal trademark rights, which is still in force. In 1988, Congress enacted a major revision, which is to allow persons to file trademark registration with "intent to use."

Likelihood of Confusion - An unauthorized use of a trademark constitutes an infringement if it creates a likelihood of consumer confusion as to source or sponsorship.

Merely Descriptive - If only one or two ways to describe something, you cannot give one a monopoly in that name or word then concurrent use of the word or name is then OK.

Non Use - No use for 3 consecutive years shall be *prima facie* evidence of abandonment.

Opposition to Trademark - If someone found the ® to be scandalous, immoral, or disparages a person someone could challenge registration in an opposition proceeding.

Ownership of Trademark - Ownership of a mark is established by priority of appropriation. Priority is established not by conception but by bona fide usage.

Patent - Provides a limited monopoly for new and inventive technological products, processes and designs.

Design - designs may be protected by a design patent if the pattern was new and required invention.

Utility - Functional features of products and processes.

Post-sale confusion - is when the purchaser is not confused about what he is buying (i.e., knows that it is an imitation), but other persons (potential purchasers) seeing the goods in the purchasers possession after the sale may be confused about their source.

Primarily Geographically Deceptive - ® is primarily geographically descriptive or deceptively misdescriptive if it conveys to meaningful segment of the purchasing public primarily a geographic connotation and those persons are likely to think that the goods come from that place.

Principal Register - Application to register a ® on the principal register established by the Lanham Act.

Prior Use - Lanham Act § 2(d) prohibits the registration of any ® that is confusingly similar to another ® that is in use and that has not been abandoned, with certain limited exceptions.

PTO - Patent and Trademark Office.

Registered Mark - The registration shall be conclusive evidence of the validity of the registered mark and of the registration of the mark.

Scandalous Mark - § 2(a) of the Lanham Act prohibits registration of Immoral, Deceptive, Scandalous, or Disparaging Matter.

Scent - A scent can also be granted trademark protection as long as it is distinctive, and not merely functional.

Secondary Confusion - Post-sale confusion is when the purchaser is not confused about what he is buying (i.e., knows that it is an imitation), but other persons (potential purchasers) seeing the goods in the purchasers possession after the sale may be confused about their source.

Secondary Meaning - In order to establish secondary meaning for a term, one must show that the primary significance of the term in the minds of the consuming public is source, not the product.

Service Mark - Identifies services.

Slogans - Can be registered and protected if it functions to identify and distinguish the ® owner's goods or services from those of others.

Sound - can be granted trademark protection as long as it is distinctive, and not merely functional.

Supplemental Register - Marks "not registrable on the Principal Register" may be registered on the Supplemental Register if they are "capable of distinguishing the applicant's goods or services."

Surnames - Lanham Act explicitly provides that surnames are registrable on the Supplemental Register. However, a surname must have acquired, through usage, a secondary meaning.

Survey Evidence - Survey evidence usually is the strongest evidence used to prove secondary meaning.

Tarnishment (Disparagement) - Creates negative image of ® in public's mind through an association with unsavory, unrelated goods or services.

Trade Dress - Trade dress is the total image of a product, the overall impression created, not the individual features.

Trademark - A word logo or package design, or a combination of them, used by a manufacturer or merchant or to be used by one who has a bona fide intention to use it in commerce to identify its goods and distinguish them from others.

Trademark Classification Act of 1984 - Congress amended the Lanham Act Sections 14(c) and 45 to protect marks for a unique product or service.

TTAB - Trademark Trial and Appeal Board.

Use in Commerce - Defined in Lanham Act § 45 as the "bona fide intent use of the mark in the ordinary course of trade, and not merely to reserve a right in a mark."

USPTO - United States Patent and Trademark Office.

Chapter 30

PATENTS

A. **Constitutional provision**

1. Patents and copyrights are protected under the Constitution, *Art I, § 8 cl. 8*, which provides:
2. "The Congress shall have the power *to promote* the progress of science and *useful arts*."

B. **Exclusivity:** "by securing for limited times to authors and inventors the exclusive right to their respective writings and discoveries"

C. **The patent laws create a number of incentives, including:**

1. an incentive to invent
2. an incentive to disclose
3. an incentive to commercialize
4. an incentive to design around

D. **What is NOT patentable subject matter?**

1. natural phenomena
2. abstract ideas
3. laws of nature

E. **The Patent and Trademark Office (PTO)**

1. **General information**
    a. The PTO exists within the Department of Commerce
    b. It is funded entirely through user fees
    c. Is a performance-based organization
    d. Is located in Crystal City, Virginia

2. **Workflow**
    a. In the year 2000,
        i. Over 300,000 patent applications were filed
        ii. Over 182,000 patents were granted

   iii. Average pendency to issue/abandonment: 25 months

b. Future projections
   i. 500,000 patent applications by 2008
   ii. average pendency: 35 to 40 months

3. **Technology Centers (TC's)**
   a. Biotechnology and Organic Chemistry – 1600
   b. Chemical and Material Engineering – 1700
   c. Communication and Information processing – 2700
   d. Physics, Electrical Components & Engineering – 2800
   e. Design patent Application – 2900

4. **Examining hierarchy**
   a. Group director
      i. Oversees group within TC
      ii. Oversee petitions

   b. Supervisory Patent Examiner (SPE)
      i. Supervises examiners in an art unit
      ii. Senior to a Primary Examiner

   c. Primary Examiners
      i. Has signatory authority (i.e., can sign off on Office Actions without approval of SPE)
      ii. Have no researchers – do their own work

   d. Junior Examiners
      i. Approximately their first four years
      ii. No signatory authority
      iii. Have no researchers – do their own work

5. **Examiner Education and Training**
   a. Engineering or Science degree required
   b. A Law degree is NOT required
   c. In-house training: The Patent Academy
      i. Patent Examiner Initial Training course (PEIT)
      ii. Introduction to Practice and Procedure (IPP)
      iii. Weekly 3 hour lectures over the first 6-8 months
   d. "on-the-job" training by Primary Examiners and SPE's

6. **Production system**
   Examiners must examine a certain number of applications in a given period - depends on the difficulty of the technology and the level of the examiner.

7. **Workflow System**
    a. Examiners must respond to amendments within a certain period of time
    b. Responding within 30 days gets an addition
    c. Failure to respond within 60 days gets a subtraction

8. **The incentive**
    a. Promotions depend on production
    b. To receive a promotion, one must work at 110% of the previous quarter
    c. Monetary bonuses
        i. Bonuses for every 10% over 110%
        ii. Earn up to 10% over salary

9. **Quality control**
    a. Junior examiners are reviewed by the primary examiners/SPE's
    b. Office of Quality Management (OQM)
    c. Office of Patent Quality Review (OPQR)
    d. Center for Quality Services (CQS)
    e. Quality Assurance Specialists (QAS)

10. **Affect of production on examination**
    a. Frequent restrictions – forces divisionals
    b. Failure to read entire specifications
    c. Incomplete searching
    d. Inadequate Office Action
    e. End-loading cases at the end of each quarter

F. **Jurisdiction over patent cases?**

1. 28 U.S.C. § 1295 grants jurisdiction over patent appeals solely to the Court of Appeals for the Federal Circuit (CAFC)
    a. The Federal Circuit was formed in 1982
    b. The Federal Circuit's jurisdiction is fixed with reference to that of the district court
        i. Turns on whether the action is one "arising under" federal patent law, 28 U.S.C. § 1338(a)
        ii. If yes, ALL patent cases will appeal to the Federal Circuit
    c. Well-pleaded complaint rule
        i. Governs whether a case arises under §1338(a)

ii. Does not allow a counterclaim to serve as the basis for a district court's "arising under" jurisdiction. ***Holmes Group, v. Vornado Air Circulation Sys.***, 535 U.S. 826 (2002).

2. There are two paths a patent applicant can take if the PTO rejects their application.

   a. **Path 1**
      i. Hearing in front of the Board of Patent Appeals and Interferences (BPAI) (no jury)
      ii. Appeal to the Federal Circuit
      iii. Appeal to the Supreme Court

   b. **Path 2**
      i. District Court (with a jury)
      ii. Appeal to the Federal Circuit
      iii. Appeal to the Supreme Court

G. **Federal preemption**

1. State law is preempted by the patent laws under the Supremacy Clause
   a. Field preemption occurs when Congress so thoroughly occupies a legislative field that it is reasonable to assume that Congress left no room for the states to supplement it
   b. Explicit preemption (17 U.S.C. § 301(a)) - any legal or equitable rights under state law equivalent to any of the exclusive rights within the general scope of copyright
   c. Conflict preemption: State laws are preempted by the Supremacy Clause if they stand as an obstacle to the accomplishment and execution of the full purposes and objectives of Congress in enacting a patent statute

2. Case law on preemption:
   a. ***Aronson v. Quick Point Pencil Co.***, 440 U.S. 257 (1979) (holding that the patent royalty agreement was held not enforceable under state law because the patent application had been denied by the PTO).

   b. ***Sears Roebuck & Co. v. Stiffel,*** 376 U.S. 225 (1964) (holding that when an article is unprotected by a patent, state law may not forbid others to copy it.)

Chapter 31

WHAT IS A PATENT?

A. A patent is an agreement between an inventor and the U.S. government which:

   1. gives the inventor the right to exclude anyone he chooses from practicing his patent (it does <u>NOT</u> give the inventor the right to practice his patent); and
   2. upon expiration (which is 20 years from date of filing), the inventor will lose his exclusive rights and the invention will be made public.

B. Intellectual Property (type) chart

Intellectual Property	Broad category; encompasses one or more of the following:
Invention	***Patent, Trade Secret***
Know-how, invention	***Trade Secret and/or Trade Secret*** *(can have both)*
Brand-name	***Trademark***
Work of Authorship	***Copyright***

C. A patent gives the right to another exclude others from making, using and selling the patented invention.

D. A patent can be:

   1. "an article of manufacture": the production of articles for use from raw or prepared materials by giving to these materials new forms, qualities, properties, or combinations, whether by hand-labor or machinery
   2. "a composition of matter": a combination of two or more substances, whether they be the results of chemical union,

or of mechanical mixture, or whether they be gases, fluids, powders, or solids.

3. ***In re Chakrabarty,*** 571 F.2d 40 (CCPA), cert. dismissed, 47 U.S.L.W. 3129 (Aug. 25, 1978) blurred the lines between whether microorganisms are articles of manufacture of compositions of matter

4. ***Diamond v. Chakrabarty,*** 447 U.S. 303 (1980)
   a. "Anything under the sun that is made by the hand of man" is patentable.
   b. includes living matter

E. Kinds of patents: five groups

1. **FIRST GROUP**
   a. Utility Patents
   b. Design Patents
   c. Plant Patents

2. **SECOND GROUP**
   a. Mechanical Patents
   b. Chemical Patents
   c. Electrical Patents
   d. Biotech Patents
      i. subspecies of utility patents
      ii. Utility models (petty patents) are non-existent in the US, but they exist in the Europe.

   e. Software Patents: Separate special category of patents

   f. Business Method Patents
      i. The newest kind of patent
      ii. See ***State Street Bank v. Signature Financial,*** 149 F.3d 1368 (Fed. Cir. 1998)
         - Narrow holding: a processing system that takes data representing discrete dollar amounts through a series of mathematical calculations to determine a final share price – a useful, concrete, tangible result – is patentable subject matter
         - Broad holding: A specific, practical application of algorithm-based software is patentable

3. **THIRD GROUP**
    a. Product Patents
    b. Composition Patents
    c. Use Patents
    d. Process Patents

4. **FOURTH GROUP**
    a. Pioneer Patents
        i. Interpreted broadly in the courts and tend to dominate over improvement patent. Starting a new industry.
        ii. They dominate all the other improvement patents in that field.
        iii. Full broad sweep of interpretation.

    b. Basic Patents: One that is instrumental in getting a whole industry established.

    c. Improvement Patents

    d. Selection Patents: for example, chemicals - if you have a broad genius covered can have a patent for a specific chemical out of that group.

    e. Dominant Patents: all improvement patents infringe this patent. Usually facilitates cross-licensing.

    f. Submarine Patents
        i. Patents which are pending in the PTO for a long time
        ii. by the time they issue they cover a whole industry and everyone has to get a license.
        iii. Eliminated by the current patent duration of 20 years after filing.

    g. Paper Patents
        i. Patent that is not commercially practiced: it covers no commercial product or process.
        ii. Are very narrowly interpreted for infringement issues.

    h. Picture Patents
        i. Very narrowly drafted claims. Like a design patents or a plant patent.
        ii. So narrow that it does not mean something; it can easily be avoided by alternatives.

i. "Poor Man's" Patents
   i. Inventors to try to establish a date of invention so the practice arose of mailing a letter describing the invention to themselves.
   ii. Disclosure document can be used as the poor man's patent: description of the invention to the PTO where the PTO kept it for two years.
   iii. Now can file a provisional patent application without any claims

5. <u>**FIFTH GROUP**</u>
   a. Petty Patent (Utility Models)
   b. Patent of Importation: based on a foreign patent
   c. Patent of Confirmation: Synonymous for Patent of importation.
   d. Use Patents:
      i. Patents that covered the use of old chemicals.
      ii. *Atrazine* patent example: new herbicidal use of an old known chemical.
      iii. Especially valuable from an international perspective.

F. Still have common law rights to practice an un-patented invention.

G. One can file a patent application without having reduced the invention to practice: *Constructive reduction*

H. Do not need to have literal infringement for patents because of the ***Doctrine of Equivalents.***

1. Definition of Doctrine of Equivalents: a rule of interpretation of a claim under which an accused infringer, although not a literal infringer, is it still infringing if it performs substantially the same function in substantially the same way to obtain substantially the same result as the claimed patent.

2. Negative doctrine of equivalents: sometimes one can copy the claims exactly but because of the way it works is different there is no infringement.

I. <u>File wrapper estoppel</u>: limitation on the doctrine of equivalents that prevents application of doctrine of equivalents when the inventor narrowed the claim to avoid cited prior art that covers crucial element of the accused product or process.

J. Patents and Monopolies

1. A patent is not a monopoly.
2. A patent is personal property under 35 U.S.C. § 261
3. Patents are pro-competitive.
4. A monopoly by definition is taking something out of the public domain that is in the public domain. Patents are not in the public domain before they are issued; they are not taken from the public domain. Patents go into the public domain because of knowledge and allowing people to practice the invention.
5. Owning a patent does not give the right to practice the invention, it just gives the right to prevent others from practicing it.
6. Patents intensify competition.

K. Domination definition: patents have different scopes.

L. How does domination work?

Ex. Cheeseburger "invention"

a. Inventor patented the Cheeseburger
b. Later on, the inventor added some more cheese and received an improvement patent on the cheeseburger
c. Then a second inventor came along and replaced the ketchup and added a special sauce. The second inventor gets a patent on this new and improved cheeseburger.
d. The second inventor is subject to the rights of the original inventor's Cheeseburger patents.

Chapter 32

PATENT SECTIONS

A. Main sections

1. § 100 – Definitions
   a. "inventions" means invention or discovery
   b. "process" means process, art or method including new uses of knows processes.
2. § 101 – Inventions patentable
   a. Patentable manner is new and useful process, machine, manufacture, or composition of matter
   b. Or, any new and useful improvement.
   c. This section was originally written by Thomas Jefferson, the father of the US patent system
   d. This section is a key, but not really very helpful, authority regarding patent subject matter and utility
3. § 102 – Conditions for Patentability; Novelty and Loss of Right to Patent
   a. ***Pennock v. Dialogue***, 2 Pet. 1, 24 (1829) (holding that an inventor who makes a discovery public or permits others freely to use it, abandons the rights a patent would have secured, had it been applied for before such use).
   b. § 102 has six main sections:
      i. SECTION a
         - whether a third party knew or used this invention in the US before the current application was filed
         - whether a third party patented or described in a publication anywhere in the world before the current application was filed
         - if rejected under (a), go to Rule 131 (Title 37)

      ii. SECTION b
         - whether the inventor or anyone else patented or described in a publication, in the US or worldwide, the invention more than a year before the filing date.

- whether the invented or anyone else offered for sale, sold, or publicly used the invention in the US one year before the filing date.
- policy behind the on-sale bar:
  - A) extension of period of protection
  - B) encouraging prompt and widespread disclosure
  - C) discouraging the removal from public
  - D) give investors reasonable evaluation time
- What is experimental use? Principles of experimental use:
  - A) Use may be public if need be (see ***City of Elizabeth v. American Pavement Co.***, 97 U.S. 126 (1878)).
  - B) Need not alter
  - C) Durability may dictate duration
  - D) No reduction to practice no guarantee
  - E) Public & patentee may incidentally benefit
  - F) Bona fide intent to test and perfect primary
  - G) Records are beneficial
  - H) Experiments must have been conducted under the surveillance of the inventor
- Main Cases
  - A) *Pfaff v. Wells Elecs.*, 142 L. Ed. 2d 261 (1998) Holding that the §102(b) on-sale bar applies when two conditions are satisfied before the critical date -
    - 1) Product subject of commercial offer for sale
    - 2) Invention must be ready for patenting
  - B) ***Metallizing Engineering Co. v. Kenyon Bearing & Auto Parts Co.***, 153 F.2d 16 (2nd Cir. 1946) Holding that "it is a condition upon inventor's right to a patent that he shall not exploit his discovery competitively after it is ready for patenting; he must content himself with either secrecy, or legal monopoly."

ii. SECTION c: if the invention was abandoned, that results in unpatentablity

iii. SECTION d
   - if the inventor patents the invention in a foreign country more than a year before the filing date, it will be rejected
   - policy behind this section is to encourage prompt filing in the US

iv. SECTION e: if a third party describes the invention in an application that is ultimately issued or published before the you invent your invention, your application will be rejected

v. SECTION f
   - if the inventor did not invent the subject matter he seeks to patent, he will not be granted a patent
   - also look to §103 for guidance when dealing with issues from this section

vi. SECTION g
   - deals with interferences
   - if a third party can prove during an interference proceeding that he invented it before you did, your patent application will be rejected
   - so, the first to reduce to practice wins, unless the second to reduce to practice can prove earlier conception AND diligence (constructive reduction to practice)
   - key cases:
     A) ***Apotex USA, Inc. v. Merck & Co.***, 254 F.3d 1031, 59 U.S.P.Q.2d 1139 (Fed. Cir. 2001).
     B) ***Dunlop Holdings Ltd. v. Ram Golf Corp.***, 524 F.2d 33 (7th Cr. 1975).

e. The inventor did not invent the subject matter results in un-patentability as well.

f. What is prior art?
   i. Prosecution context: §§(a), (b), (e), and (g) are the "prior art" provisions
   ii. Litigation context: § 102 plus anything else, including the knowledge of those of ordinary skill in the art, that bears of the patentability of the claims at issue

g. Conception: "the formation in the mind of the inventor of a permanent and definite idea of the complete and operative invention as it will thereafter exist." ***Mergenthaler v. Scudder***, 11 App. D.C. 264, 276, 1897 C.D. 724, 731 (1897).

h. Anticipation
   i. §§(a), (b), (e), and (g)
   ii. whether the claims reads on product or process
   iii. every element and limitation of the claim must be found in a single reference either explicitly or inherently
   iv. is not shown even if the difference between the claims and the prior art reference are insubstantial; and the missing elements could be supplied by the knowledge of one skilled in the art

4. § 103 – Conditions for Patentability; Non-obvious Subject Matter
   a. As was noted by Professor Craig Jepson, "Barbed wire was invented *after* the electric light and *after* the air brake"
   b. The invention sought to be patented must *not* have been obvious to a person having ordinary skill in the art at the time the invention was made.
   c. Can only patent when the subject matter was non-obvious "at the time the invention was made to a person having ordinary skill in the art to which the patent pertains."
   d. Biotechnology processes are patentable.
   e. What determines the level of ordinary skill in the field of invention?
      i. Education of the inventor
      ii. Type of problems encountered in the art
      iii. Prior art solutions to those problems
      iv. Rapidity with which innovations are made
      v. Sophistication of the technology
      vi. Education of active workers in the field
   f. Secondary considerations
      i. Commercial success
         - Failure of others to commercialize
         - Chain of inferences
      ii. Unexpected results
         - Operates during prosecution
         - Danger of hindsight change in expectations
         - Reinforces presumption of validity

- iii. Copying
  - Flattery
  - Design around
  - Must be identical
- iv. Failure of others
- v. Long-felt and unmet need
- vi. Praise from experts
- vii. Acquiescence and licensing
  - Acknowledgement
  - Fear of litigation

g. Key cases
- i. *Hotchkiss v. Greenwood*, 52 U.S, 248 (1851) (the porcelain door knob case finding the porcelain knob obvious in light of prior art metal knobs).
- ii. ***Cuno Eng'g Corp. v. Automatic Devices Corp.***, 314 U.S. 84 (1941) (holding that a new device must reveal a "flash of creative genius").
- iii. ***Great Atl. & Pac. Tea Co. v. Supermarket Equip. Corp.***, 340 U.S. 147 (1950) (holding that the patentee had added nothing to the total stock of knowledge, but had merely brought together segments of prior art and claimed them in congregation).
- iv. ***Arkie Lures, Inc. v. Gene Larew Tackle***, 19 F.3d 953 (Fed. Cir. 1997) (the flavored fishing lure case)

h. Seminal modern nonobviousness cases:
- i. ***US v. Adams***, 383 U.S. 39 (1966), (holding that "despite the fact that each of the elements of the Adams battery was well known in the prior art, to combine them as did Adams required that a person reasonably skilled in the prior art must ignore long-accepted factors").
- ii. ***Graham v. John Deere***, 383 U.S. 1 (1966).
- iii. ***Calmar v. Cook***, 86 S.Ct. 684 (1966).

5. § 112 – Specifications of a patent

a. This section requires patentees to disclose to the PTO how to practice their invention, and the best method of doing so.

b. Disclosure requirements
- i. Notice
- ii. Dissemination
- iii. Avoid infringement and design around

c. Filing date satisfaction
    i. The application must be enabling as of the filing date
    ii. The best mode requirement must be satisfied upon filing
    iii. The subject matter of later-added claims must be supported and described as of the filing date

d. Six paragraphs to § 112
    i. Paragraph 1: Enablement.
        - The specifications need to be a written description of the invention and its making & use.
        - Best mode requirement:
            A) The specification must describe the best mode contemplated by the inventor of carrying out his invention
            B) Public policy behind this is to prevent inventors from obtaining patent protection while concealing preferred embodiments of their inventions
            C) A well-done enabling disclosure enables a person of ordinary skill in the art to make and use any embodiment of the invention
            D) If better modes are discovered later on, that's OK. But at the time of filing, the best mode must be set forth.
            E) Is violated in two situations:
                A) If the inventor does not adequately disclose a preferred embodiment of the invention. See ***Northern Telecom, Inc., v. Datapoint Corp.***, 908 F.2d 931 (Fed. Cir. 1990) and ***Chemcast Corp. v. Arco Indus. Corp.***, 913 F.2d 923 (Fed. Cir. 1990).
                B) If the inventor fails to disclose aspects of making or using the claimed invention and the undisclosed matter materially affected the properties of the claimed invention. See ***Great Northern Corp. v. Henry Molded Products***, 94 F.3d 1569 (Fed. Cir. 1996) and ***Dana Corp. v. IPC Ltd. Partnership***, 860 F.2d 415 (Fed. Cir. 1988).
            F) Other cases
                A) ***Peabody v. Norfolk***, 98 Mass. 452 (1868) (best mode of making gunny

sacks – the world of trade secrets arose from this case).

B) ***Kewanee Oil v. Bicron Corp.***, 416 U.S. 470 (1974).

C) ***Bonito Boats v. Thunder Craft Boats***, 489 U.S. 141 (1989).

- The scope of enablement is Everything disclosed in the Specification AND everything known to a person of ordinary skill in the art without undue or unnecessary experimentation

ii. ¶ 2 Definiteness.

- "the specification shall conclude with one or more claims *particularly pointing out* and *distinctly claiming* the subject matter [of the] invention."
- The specification has to include one or more claims about the subject matter of the patent

iii. ¶ 3 Independent claims. A claim may be written in dependant, independent or multiple forms.

iv. ¶ 4 Dependent claims. A claim in dependant form has to reference the previous one

v. ¶ 5 Multiple dependent claims. A claim dependant in multiple form shall have a reference

vi. ¶ 6 Means plus function language.

- The elements in a claim for combination may be expressed as a means or step for performing a specific function.
- For literal infringement, one needs to show: Identical function AND equivalent structure

6. § 119 – Benefit of Earlier Filing Date
   a. if you first file for a patent overseas, you get that same filing date in the US
   b. <u>Important</u>: Be mindful of the one-year bar.

7. § 121 – Divisional Applications
   a. if the examiner thinks that your application has more than one "independent or distinct" inventions, he may restrict the application to only one invention

   b. should you desire to proceed with the other patent(s) that were restricted out of this application, you may do so. Those applications will then be called *divisionals*.

8. §133 – Time for Prosecuting Application
   a. if you fail to act within six months on any action you receive from the PTO, the PTO will consider your application abandoned.
   b. Unless you prove that the delay was unavoidable

9. § 145 – Civil Action to obtain a patent. One can file civil action to challenge PTO's decision but will have to pay the costs.

10. § 154 – Contents and terms of a patent; provisional rights
    a. a patent grants an exclusive right that lasts for 20 years after date of filing.
    b. A patent must contain specifications and a drawing.

11. § 161 – Plant patents
    a. asexual reproducing plants only, must not be found in nature
    b. there are currently over 12,000 plant patents
    c. important case is ***J.E.M. Ag Supply, Inc. v. Pioneer Hi-Bred Int'l, Inc.***, 534 U.S. 124, 60 U.S.P.Q.2d (BNA) 1865 (2001) (holding that newly developed plant breeds fall within the subject matter of §101, and neither the Plant Protection Act (PPA) nor the Plant Variety Protection Act (PVPA) limits the scope of §101's coverage).

12. § 171 – Design patents
    a. patent term is 14 years
    b. anyone can patent new, original ornamental features

13. § 251 – Reissue of defective patents
    a. A patent can be reissued because of error; *but*
    b. A reissued patent cannot enlarge the scope of the original patent *unless* it is applied for within 2 years of issuance

14. § 252 – Effect of Reissue
    a. Period continues to run and it has the same effects as the original patent; ***except***
    b. that it cannot abridge or affect the rights of any users prior to the reissuing.

15. § 261 – Ownership; Assignment
    a. This section makes it clear that patents have the attributes of personal property.
    b. A patent can be assigned, conveyed or granted, but it needs to be recorded within 3 months.

16. § 271 – Infringement of Patent
    a. liability from infringement results when someone makes, uses, sells or imports a patented invention without permission
    b. inducing infringement also results in liability.
    c. selling or important the functional part of a patented machine without permission is infringement unless that part is a *staple* (i.e. has non-infringing uses as well).
    d. Recall: a patent gives the patent holder the exclusive right to exclude others from making, using, or selling the patented invention.
    e. See ***Deepsouth Packing Co. v. Laitram Corp.***, 406 U.S. 518 (1972).

17. § 273 – Defenses to infringement based on earlier inventor. The defense for patent infringement is: reduction to practice for more than one year before filing.

18. § 282 – Presumption of validity; defenses
    a. a patent shall be presumed valid
    b. each claim of a patent shall be presumed valid independently of the validity of other claims
    c. dependent claims shall be presumed valid even though dependent upon an invalid claim
    d. the burden of establishing invalidity of any claim rests on the party asserting invalidity

19. § 284 – Damages
    a. the court shall award damages adequate to compensate for the infringement
    b. that in no event shall be less than a reasonable royalty
    c. court may hear expert testimony on what a reasonable royalty would be
    d. important cases:
        i. ***Rite-Hite Corp. v. Kelley Co.***, 56 F.3d 1538 (Fed. Cir. 1995) (en banc) (holding that to recover lost profits, the

patent owner may establish "but for" causation, or, may show causation by establishing that infringer should reasonably have foreseen how infringement would cause the loss).

ii. ***Upjohn v. Riahom***, 641 F.Supp. 1209 (D. Del 1986).

iii. ***Panduit Corp. v. Stahlin Bros. Fibre Works, Inc.***, 575 F.2d 1152 (6th Cir. 1978). *Panduit* test requirements:

- A demand
- Absence of acceptable noninfringing substitutes
- Manufacturing and marketing capability
- Amount of lost profit
- Exception to this test: all elements need not be proven when the patentee is in a two or three supplier market

e. Enhanced damages:
Patent owner may receive enhanced damages if they can prove the infringer acted:

- by copying;
- to conceal;
- with intent; and
- in bad faith

20. § 285 – Attorney Fees: the court may, in exceptional circumstances, award reasonably attorney fees to the prevailing party.

Chapter

33

PATENT REQUIREMENTS

A. Four substantive requirements for patentability
   1. Subject matter § 101
   2. Utility § 101
   3. Novelty § 102
   4. Nonobviousness § 103

B. Four formal requirements for claim validity
   1. Definiteness § 112 ¶2
   2. Enablement § 112 ¶1
   3. Written Description § 112 ¶1
   4. Best Mode § 112 ¶1

C. Types of patents:
   1. Utility patents
      - focus on technology; can only issue for a new means of achieving a useful end or result
      - Is there a well-established utility? Ask: Can one of ordinary skill immediately appreciate why the invention is useful? Also ask: Is the utility is specific, substantial and credible?
      - The PTO has the initial burden of challenging and providing evidence showing that one of ordinary skill in the art would reasonably doubt the asserted utility. An inherently unbelievable undertaking. Implausible scientific principles.
      - Burden shifts to applicant to provide rebuttal evidence
   2. Designs or articles of manufacture
   3. Plant varieties

Chapter

34

PATENT MECHANICS

A. Allowance: i.e. Allowable subject matter

1. Notice of Allowability: Indicates all pending claims are allowable
2. Notice of Allowance and Payment of Issue Fee: 35 U.S.C. § 151, 37 CFR 1.31 - Issue must be paid within three months.
3. Amendments after Allowance: 37 CFR 1.312
   - prosecution on the merits is closed
   - amendments may be made as t formal matters
   - other amendments must show why they are necessary and were not presented earlier in prosecution

B. Appeal

1. Applicant can appeal a rejection to the Board of Patent Appeals and Interferences (BPAI) under 35 U.S.C. § 134
2. Applicant needs to file
   - A notice of appeal; and
   - An appeal brief

C. Abandonment

1. When?
   - Failure to take appropriate action within the statutory period
   - Express abandonment by applicant
2. Revival: 37 CFR 1.137

   An applicant may petition to revive if the delay in responding was unavoidable or unintentional.
   - unavoidable: office action was lost in the mail
   - unintentional: you'll still have to pay a higher fee

D. Claiming Priority under 35 U.S.C. § 120

(Benefit of earlier filing date of a US non-provisional application)

- Same invention disclosed in earlier application pursuant to §112 first paragraph
- Filed during pendency of parent application - there needs to be codependency

- Reference to earlier filed application - In the specification, "the present application is a continuation of application #, filed on ..."
- One or more common inventors

E. Types of Related Applications for claiming priority

1. continuation application: 35 U.S.C. § 120
   - no new subject matter
   - no new oath/declaration
2. divisional application: 35 U.S.C. §§ 120, 121
   - application field on non-elected claims pursuant to a restriction requirement
   - no new subject matter
   - no new oath/declaration
3. continuation-in-part application (CIP): 35 U.S.C. § 120
   - new subject matter is added
   - benefit of priority for common subject matter but not new subject matter
   - new oath/declaration required

F. Filing Procedures for Related Applications

1. standard filing procedures under 37 CFR 1.53(b)
2. new specifications, claims, and drawings
3. copy of oath/declaration (if continuation or divisional)
4. new oath/declaration (if CIP)
5. continued prosecution application

G. Claiming Priority under 35 U.S.C. § 119

1. Benefit of earlier filing date of a foreign patent application (§119(a))
   - If filed within 12 months
   - Claim made in oath or declaration
   - Certified priority document
2. Benefit of earlier filing date of a provisional application (§119(e))
   - If filed within 12 months
   - Common inventorship
   - Reference in the specifications
   - Can add new subject matter. New subject matter does not get benefit of filing date

H. Patent Term and Priority

1. 35 U.S.C. § 154
2. begins on the day that the patent issues and ends 20 years from the filing date
3. measured from the earliest date entitled to priority under 35 U.S.C. § 120
4. priority under 35 U.S.C. § 119 (foreign and provisional applications) does not start the 20 year patent term

I. Patent Term Adjustment

1. Three bases for adjusting the patent term
   - PTO fails to take certain actions within specified timeframes
   - PTO fails to issue patent within three years of actual filing date of the application
   - Delay due to interference, secrecy orders, or successful appellate review
2. reduced by period equal to the period during which an applicant failed to engage in reasonable efforts to conclude prosecution of the application.

J. Title of the Invention- 37 CFR 1.72 (a)

1. may not exceed 500 characters in length
2. must be as short and specific as possible
3. do not want it to be too narrow: do not want the title to limit the scope of the claim.
4. do not want the title to be overly broad because of obviousness (might bring in prior art).
5. should contain reference to federally-sponsored research, if any
6. reference to a "Sequence Listing," a table, or a computer program listing appendix submitted on a compact dist and an incorporation-by-reference of the material on the compact disc
7. avoid giving the invention a title that might contain a future trademark as you risk genericism and the loss of your name upon expiration of the patent term. (*See* Singer).

K. Cross-Reference to Related application - 37 CFR 1.78

1. Used to claim priority under 35 U.S.C §§ 120 or 119(e)
2. Cross-reference to prior parent application.

L. Technical field - A statement of the field of art to which the invention pertains:
   1. "The present invention relates to __ and more particularly, __."
   2. As a rule of thumb a narrower field corresponds to the broadest claim

M. Background of the Invention – 37 CFR 1.97-1.98
   1. Description of the state of the related art or other information known to the applicant, including references to specific patents where appropriate.
   2. Sets forth the problems involved with the prior art that are solved by the invention
      - Avoid using "invention" because claims change during prosecution.
      - Avoid the word prior art because of the special meaning (it could be used by the examiner as a prior art reference under § 102)
      - Leading up to some statement that is a transition to the invention: set the stage for the rest of the application.
      - Refrain from characterizing prior patents.
      - Avoid absolutes especially when characterizing prior Arts
      - End it with a sales pitch: here is the problem and here is why you need the invention

N. Summary of the Invention - 37 CFR 1.73
   1. Brief summary of the invention indicating its nature and substance
   2. Should be directed to the specific invention being claimed
   3. Typically tracks the language used in the claims (the broadest claim) without the legal terminology
   4. May include a statement of the object(s) of the invention.
   5. Object of the invention can be used to imply the doctrine of equivalents against the patentee.
   6. Reason for summary is to provide antecedent basis for the language in the claims.
   7. Make it clear and understandable in the event that someday you might want a jury to read and comprehend what your invention is

O. Brief Description of the Drawings - 37 CFR 1.74a-c
   1. A brief description of the several views of the drawings.
   2. Examples:

- "Fig. 1 is a perspective view of ... according to one embodiment of the present invention" - Use the language to broaden the invention
- "Fig.2 is a cross-sectional view taken long line 1-1 of Fig. 1" - for cross-sectional might want to review to prior Figure.
- "Fig. 3 is a functional block diagram..."

P. Detailed Description of Preferred Embodiments

1. 37 CFR 1.71
   - A written description of the invention and of the manner and process of making and using
   - The best most contemplated by then inventor must be set fourth

2. 37 CFR 1.74
   - When there are drawings, refer to the different views by specifying the numbers of the figures and to the different parts by use of reference numerals.
   - Reference numeral in the figure and the detailed description; describe how the elements are related, what shape, size, configuration they have.
   - When using reference numerals, skip some numbers so you can number the elements consecutively.
   - Don't give the same part different reference numbers.

3. Other guidelines
   - Avoid absolutes unless the inventor told you otherwise.
   - Use the present tense, active voice.
   - Be concise, keep in mind the audience.

4. Should include in specification
   - Definitions of the claim terminology (to avoid § 112 problem)
   - When you define structure in the specifications, define them broadly. If a term is not defined in the specifications, the court will interpret the claim narrowly based on the drawings in the specifications. Provide a broad definition what characteristics an element has.
   - Give standards in the specifications that allow one skilled in the art to determine the scope of the claim that is otherwise vague or indefinite: *e.g. "essentially free of alkali metals"*
   - Be sure that any time means-plus-functions language is used that there is adequate support in the specification for the means and define the structures broadly.

- Write the specifications so that they are broad enough to encompass alternate forms of the inventions.
- In the detailed descriptions you can also have examples. These examples do not need to be working examples.
- Don't need to include in the specification: Structures, components related to the invention that one skilled in the art would know how to practice them.

Q. Abstract of the Disclosure

1. 37 CFR 1.72 (b)
2. A brief abstract (no more than 150 words) of the technical disclosure of the patent set forth on a separate sheet.
3. Purpose: to determine quickly from a cursory inspection the nature and gist of the technical disclosure.
4. Cannot use legal language in it.
5. Write in active voice.
6. Begin all paragraphs with a topic sentence.
    - Expand on the topic sentence in the body of the paragraph.
    - Limit the paragraph to that topic.
    - Conclude the paragraph with a concluding sentence.
    - Your topic sentence or concluding sentence must transition from one paragraph to the next, unless you have concluded the section.
7. The abstract will not be used for interpreting the scope of the claims (only applies to PTO)
8. Good case: ***Hill-Room Co. v. Kinetic Concepts, Inc.*** 209 F.3d 1337 (Fed. Cir. 2000) (the Federal Circuit used the abstract to interpret scope of the claim).

R. Drawings

1. All the claimed features must be shown in the drawing (37 CFR 1.83)
2. Formal patent drawings must comply with 37 CFR 1.84
3. Informal drawings accepted for examination.
4. All drawings must be capable of reproduction - Follow margin requirements.

S. Oath or declaration

1. 35 U.S.C. § 115; 37 CFR 1.63-1.69
2. The applicant must state:
    - that they believe they are the original and first inventor

- that they have reviewed and understand the contents of the application, including the claims
- acknowledge the duty to disclose to the PTO all information known to the person to be material to patentability
- acknowledge that willful false statements may jeopardize validity of the application

3. Joint inventorship: 35 U.S.C. § 116, 37 CFR 1.45
   - Applications must be filed in the names of the inventors
   - Do not need equal contribution but there is some level of collaboration

T. Filing Fees – 37 CFR 1.16-1.18

1. Base filing fees:
   - 3 independent claims
   - 20 Total Clams
2. Additional fee for multiple dependent claims
3. Small entity status 37 CFR 1.27: 50 % discount on filing fees for:
   - Independent inventors
   - non-profit organizations
   - small businesses with less than 500 employees

U. Notice to File Missing Part:

1. no filing fee or signed oath./declaration has been filed
2. filing date granted
3. Filing fees and Signed Declaration identifying the inventors must be filed within a specified time or the application will be abandoned.
4. have two months to correct

V. Notice of Omitted items

1. missing pages of specifications/drawings but the disclosure is otherwise adequate
2. filing date still granted.

W. Notice of Incomplete Application

1. description, claims, or drawings have not been filed
2. will <u>not</u> be granted a filing date.

X. Power of attorney

1. 37 CFR 1.31
2. Applicant may file and prosecute own application or may appoint a registered agent or attorney

Y. Assignment
3. 35 USC § 261, 37 CFR 3.1 et seq.
4. all or part(s) of the rights, title and interest to a patent application can be transferred
5. However, the application still must be filed in the name of the inventor(s)
6. one should record the assignment with the PTO.

Z. Express Mail Procedure
- i. 37 CFR 1.10
- ii. all patent applications are considered filed in the patent office as of the day they are deposited with the "Express mail service" of the U.S. Postal Service.
- iii. Anything else it gets the filing date the PTO receives it.

AA. Duty to Disclose
- i. 37 CFR 1.56: "Each individual association with the filing and prosecution of a patent application has ... a duty to disclose all information <u>known</u> ... to be <u>material</u> to patentability."
- ii. When in doubt disclose

BB. Information Disclosure Statement
- i. When to file: 37 CFR 1.97
  1. preferably when you file the application
  2. can be filed later (3 months plus) you may have to pay a fee and/or file a petition
- ii. What to file: 37 CFR 1.98
  1. a list of all patents, publications, or other information
  2. a copy of each & a concise explanation of those not in English.

CC. Request for Non-publication
- i. Applicant may request that an application not be published if the invention has not been and will not be the subject of an application filed in another country (or under international agreement) that require 18 months publication – 35 USC § 1.122 (b)(2) B (I)
- ii. Request must be made at the time of the filing
- iii. Request must have a signed certification and must be conspicuous – 37 CFR 1.213

DD. Application Data Sheet

i. An application data sheet is a sheet or sheets that may be *voluntarily* submitted in either provisional or non-provisional application, which contains bibliographic data, such as applicant, correspondence address representative, domestic priority claim, and foreign priority claim information.
ii. Assists PTO in capturing data

EE. Provisional Patent Applications 35 U.S.C. § 111 (b)

i. What is needed for a filing date? 37 CFR 1.53 (c)
    1. Do not need claims
    2. a description pursuant to 37 CFR 1.71
    3. any drawing required by 37 CFR 1.81 (a)
    4. cover sheet identifying the application as a non-provisional application as required by 37 CFR 1.51 (c) 1
ii. What is needed to keep the filing date? 37 CFR 1.53 (g)
    1. Filing fee
    2. Cover sheet with inventor name(s)
    3. No information disclosure sheet
iii. Advantages and Strategies
    1. Secures a filing date without starting the 20 year patent term
    2. Can be prepared and field more quickly to prevent a statutory bar
        a. Do not need to prepare and file claims
        b. Does not require signed declaration
    3. Relatively less expensive.
iv. Disadvantages and Pitfalls
    1. does not get examined and cannot issue as a patent
    2. a formal application must be filed within one year with full filing fee.
    3. Disclosure may not comply with 112, 1st paragraph
        a. Not detailed enough to be enabling
        b. Not broad enough to provide written description to support broad claims.
    4. Foreign PCT application must be filed within one year to claim priority.

5. Include summary of the invention that describes the invention broadly to support broad claims in the later non-provisional application.

FF. Responding to Office actions

i. Amendment practice
   1. A response to an office action is a response. If the document includes amendments to the claims it is an "AMENDMENT" or "AMENDMENT IN RESPONSE"
   2. Do not call it remarks. Can have remarks section in the document.

ii. First Office Action
   1. Take care of long lead time matter
   2. Restart the response clock
   3. Get the client on board
      a. If you get a first office allowance, you have WAY too narrow of claims.
      b. If the PTO misses some papers can call the examiner to send all the papers and restart the time. Ask the client to have look at references and have them distinguished.
   4. Check the dates!
      a. Prior art might not be prior art
      b. Divisional
      c. Provisionals
      d. Foreign Priority
      e. Reference Date
   5. Do not make unnecessary amendments
      a. Do not change claims unless you have to.
         - Potential Prosecution History/Estoppel
         - Warranted or Not
         - State when not an art related amendment to avoid prosecution history estoppel.
      b. DO NOT MAKE UNNECESSARY AMENDMENTS
      c. Any facts/statements create prosecution history. Narrowing amendments designed to comply with patentability requirements bars access Doctrine of Equivalents. Bar or not, acts and amendments during prosecution can create Prosecution history estoppel

6. Do not make unnecessary arguments or statements
    a. Any prosecution document can result in history/estoppel/bar
    b. Warranted or not
    c. Always consider arguing alone instead of amending first. Use as view of arguments as possible and only one of them will get the claim allowed in the PTO. Make your choice and take the stance.
7. Be economical
    a. Say as little as you have to say
    b. Keep arguments to the point: short and crisp.
    c. Arguments to the pint are more persuasive than those that ramble.
    d. Arguments to the point are less limiting
    e. Only argue what is necessary, and only make necessary amendments.
    f. Clarifying amendments may present opportunity to distinguish
    g. Only arguments on the Record to examiner can be considered on appeal: might be good to have examiner put the material on record
8. Tailor the response to the rejection
    a. <u>GENERAL RULE</u>: Do not argue about the claims argue about prior art. Do not argue limitations, argue problems. The further away the art is away from the claim the more abstract the arguments can be requiring less detail. The further away the art is the less need to say about it. Think about the big picture.
    b. Concepts are better than details.
    c. Problems are better than comparisons
    d. Art better than invention: Talking about art is better than talking about the invention
9. Rely on earlier invention date to eliminate prior art if you MUST:
    a. 1.131 Affidavits to swear back
    b. § 119 foreign priority & priority to provisional
    c. 35 USC § 120
    d. Distinguish on the Merits (if that is a better idea)
10. DO NOT MAKE ADMISSION OF PRIOR ART STATUS
11. Do not argue unclaimed features

a. Unproductive
b. Alerts examiner that critical features are not claimed
c. Distracts from the patentablity of the claimed features
d. Have multiple independent claims

12. 35 U.S.C. § 102 Anticipation Language

a. Apply claim language on an element by element basis
b. To be anticipating, a prior art reference must disclose each and every limitation of the claimed invention, must be enabling, and must describe the claimed invention sufficiently to have placed it in the possession of a person of ordinary skill in the field of the invention.
c. Look at the specifications of the prior art.
d. If examiner is using more than one reference, is second reference to explain, or to expand?
e. Three instances when more than one reference can be used to show anticipation
    - Explain a term in a reference
    - Establish a date
    - Show what a person of ordinary skill in the art knows
f. If the claim at issue has an element or limitation in preamble that limitation may be a limitation not a preamble.
g. Is the reference enabling?
    - Reference has to enabling to anticipate
    - Does it enable the claim that is supposedly anticipated?
    - Most applicable to chemical & biochemical inventions
    - Anticipatory reference must be enabling
    - The prior art most enable one skilled in the art; enable that person to understand

Chapter 35

PATENT CLAIMS

A. Claims must be patentable over the prior art.

B. Function of Claims
   1. To define the exclusive right
   2. Are interpreted in light of the specifications
   3. Notice: *patent claim* must put the public on notice what the exclusive right is
   4. What the claim should do
      a. Particularly point out the subject matter which the applicant considers to be the invention
      b. This notion is a shift from the earlier practice of having claims incorporate the specifications and letting the courts figure it out

C. Claim categories (35 U.S.C.§ 101)
   1. Machine claims (apparatus) claims. Apparatus is something that has multiple components that cooperate together in some way.
   2. Manufacture (or article) claims - difference between machine and manufacture is purely academic
   3. Process (or method) claims
      a. Method of making
      b. Method of using
      c. Defining the steps that are performed.
      d. Each sub-paragraph begins with a verb in "-ing" form. Ex: A method of making a widget comprising the steps of: Obtaining; Mixing; and Layering.
   4. Composition claims - define the chemical composition

D. Claim interpretation
   1. is for a judge to decide in a *Markman* hearing.
   2. intrinsic evidence
      a. claim language
      b. written description
      c. prosecution history

3. extrinsic evidence
    a. technology and interpretation
    b. dictionaries and treatises
    c. expert testimony

E. ***Fressola v. Manbeck,*** 36 U.S.P.Q.2d 1211 (D.C. 1995**)**
1. Contained a claim with multiple sentences.
2. In patent claim drafting, claims are to be drafted with one single sentence.
3. Source of this is the Manual of Patenting Examination Procedure (MPEP)
4. The claim was objected to by PTO because it contained multiple sentences – a violation MPEP 608.01 (m)
5. Applicant argued that
    a. the rule was not created properly
    b. the one sentence rule is incompatible with 35 U.S.C. § 112 ¶ 2
    c. the one sentence rule is arbitrary, rule was not created using the proper procedure
6. Court ruled that the rule was sufficient:
    a. held under 35 U.S.C. § 112 ¶ 2 and may even advance the goals
    b. One sentence rule is procedural and exempt from notice and comment rulemaking requirements.

F. Claim Structure and Format
1. Guidelines may be found in:
    a. 35 U.S.C. § 112
    b. 37 CFR 1.75
    c. MPEP 608.01 (m)
2. Parts of claims:
    a. Preamble
        i. names the invention
        ii. does it limit scope of claim?
        iii. rule: if limitation in preamble is intended to limit scope of claim, limitation should be repeated in the body of the claim
        iv. rule if not intended to limit scope, should be deleted from preamble
    b. Transition
        i. introduces the elements and limitations that make up the invention

ii. word phrases
- comprising (open)
  - A) ex: "A widget *comprising* [at least] A, B, and C [plus any other elements or ingredients]."
  - B) Eliminating a claimed element or limitation may avoid infringement
  - C) Adding an element or limitation will not avoid infringement
- consisting of (closed)
  - A) ex: "A widget *consisting of* [only] A, B, and C [and no other elements or ingredients except for impurities]."
  - B) Eliminating a claimed element or limitation may avoid infringement
  - C) Adding an element or limitation not claimed may also avoid infringement
- consisting essentially of:

b. Body (for independent claims)
  i. Recites the elements and limitations
  ii. Positively recites elements v. inferential claiming
  iii. Provides an antecedent basis
  iv. Provides relationship between the elements
  - Element is thought of a structural feature
  - Each element is recited separately in its own indented sub-paragraph.
  - For elements need *antecedent basis*: when introducing an element use the terms a, afterwards use "said"

  v. Elements should be interrelated. Each element should be related to one of the elements defined previously.

G. Types of claims

a. ***Independent Claims***
  i. 35 U.S.C. § 112 ¶ 3
  ii. Does not refer to another claim
  iii. Stands alone
  iv. Basic parts – Preamble; Transition and Body of claim

b. ***Dependent Claims***
  i. 35 U.S.C. § 112, 37 CFR 1.75 (c)
  ii. Refers to previous claims and specifies further limitations

iii. Incorporates by reference all the limitations of claim to which it refers.

iv. Further limits what is recited in limited claim - By further defining an element; a shortened way of further defining the invention

v. Use preamble consistent with the previous claim

vi. Adds another element - "including" or "comprising"

vii. Example:

1. A widget comprising A and B.
2. The widget of claim 1 further including C.
3. The widget of claim 2 further including D.
4. The widget of claim 3 further including E.

c. ***Multiple dependent claims***

i. Any dependent claim which refers to more than one other claim shall refer to such other claims in the alternative only – 35 U.S.C. § 112 ¶ 5; 37 CFR 175 (c)

ii. A multiple dependent claim cannot depend from another multiple dependent claim – 35 U.S.C. § 112 ¶ 5; 37 CFR 1.75 (c)

iii. Acceptable wording: "according", "as in any of the preceding claims", "as in either claim ... or ..." , "as in claims..."

2. Claim Format rules

a. Claim section starts on separate page beginning

b. "I" or "we" "claim" or "The invention claimed is"

c. 37 CFR 1.75 (h); MPEP 608.01 (m)

d. One Sentence rule MPEP 608.01 (m)

e. Each element recited in a claim should be indented – see 37 CFR 1.75 (i)

3. Antecedent Basis

a. Use "a/an" when element is introduced in the claims for the first time

b. Use "the/said" once element has been introduced

c. Lack of antecedent basis if:

i. not described at all in the specification

ii. description claim inconsistent with that in specification

iii. language used to describe element is misdescriptive

iv. no clear element in specification is referred to

v. drawing must support claims by presenting every element claimed

H. Other formats of claims

1. Markush groups
    a. Must have the language "from the group consisting of"
    b. Remember: the phrase "consisting of" is a closed term that is not desirable for other claims, but IS desirable when writing Markush claims
    c. Most commonly used in the chemical arts, though acceptable in other arts
    d. The materials or elements in the group must belong to a recognized art or have at least one property in common

2. Jepson claims
    a. 37 CFR 1.75(e) – suggested format for independent claims on an improvement
    b. Must have the language "the improvement comprising" somewhere in the claim
    c. Notice: the open phrase "comprising" is the preferred terminology
    d. Some practitioners do not like Jepson claims because they acknowledge prior art, and therefore only attempt to claim a narrow improvement.

3. Product-by-Process claims. Ex: A resistor [the product] comprising: a ceramic core; and a coating of carbon deposited on the core by decomposition of a hydrocarbon gas in the presence of the core [process].

4. Kit claims
    a. for products that are sold unassembled or contain a variety of parts
    b. Structure:
        i. Preamble: use "kit", "assembly", or other term that indicates interrelated parts that are not yet connected.
        ii. Body: use "adapted to" to define the interrelationships between the parts
    c. Advantage: Claim can be directly infringed by making, using, or selling unconnected part as a kit.

I. Functional language

Purpose:
    a. To stop infringers, as functional language might allow to define a structure more broadly.
    b. Define the properties of the pipe lagging.

c. In ***In re Stencel***, 828 F.2d 751 (Fed. Cir. 1987), functional language was used to define the dimensions of the driver without giving specific measurements.
d. It is also useful to fill out the claim, to make it more readable.

J. Means plus function language

1. 35 U.S.C. § 112 ¶ 6
2. ***Ex Parte Roggenburk:*** Means plus function language. Supreme Court case saying that means plus function language was not patentable and subsequently § 112 was amended to reverse the Court's decision
3. Modified by 35 U.S.C. § 112 3rd ¶ (now 6th ¶)
4. Means plus function limitation should be given patentable weight to define over prior art.
5. Means/Step plus function 35 U.S.C. § 112, 6th paragraph
   a. "An element in a claim for a combination may be expressed as a means or step for performing a specified function without the recital of structure, material, or acts in support thereof, and such claim shall be construed to cover the corresponding structure, material, or acts described in the specification and equivalents thereof."
   b. Specifically tells how to interpret the language and how to use it.
   c. At first, means plus function language was thought to broaden some claims.
   d. Do not recite structure or material
   e. Examples:
      i. In an apparatus claim to a steam iron: Means for supplying steam."
      ii. In a claim to a method for ironing: Step for supplying steam.
6. How is means plus function language interpreted under 35 U.S.C § 112 paragraph 6?
   a. Patent examiners are entitled to give the claims the broadest reasonable interpretation.
   b. To cover any structure capable of performing the stated function, i.e. moving particulate matter in a downward direction.

c. Statute says to look at the *specifications and equivalents thereof*
d. PTO made argument that means plus function only applies to infringement
e. Means plus function limitation should be construed to cover the structure or material described in the specifications and the equivalents thereof.

K. Reissuing patents
1. Most common bases for submitting a reissue application
   a. Claims are too narrow or too broad
   b. Disclosure contains inaccuracies
   c. Failed to or incorrectly claimed priority
   d. Failed to make reference to or incorrectly made reference to prior co-pending applications
2. Five requirements for reissue:
   a. defect – the patent must be invalid or inoperative in some way
   b. error without deceptive intent
   c. applicant discloses no new matter
   d. applicant files application within two years if desiring to broaden scope of original patent
   e. the subject matter must still be patentable

L. The Doctrine of Equivalents (DOE):
1. Literal infringement is when the accused invention reads literally word-for-word on the claimed structure
2. Equivalents infringement is when the courts will find an accused invention infringes the claimed structure even though the infringement is not literally word-for-word (i.e., a Ph level of 7.8 vs. 7.7).
3. Key cases upholding the DOE:
   a. ***Graver Tank & Mfg. Co. v. Linde Air Prods.***, 339 U.S. 605 (1950). Held that "one may not practice fraud on a patent." And that things equal as to one thing may not be equal to each other; things different for most purposes may sometimes be equivalent.
   b. ***Warner-Jenkinson Co. v. Hilton Davis Chem. Co.***, 520 U.S. 17 (1997) (DOE upheld even though the accused process was developed independently and without knowledge of the patentee's work).

c. ***Festo Corp. v. Shoketsu Kinzoku Kogyo Kahushiki, Co.***, 122 S. Ct. 1831 (2002) (Supreme Court upheld *Warner-Jenkinson* and reinforced Prosecution History Estoppel: that one who takes a position in order to obtain a benefit cannot later try to take a different position after the requested benefit is obtained based on the original position asserted.)

4. Arguments against the DOE
   a. §112 clearly states that the invention is what has been distinctly claimed
   b. it undermines reissue
   c. it undermines examination

M. <u>Licensee/Assignor Estoppel</u>
   1. policy reasons
      a. prevents unfairness and injustice
      b. prevents people from benefiting from their own wrong
      c. analogy to 'estoppel by deed' in real estate
      d. analogy to a landlord-tenant relationship
   2. See ***Scott Paper Co. v. Marcalus Mfg. Co.,*** 326 U.S. 249 (1945).

N. <u>Laches</u>. Presumption of laches arises six years after the patentee *should have known* of the infringer's activity(ies).

O. <u>Equitable estoppel</u>
   1. patentee's conduct leads infringer to believe, mistakenly, that the patentee does not intend to enforce patent against infringer
   2. infringer reasonably relies on the conduct
   3. infringer will be materially prejudiced if patentee is allowed to proceed

P. <u>Patent Misuse</u>
   1. occurs when the patent holder impermissibly broadens the scope of his patent with an anticompetitive effect
   2. traditional patent misuse occurs if there is
      a. tying to another product
      b. post-patent royalties
      c. package licenses with covenants not to deal
      d. price restraints
   3. Key case: ***Morton Salt v. Suppiger***, 314 U.S. 488 (1942) (holding barred prosecution of a suit against an infringer who

was not a competitor with the patent owner in the sale of the unpatented product).

4. Indirect infringement - Inducement § 271(b)
   a. Actual intent to cause the acts which constitute the infringement
   b. Specific intent to induce infringement
   c. Direct infringement

5. Indirect infringement – Contributory § 271(c)
   a. Knowledge that the combination for which component was especially designed was patented and infringing
   b. The component at issue must have no substantial non-infringing uses

Q. Remedies – 35 U.S.C. § 281

1. Preliminary injunction
   a. Reasonable likelihood of success
   b. Irreparable harm
      i. Lost jobs
      ii. Lost market share
      iii. Length of remaining term
      iv. Other infringers will be encouraged
      v. Market of product is short
      vi. Infringer has a big presence
   c. Balance of hardships
      i. Willful infringement
      ii. Smaller company
   d. Impact on public interest

2. Permanent injunction

Chapter 36

DESIGN PATENTS

A. 35 U.S.C. § 171
   1. "whoever invents any new, original, and ornamental design for an article of manufacture ..."
   2. if the item sought to be patented is primarily ornamental, can receive a design patent
   3. if the item sought to be patented is primarily functional, cannot receive a design patent.

B. How design patents differ from utility patents:
   1. the term is for 14 years
   2. design patents have no maintenance fees
   3. design patents contain only one claim,
   4. no provisionals in design patents

C. What is design patent subject matter?
   1. Appearance
   2. Must be:
      a. embodied in, or applied to, an article of manufacture
      b. surface ornamentation, configuration, or both
      c. inseparable from the article; i.e., cannot exist on its own

D. What the MPEP says about design patents:

   A patentable design of an article of manufacture includes "the visual characteristics of aspects displayed by the object. It is the appearance presented by the object that creates an impression, through the eye upon the mind of the observer." MPEP 1502.

E. Infringement: the accused design must also contain substantially the same points of novelty that distinguished patented design from prior art

F. Some important design patent cases:

1. ***Gargoyles, Inc. v. Aero Corp.***, 49 U.S.P.Q.2d 1556 (D. Mass. 1998).

2. ***TrafFix Devices, Inc. v. Marketing Displays, Inc.***, 532 US 23 (2001) (holding that because the central advance claimed in the expired utility patent was the dual-spring design, which was an essential feature of the trade dress, Marketing Displays had not carried the burden of overcoming the strong inference of functionality based on the disclosure in the expired patents).

3. ***Vornado Air Circulation Systems, Inc. v. Duracraft Corp.***, 58 F.3d 1498 (10th Cir. 1995) (Vornado I).

Chapter

37

LICENSING PATENTS

A. License - generally. To give permission to someone else to use your Intellectual Property right.
   1. A license is conditional, title remains with the owner.
   2. One can sell the patent or assign it (assign = transfer of title)

B. Types of License Transactions
   1. *Assignment* is an outright sale; a transfer of title
      a. sell, transfer, convey and assigns to B *all its rights, title, and interests*
      b. Assignment gives *transfer of title*
         i. Therefore, need to have a provision for reversion of title if royalties are not paid
         ii. otherwise assignor (seller) would have no rights in case of non-payment.
   2. *Exclusive license*: permission given to one party only
      a. More than a mere license, it conveys positive affirmative rights
      b. Less than an assignment or full-ownership because *title does not transfer* from patent holder to licensee as in assignment.
      c. From a tax law perspective, assignments and exclusive licenses are the same: they are considered *assets.*
      d. The right to *exclude* is an essential part of an exclusive license.
      e. A co-owner could grant an exclusive license to the other co-owner to avoid 35 U.S.C. § 262.
      f. An exclusive license is not an all-inclusive exclusive license which extends to the entire world market
      g. One can grant an exclusive license to a specific *territory.*
      h. One can grant exclusive licenses for *fields of use.*
      i. Can have an exclusive license subject to non-exclusive license: a *sole/semi-exclusive license*

   i. licensor may retain a right or may have previously granted a non-exclusive license to another party;
   ii. there may have been an option promise;

j. a penalty on an exclusive license could convert an exclusive license to a non-exclusive license.

k. an exclusive licensee can sue the infringer but a non-exclusive licensee cannot. The exclusive licensee can sue in his or her name but can and as a rule *must* join the *licensor*.
   i. Exceptions:
      - a licensee who threatened to sue an alleged infringer - the licensee can be subject to a *directed judgment*.
      - If the licensor sues, the licensee must be *enjoined* as well if the rights of the licensee are affected.
   ii. One can however provide in an agreement for the payment of the litigation by specific parties or specify how the litigation expenses and damage awards must are shared.
   iii. Normally "no standing" denotes dismissal. However, in some jurisdictions a licensee is allowed to amend the complaint to join the patentee.
      - Oral licensee cannot confer standing.

l. Examples:
   i. Exclusive licensee does not exercise his rights and does not maximize profits.
   ii. Licensor cannot do anything unless they specified a *best efforts clause, minimum payment clause, termination or modification clause,* or convert the exclusive license to a non-exclusive license.

m. Antitrust aspects of exclusive licenses
   i. Antitrust law is implicated because exclusive licenses are considered assets; therefore they fall under § 7 of the Clayton Act.
   ii. One needs to include *sub-licensing rights* in an exclusive license to avoid antitrust conflicts (because an *exclusive license* creates a monopoly).

   iii. In a non-exclusive situation, the licensor can grant additional licenses, which is preferable to giving non-exclusive licensees sub-licensing rights.

3. *Sole (semi-exclusive) license*: permission to one other party
4. *Non-exclusive:* permission to one or more parties
   a. No statutory basis
   b. Immunity from suit
   c. No affirmative rights go with it: e.g. re-enforcement of licensed patent
   d. No freedom from competition if there is infringement

C. Why license?

1. Licensing, technology, and investments are much easier to carry out and accomplish via patents and other Intellectual Property rights as vehicles or bases.
2. Importation of technology not only leads to export of products of that technology but also the exporting of technology – *reverse technology transfer* is the name of this process.
3. Days of abuse of technology transfer owners are gone – viable licenses are win-win and need to pass the *fairness test:*
   a. must be able to sit in the other party's shoes; and
   b. must still be willing to sign the agreement from that party's perspective.

D. Title 35 sections pertaining to patent licensing

1. 35 U.S.C § 261: Ownership; assignment
   a. Patents have the attributes of *personal property*.
   b. Patents as well as patent application and any interest therein is assignable by an instrument of writing.
   c. Applicant, assignee can grant an exclusive right for part of the United States.
   d. Exclusive licensing is recognized by § 261.
   e. Race notice with look-back recording for patent assignments.
   f. Now you can record in the PTO security interests.

2. 35 U.S.C. § 262: Joint owners
   a. No duty to account among co-owners (not true in ©)

   b. Each joint owner may make, use or sell the patented invention without consent and without accounting.
   c. First rule: for joint inventions need contracts outlining the partnership

E. The Range of Licensing

1. *Option* to have a license, so that one can analyze the technology and its value. One does not want to commit to a high royalty bearing payment at the start.3 to 6 months.
2. Option/License: option can be combined with an agreement.
3. Non-exclusive licenses
4. Exclusive licenses are the most predominant.
5. ***Assignment:*** if you want to buy the invention or the patent rights, Trademark rights.
6. ***Acquisition:*** buying the whole company.

F. Developments and Trends in Licensing/Technology

1. There was a time when there was no licensing, now licensing is the norm.
2. Licensing arose because of the high value of IP.
3. Royalties exploded during the 1990's
4. Option agreements are increasing because of the high value and the high royalties: options are used to test a product before committing to a license.
5. Cross-licenses
   a. One receives more than money in return
   b. In essence, a license for license.
6. No longer just licensing one thing. It is a strategic alliance.
7. Vast changes of antitrust.

G. Kinds of Licenses

1. Patent or Trademark license
2. Degree of exclusivity
   a. exclusive, non-exclusive, semi-exclusive (sole)
   b. Degree of exclusivity determines the royalty
3. Royalty free license may be much more valuable.
4. Sublicense
5. Label license: label on the product for use in a patented product.
6. Shrink-wrap/click-wrap licenses

  a. license created by opening "shrink-wrap" of computer software and likes
  b. license created by clicking on OK when installing computer software

7. Grant-back licenses
   a. I license you and you pay me but if you improve the invention I (the licensor) want the ability to practice the improvement.
   b. Grant-forward is the opposite.

8. Implied licenses:
   a. licenses implied from a parties' conduct
   b. *Shop right* if while working for a company you use that company's resources for an invention that company will have the right to use that invention for its own purposes.

H. Reasons for Licensing

1. Unblock interlocking Intellectual Property Rights (IPRs)
2. Settle IP litigation, interferences
3. Grow and diversify product: cannot grow the product without licensing.
4. Deal with outside idea submission
5. Convert dormant IP portfolios into profits.
6. Also suggestions companies receive from outside customers.
7. *Royalty free licenses:* tie use of IP to buying something else and giving the IP for free in that regard.

I. Granting Licenses

1. When can a license be granted?
   a. Under the issued patent during the patent life. One can now have liability for infringement during patent dependency after publication providing the patent is issued.

   b. Under pending application
      i. After publication have rights.
      ii. Rationales: Have trade secret or License becomes effective upon patent issuance.
      iii. Pending application does not grant any exclusion

iv. Cannot get royalties after the patent term but can have royalties before the patent term starts.

c. Before filing patent application based on Trade Secrets

d. After patent expired have a right of up to six years to sue for infringement that occurred during the patents life

2. Granting licenses
   a. Formal written agreement:
      i. Formal agreement
      ii. Letter agreement
   b. Informal written agreement
      i. Informal correspondence
      ii. Letter of intent
      iii. Memorandum of Agreement
      iv. Depending on the circumstances may end up with an agreement if there is intent.
   c. Oral or parol agreement
      i. Only if valid for < 1 year
      ii. Void if within Statute of Fraud
   d. Implied Licenses as consequence of conduct or relationship of parties.
   e. Sample license: A grants to B (and its affiliates and subsidiaries) (or "agrees to grant" or "grants and agrees to grant"), a license to Intellectual property rights, to make, use, offer, sell or import (or to practice Licensed Methods), throughout the US (*its territories and possessions*), for the duration of the Agreement.

J. <u>Implied Licenses</u>

1. First rule in *drafting licenses* and *license agreements* is to leave nothing to implication because very little is implied in contract and parol evidence rarely applies.
   a. Because of the freedom of contract, the Courts are unlikely to find implied parties unless there is strong evidence that the parties *intended* to have a contract manifested by *meeting of the mind*.
   b. Rights not granted in the license remain in the licensor.

2. No *implied license* springs from a written agreement that specifies the use of a certain patent rather than a *certain activity* (if there is an activity might *imply* other patents as well). Only if the license fails to mention patents covering the activity an implied license can be *implied* for the activity as specified by the license.

3. Shop Right
    a. In corporate settings have R&D, or corporate employees making invention in the absence of an agreement that requires the employee to assign the patent right the employee owns the patent, but the company has an *implied license* under a Shop Right providing the employee did not use company resources.
    b. Company cannot sublicense the invention; just for limited internal use.

4. Laches
    a. Sitting on one's rights can create a license.
    b. Have to enforce one's patent rights, otherwise after six years there is a presumption of a license.

K. Compulsory Licenses
1. Not likely to be found in the U.S., still rare in other countries.
2. In foreign countries
    a. Compulsory license provisions are universal
    b. *Paris Convention*: Art 5: 5 years of non-use of patent annuls the patent.
    c. *GATT TRIPS*: Art. 31 (very restrictive use): compulsory license will be granted after 4 years if a party does not use the patent in the industry.
    d. For *non-working patents*.
    e. For *dependent patent*: In Japan you have the right to use a patent but not the right to exclude. A Japanese improvement patentee can legally get a license for the dominant patentee.

3. In United States
    a. No duty to use the license.
    b. Can force the patentee to license.
    c. Can deny patentee injunctive relief.
    d. *Compulsory license* under:
        i. Atomic Energy Act

  ii. Air Pollution Control Act
  iii. Plant Variety Protection Act.
  iv. Relief in Antitrust case
  v. Public Health and Safety reasons.

L. How to Face Third-Party Patents
1. Consider licensing
2. Check the scope of the claims
   a. If you are outside the claim there is no problem.
   b. What the claims cover is important - one may not literally infringe, but there might still be infringement by the *doctrine of equivalents*
   c. Companies have policies not to infringe *valid* patents.
   d. Determine validity by doing a prior art search. If the stakes are high, make at least three validity searches anywhere in the word.
   e. If the patent is valid, if one can modify the embodiment of the patent, one can avoid infringement.
      i. Design, invent, work around it.
      ii. Case law says that if you come up with an improvement patent, one might be able to practice the improvement without infringing the original patent.
      iii. One can also wait for the patent to expire. This is the *best alternative*. Matters if you have a pioneer or paper patent in that context.
   f. Could also buy the patent or business.

M. Reluctance to license
1. In spite of innate reluctance of licensing, it is still beneficial.
2. When one licenses, one creates *ipso facto* a competitor
3. Subsidiaries are legally separate entities and hence need to have licenses.
4. Associated Companies
5. Joint Ventures: diminish reluctance as well
6. Cross-Licenses

N. Drafting Licensing Agreements

1. Overview
    a. There is no such thing as standard patent licenses.
    b. Don't ever rely on boiler plate contracts.
    c. Design the license specifically for the field.
    d. It is a branch of contract laws.
    e. The important elements of a license are:
        i. The most important clause is the *granting clause*
        ii. The second most important clause is the *definition clause*
        iii. Always have a *termination clause*.
    f. Best Efforts Clauses
        i. Merely "best efforts to exploit" the inventions is useless.
        ii. Courts have deemed that to be poor language: it has been interpreted strictly or lenity.
        iii. Define best efforts as "reasonable diligence consistent with the interests of the business" or add objective criteria of performance.
        iv. Best efforts may not be the best advice.

2. Required elements of an Agreement
    a. Heading
        i. Parties Names and State/ Country of Incorporation.
        ii. Parties need to have the power to enforce the agreement.
        iii. Parties need to be empowered to execute the agreement especially for multidivisional companies. Parent companies are not bound if only one subsidiary is involved.
        iv. Effective Date: needs to be a stated in the definitions: if not it is presumed to be the date when the last party necessary for the agreement executes the agreement. Use language "*effective on*" (starts on that date) but not "*effective as of*" which is used when the effective date is retroactive or perspective.

b. Recitals
    i. "Whereas" clauses
    ii. History prior agreement, subject matter
    iii. Important because of the fluidity of companies.
    iv. No operative language is allowed.
    v. Modern Style: entitled "*Background*"
    vi. Rules: if the recitals are clear and the main body is ambiguous, the recitals will govern and vice versa. If both are clear but inconsistent with each other, the main body will govern.
    vii. If the agreement is simple do not need a structure, if is complex need organization: Title, numbering.

c. Definitions
    i. Follows the recitals and precedes the operative language (grant clause)
    ii. Need them because of the uncertainty principle when drafting agreements.
    iii. Can be own lexicographer in licensing agreements.
    iv. Necessary because there might be long terms and as such definitions can be used to simplify the agreement.
    v. If you have a very lengthy definition put it in as an Appendix.
    vi. Defined terms have to be in CAPS throughout the agreement.
    vii. Can put in alphabetically or hierarchically – i.e. defining the terms in order of how they show up in the agreement as some defined terms depend one ore more defined terms

d. Grant clause
    i. Need all the elements - the grant clause controls the entire agreement – one can only use a licensed method.
    ii. Different IP rights last for a different duration
    iii. Grant rights under patents: for a pending patent application *agree to grant*. Agree to

grant refers to a future right and grants a present right.

iv. May want to include subsidiaries and affiliates for corporations for corporations, otherwise these are not part of the agreement. To avoid vagueness need to define the affiliates and subsidiaries in the agreement.

v. If sub-licensees are granted a separate operate language needs to be present.

vi. Statute gives only the right to exclude others
- This goes back to Statutory and common law patent laws.
- Under the common law, do have the right to make, use, offer and sell but under the Statute can only exclude others from doing so.
- Patentee's rights are: *common law* and *statutory right*. In essence, that common law patent right is a trade secret.

vii. Do not use "*indivisible*," "*irrevocable*" and "*non-transferable*"
- *Irrevocable* is operative language and if there are conditions of revocability it goes with the termination clause.
- *Indivisible* means that you do not have a right to make. Indivisible precluded allowing the licensee to sub-licenses, affiliates and subsidiaries.
- *Non-transferable:* does not belong in the granting clause. If it is important, put it in the operative clauses. Runs against to sell.

e. Termination Clauses

i. Have to specify term and termination and what terminates when.
- Never is the termination sudden.
- Terminates over a period of time: different obligations and rights continue.
- *Multi-pronged concept*: several rights and obligations go on
- Licensee will have to pay accrued royalties.

  - Licensee will have to provide reports
  - Confidentiality continues (obligation to return confidential papers)
  - Each of the prongs has to be defined separately.

ii. Sub-licensing rights: Have to provide separately for termination of sub-licenses.

iii. Licensor will have rights to audit for royalties (usually specify 2 years).

iv. Disposal of inventory

v. Cessation of use of technology.

f. Execution

i. Have to make sure that all the parties signing the agreement have indeed the power to execute it.

ii. Might need to consult the bylaws of a company to verify authority to execute an agreement.

iii. Sign as: *"ABC Corporation by John Doe President"*

iv. Authentication is important so that the agreement is self-executing. If there is an authentication then the agreement is self-executing. Having a witness or two to co-sign or notarization best does this. A corporate secretary will separately attest the agreement. This serves as *prima facie* evidence.

g. Royalties

i. In general:

  - The *royalty rate, royalty base* and *duration of the agreement* determine the royalty income. Usually it is a combination of lump sum payment and sliding scale. The royalty is best based on the *net* sales. Net sale is the basis because of inflation. If it is based on a fixed sum, have to worry about inflation. For fixed lump sum payments (fixed royalty) need an inflation clause. Net sales have to be carefully defined in a definition that stipulates payment. Net Sales = Gross sales – overhead.

- Minimum royalty payments that is separate from the running royalty to motivate the licensee. It becomes mute if the running royalty is greater than the minimum amount set fourth.
- Have to have provision that obligates the licensee to keep careful records as to net sales and submit those reports periodically for the licensor accompanied by payments.
- If the royalty payments are large, parties can go down to monthly payments.
- There is always a provision for inspection of the licensee's books. Usually an outside accountant up to two years after the agreement's termination does this.
- Use "*shall pay*"
- Never use gross profits because accountants can be creative in making the profit disappear.
- Payments clause always comes after the grant clause and then the rest of the provisions.

ii. Payments

- Lump sum: the best resolution because have no further concerns if the licensor will pay again. Can be one single payment or installments over a period of time. If lump sum payments and running royalties are tied together, the lump sum usually is 10% of the running royalty.
- For lump sump payments, the term "*present value*" is used to account for inflation. Present value is beneficial for large corporations who can afford to pay in the present rather than having a payment schedule.

iii. Royalty base: can be used to introduce flexibility to the royalty rates. Royalty base is separate from the royalty rate.

iv. Misconceptions about Royalties
- Licensor cannot take the position that he controls the license. The economics of the licensee determine what the royalty rate will be. The licensor's investment cost has no influence on the royalty rate (*sunken expenses*).
- Royalty standards are usually viewed as industry standards: royalty figures in a given industry are always a range. Therefore, need to consider a series of applicable factors. Standards for exclusive licenses are higher.
- The average royalty rate is about 5 % of net sales (in 90% of licenses royalty rate is phrased in terms of net sales).

v. Factors to consider for royalties
- The degree of exclusivity: For an exclusive license can charge up to 50 % (considering the other factors as well) for pharmaceuticals it is 300 %. In some industries there is a greater need for exclusive licenses the average is 53.5%. There is no standard royalty rate.
- Strength of the IP Right
- Ease to design around and *vel non*
- Strong patent or weak patent
- A valid patent that has been tested in court or one that has already been licensed.
- State of the Development of the subject technology
- Pay more if the license is exclusive or the field of use is unrestricted.
- May have lower royalties if the agreement involves grant back clauses.
- Warranty clauses: if the licensee has to give large warranties will not have to pay as much.

- Most Favored License clause

3. Optional elements of an Agreement
   a. Most Favored Licensee (MFL) Clause
      i. MFL clauses are moot in exclusive license.
      ii. Scenario arises if there are more than one licensee, subsequent licensees may have advantages.
      iii. Provides for the fact is subsequently to the first license, licensor grants a license on better (money) terms, that license with more favorable terms should be extended to the first licensee or it obligates the licensor not to grant a more generous licensee.
      iv. Troublesome for licensor, as there might a different scenario during the granting of a license.
      v. Should include escape clauses or exceptions
      vi. Stay away from vague phrases
      vii. Advisable to give licensee the right to terminate and negotiate the license.

   b. Warranties and indemnification clauses
      i. Found in most agreements even though licensor is reluctant to give warranties to the licensee: Licensee will want warranties that there are no other patents that are being infringed.
      ii. All licensee can expect is a warranty that the licensor is aware that there are no infringing patents.
      iii. Warranties and indemnifications clauses
         - have to be explicit
         - have financial value.
      iv. Can minimize the cost of warranties by controlling how the licensee can use the patented invention.
      v. *Hold harmless* is an important phrase as well.
      vi. Can agree to *share costs if there is litigation* (up to 50% of royalty paid).

4. Improvements
    a. Very often research is done on the licensed subject matter and come up with improvements which are not covered by the original license.
    b. *Grant backs* and *grant forwards*.
        i. If the licensor makes improvements there has to be a *grant forward* from licensor to licensee and vice verse for *grant back*.
        ii. Grant forward and grant back need to be non-exclusive because otherwise have anti-trust problems.
    c. Improvements have to be defined what they mean in relation to the license.
    d. Need to have a *definition of improvements* and a *definite period of duration* of the improvements.
    e. Can define improvement as something that has a beneficial function or best "*anything under the scope of the patent*"

O. <u>Antitrust and Intellectual property misuse</u>
1. Every antitrust violation is IP misuse but not every IP misuse is an antitrust violation.
2. Misuse came out up from *unclean hands* from *Morton Salt*.
3. Antitrust violation has to be an activity outside the scope of the term of the patent or acts that are not covered by the claims of the patents and *market power*. Still can have misuse.
4. Can purge/correct intellectual property misuse by (1) abandonment of the misuse and (2) dissipate the consequences.
5. Per se violation of anti trust.
6. Things to Avoid
    a. Tie-Ins
    b. Grant Backs: Nothing illegal about grant backs as long as they are non-exclusive.
    c. Restrictions
        i. On resale
            - Still legal if for public health reason.
            - freedom to deal outside scope of patent
        ii. on products made by patented process
        iii. on price
    d. Licensee veto of other licenses
    e. Mandatory package licensing

f. Conditioned royalties on unpatented items

7. Patent Misuse Reform Act of 1988 - 35 U.S.C. § 271 (d)
   a. In every antitrust violation where intellectual property is involved there is misuse.
   b. Classic example of a misuse intellectual property is a tie-in where the licensee is forced as part of the license to take un-patented products
   c. § 271 (d): a patent owner is entitled to relief in an infringement action by refusing to license or use any rights of the patent.

P. Due Diligence

1. Due diligence is an investigation undertaken in the course of an intellectual property to verify and determine ownership and scope of the intellectual property right being sold, licenses, or used as collateral.

2. Purpose of due diligence investigation is to provide data needed to analyze and assess the business and legal risks associated with the IP rights that are subject of the transaction.

3. Open good faith cooperation on the part of the seller or licensor with buyer or licensee.

4. Means of evaluating the technology in a short time – a term used by invest bankers.

5. Also known as a *patent clearance*.

6. Due diligence procedure may include, among other things:

   a. Identification of all IP involved in the transaction
   b. Verification of IP ownership
   c. Determination of enforceability or strength of IP
   d. Review and verification of all the documents associated with the IP including registrations, licenses, security, liens, file wrappers, and claims of infringement
   e. Interviews of those persons with knowledge of the IP

7. "Due Diligence" is not the same as "diligence" and "best efforts."

Appendix A

OVERVIEW OF KEY PATENT CASES

Amgen v. Chugai, 927 F.2d 1200 (Fed. Cir. 1991)

Erthropoietin (EPO) Patents (EPO is a protein that stimulates the production of red blood cells)

Ruling:

No prior art anticipation. Claims were not obvious. Best mode was present even though the organism was not deposited. No inequitable conduct. No enablement for isolation claims. Affirmed in part, reversed in part, vacated in part.

AT&T v. Excel Communications, 172 F.3d 1352 (Fed. Cir. 1999)

Method for message records for long distance phone bills allowing for differential billing treatment.

Ruling:

Mathematical concepts reduced to a practical application are useful and patentable. Any transformation of data is sufficient to create patentable subject matter.

Brenner v. Manson, 383 U.S. 519 (1966)

Patent to chemical process.

Ruling:

A chemical process satisfies the utility requirement if it is useful in industry. Until a process claim has been refined and reduced to production of a useful product it is not patentable.

Bristol-Myers Squibb Co. v. Ben Venue Laboratories, Inc., 246 F.3d 1368 (Fed. Cir. 2001)

Antitumor paclitaxel.

Ruling:

Antineoplastically effective amount is was non-limiting in the claim. Prior art anticipates claims from the patent. (Definition of antineoplastic: acting to prevent, inhibit or halt the development of a neoplasm (a tumor)).

Compco v. DayBrite Lighting, 376 U.S. 234 (1964)

Competing fluorescent bulb manufactures with one having a design patent on a fixture similar to one used by the other's predecessor.

Ruling:

If design is not patented it can be copied. State trademark law cannot preempt federal patent law.

Continental Paperback v. Eastern Paperback Co., 210 U.S. 405 (1908)

Non-use of patent for paper bag.

Ruling:

Non-use in not sufficient to void the patent. A patentee's right to a patent is not voided by non-use.

Diamond v. Chakrabarty, 447 U.S. 303 (1980)

Chakrabarty tried to obtain a patent for bacteria, but the PTO refused.

Ruling:

Microorganisms are patentable subject matter under 35 USC § 101 as "manufacture" or "composition of matter."

Diamond v. Diehr, 450 U.S. 175 (1981)

Process for curing rubber that involved a mathematical equation.

Ruling:

Process as a mode of treatment is patentable even when it involves laws of nature. However, laws of nature, physical phenomena, and abstract ideas are not patentable.

Ethicon, Inc. v. U.S. Surgical Corp. 135 F.3d 1456 (Fed. Cir. 1998)

U.S. Surgical, alleged infringer, obtained license from co-inventor that was not mentioned in the patent application.

Ruling:

As one co-inventor of the patent refused to join the others patent infringement suit, the case had to be dismissed. Contributor of any claim element is a co-owner of the entire patent not simply of that claim. All co-owners of a patent must consent to file an infringement suit.

Evans v. Eaton, 20 U.S. 356 (1822)

Eaton made an improvement to Evan's patent for a Hopperboy.

Ruling:

Patent is invalid as it did not distinguish from the prior art. Hence, once a patent expires, it becomes public property. 35 U.S.C. § 112: specifications need to list claim.

Festo Corp. v. Shoketsu Kinzoku Kogyo Kahushiki, Co., 122 S. Ct. 1831 (2002)

Rodless cylinder – infringement only under the doctrine of equivalents.

Ruling:

Patentee has the burden to show that an amendment in prosecution does not surrender the particular equivalent in question. Narrowing amendments may be presumed to be a disclaimer of the territory surrendered by the amendment. When (1) the equivalent was "unforeseeable" at the filing of the application, (2) the amendment bears only a "tangential" relation to the equivalent or (3) other reasons suggest the applicant "could not *reasonably* be expected to have described the insubstantial substitute in question," the applicant may overcome the presumption of prosecution history estoppel.

Flick-Reedy v. Hydro-Line Mfg., 351 F.2d 546 (7th Cir. 1965)

Invention to a cylinder, but failed to disclose the special tool.

Ruling:

Since the special tool is necessary to practice the invention, the inventor failed to disclose the best mode and hence the patent was invalid.

Fregeau v. Mossinghoff, 776 F.2d 1034 (Fed. Cir. 1985)

Method using magnetic field to improve the flavor of a beverage

Ruling:

Need to have actual evidence to prove utility. Thus, invention was not deemed patentable for lack of utility.

Funk Bros Seed v. Kalo Inoculant, 333 U.S. 127 (1948)

Patents to methods to inoculate bacteria

Ruling:

Cannot patent a phenomenon of nature and hence patent was invalid. Patent invalid as there is no clear description of what was invented.

General Talking Pictures v. Western Electric, 305 U.S. 124 (1938)

Restriction of amplifier manufacture to either commercial or private use via a license.

Ruling:

Patent infringement based on *prima facie* evidence since both parties were aware of the violation of the license. Patentee may grant licenses to a field and restrict usage of the item. Buyers of goods covered by a restrictive license cannot use those goods in a way that would violate the license.

Graham v. John Deere, 383 U.S. 1 (1966)

Improvement to plows by adding a spring.

Ruling:

Adding a spring to a plow was deemed to be obvious under the test for nonobviousness set fourth by the Supreme Court. Test for Nonobviousness: (1) scope and content of patent (2) difference between what is claimed and prior art (3) ordinary skills with pertinent art (4) secondary indica of non-obviousness.

Holmes Group, v. Vornado Air Circulation Sys., 535 U.S. 826 (2002)

Fans.

Ruling:

For the Court of Appeals for the Federal Circuit to have jurisdiction *arising* under patent law, the complaint needs to have a cause of action routed in patent law. Asserting a counterclaim routed in patent law is insufficient for the Federal Circuit to have jurisdiction.

In re Cortright, 165 F.3d 1353 (Fed. Cir. 1999)

Applying *Bag Balm* to human scalp as a treatment for male pattern baldness.

Ruling:

Fails under § 112 ¶ 1 enabling provision, do not know how it treats baldness. Novelty under 35 U.S.C. § 101 is only the first hurdle to patentability.

In re Deuel, 51 F.3d 1552 (Fed. Cir. 1995)

Heparin Binding Growth Factor with the 168 amino acids.

Ruling:

Review obviousness *de novo.* Prior art did not disclose the molecule hence it is not obvious. None of the references suggest or imply the cDNA molecule.

J.E.M. Ag. Supply v. Pioneer Hi-bred, Intl, 534 U.S. 124 (2001)

Patented inbred and hybrid corn.

Ruling:

One can receive a utility patent to a plant. Granting utility patents on plants does not violate the Plant Variety Protection Act , 7 U.S.C. 2321, and the Plant Patent Act, 35 U.S.C. 161-164.

Juicy Whip v. Orange Bang, 185 F.3d 1364 (Fed. Cir. 1999)

Juicy Whip had a patent for a post-mix beverage dispenser which mixed the syrup and water as the beverage was dispensed to the customer.

Ruling:

"The fact that one product can be altered to make it look like another is in itself a specific benefit sufficient to satisfy the statutory requirement of utility."

Keeler v. Standard Folding Beds, 157 U.S. 659 (1895)

Standard's beds were bought in one licensed area and resold in another.

Ruling:

Once a patented device is sold without any restrictions, its buyer is free to do as he/she pleases. An authorized unrestricted sale of a patented good enables the buyer to use or resell the good.

Kellogg v. Natl. Biscuit, 305 U.S. 111 (1938)

Kellogg and Nabisco manufacturing shredded wheat.

Ruling:

Nabisco could not enjoin Kellogg from producing *wheaties* because part of public domain and they were differentiated. Once a patent expires it is part of the public domain and the ex-patentee cannot enjoin anyone from using it but can try to prevent source confusion.

Kendall v. Winsor, 62 U.S. 322 (1858)

Invention kept secret in the U.S., defendant stole the invention and patented it in the U.K.

Ruling:

If an inventor withholds his invention from public, he comes not within the objectives of the Congress and the Constitution. Important case as it is the first case to discuss the 35 U.S.C. § 102 (b) on sale bar.

Larsen v. Terk Tech. Co., 151 F.3d 140 (4th Cir. 1998)

Terk was selling a knock-off of Larsen's CD holder.

Ruling:

Court imposed liability under Lanham Act § 43 (a) for willful copying even when there was no patent on the CD holder in the US. Assertion of infringement of trade dress may provide an alternate route of enforcing the rights in one's invention.

Lifescan v. Can-Am Care, 859 F. Supp. 392 (N.D. Ca. 1994)

Patented glucose meter and strips; competitor sold strips for patented glucose meter.

Ruling:

Strips were found to be infringing unless warning was given. Sellers of patented goods may sometimes condition patent use on purchases of needed supplies.

Mallinkrodt v. Medipart, 976 F.2d 700 (Fed. Cir. 1992)

Remanufactured patented good sold.

Ruling:

A remanufacture is infringement where the good is sold. A purchaser of patented items with a single use restriction has no rights to the otherwise presumed right to reconstruct.

Midwest Indust. v. Karavan Trailers, 175 F.3d 1356 (Fed. Cir. 1999)

Patent for a hitch-mount design on a trailer.

Ruling:

It is possible to have patent protection and trade dress protection for a patented device.

Morton Salt v. Suppiger, 314 U.S. 488 (1942)

Conditioned sale of patented canning machine to use of non-patented proprietary salt chips.

Ruling:

"[A] patentee who has granted a license on condition that the patent invention is used by the licensee only with unpatented material furnished by the licensor, may not restrain as a contributory infringer one who sells to the licensee like materials for like use."

O'Reilly v. Morse, 56 U.S. 62 (1853)

Morse had a patent for a telegraph that claimed to send signal *at any distance* Claimed the *exclusive right* to every improvement.

Ruling:

Whoever discovers that a new and useful invention within the meaning of 35 U.S.C. § 101 is entitled to a patent, provided the means used in an exact manner as specified such that it enables someone else to build the invention – otherwise the patent is void. The patent only covers the exact manner specified.

Oddzon v. Just Toys, 122 F.3d 1396 (Fed. Cir. 1997)

Patented Vortex tossing ball.

Ruling:

35 U.S.C. 102 (f) creates prior art for obviousness determinations.

Pfaff v. Wells Electronics, 525 U.S. 55 (1998)

Computer chip socket sold in the market before patented.

Ruling:

Patent invalid under 35 U.S.C. § 102 (b). On-sale bar applies when (1) product was subject of a commercial offer and (2) the product was ready for patenting.

Scott Paper v. Marcalus, 326 U.S. 249 (1945)

Asserting infringement suit against assignor.

Ruling: The Court declared the patent invalid as it was the same as an expired patent and hence Scott could not enforce the patent.

Sears, Roebuck v. Stiffel, 376 U.S. 225 (1964)

Stiffel had design and mechanical patents for a pole lamp and Sears started selling knock-offs.

Ruling:

Since the patent was invalid, Sears was free to copy the light fixture design. State law cannot expand the monopolies of the Federal Patent law.

Singer Mfg. v. June, 163 U.S. 169 (1896)

Singer patent expired; knock-offs used Singer name that was used in the patent.

Ruling:

Once patent expires it is part of public domain and so it the patent's name.

State St. Bank v. Signature Financial, Inc., 149 F.3d 1368 (Fed. Cir. 1998)

Patent to a business method: system involving computers that allowed efficient stock trading with daily calculations including the taxes.

Ruling:

Computer programs are patentable subject matter under § 101 as a machine for data processing.

Tilghman v. Proctor, 102 U.S. 707 (1880)

Tilghman invented a process of separating fats from oils.

Ruling:

Processes are patentable subject matter.

U.S. v. Adams, 383 U.S. 39 (1966)

Wet cell battery using water as an electrolyte.

Ruling:

Invention was nonobvious and hence the patent was valid. The non-obviousness in the invention was based on nothing in the prior art spoke on using wet cells.

Warner Jenkinson v. Hilton Davis Chem. Co., 520 U.S. 17 (1997)

Ultra-filtration of dyes; added pH range limitation during prosecution.

Ruling:

Patentees have the burden to establish the reason for an amendment during prosecution. A court then has to decide the reason's sufficiency to overcome prosecution history estoppel as a bar to doctrine of equivalence assertion for elements added by amendment.

White v. Dunbar, 119 U.S. 47, 52 (1886)

Nose of wax case.

Ruling:

Claims are like a nose of wax, the patentee needs to interpret them consistently in prosecution and litigation.

Yamanouchi Pharm. v. Dambury Pharm., 231 F.3d 1339 (Fed. Cir. 2000)

Patent on gastric acid inhibition in 1981, Dambury filed ANDA. Under ANDA, Yamanouchi sued and won on JMOL.

Ruling:

CAFC said Patent was not obvious for that was no motivation or indication to combine the prior art references. No clear and convincing case to prove obviousness. DC properly awarded attorney fees under the ANDA in light of weak case leading to JMOL and non-obviousness.

Appendix B:

TOP TEN U.S. SUPREME COURT PATENT CASES*

Updated November 29, 2005

1	***eBay Inc. v. MercExchange LLC***, Supreme Court No. 05-130: Certiorari was granted November 28, 2005
2	***Federal Trade Comm'n v. Schering-Plough Corp***, Supreme Court No. 05-273: CVSG outstanding
3	***In re Tamoxifen Citrate Antitrust Litigation***, 2005 WL 21 864654 (2nd Cir. 2005)
4	***KSR Intern. Co. v. Teleflex Inc.***, Supreme Court No. 04-1350: Order outstanding asking the Solicitor General for the opinion of the United States whether to grant certiorari
5	***Laboratory Corp. of America Holdings v. Metabolite Laboratories Inc.***, Supreme Court No. 04-607: Briefing schedule through January 2005, Hearing February-April 2006; decision by June 2006.
6	***Unithern Food Systems Inc. v. Swift Eckrich Inc.***, Supreme Court No. 04-597: A decision is expected before the end of 2005
7	***Illinois Tool Works Inc. v. Independent Ink Inc.***, Supreme Court No. 04-1329: Argument was held November 29, 2005; a decision is expected by the end of January 2006.
8	***Research In Motion Ltd. V. NTP Inc.***, certiorari petition due January 2006.
9	***Lemelson Med. Ed. & Res Found v. Symbol Technologies***, petition due February 14, 2006.
10	***AWH Corp. v. Phillips***, App. No. 05-602: Cert. petition filed.

* compiled by Harold C. Wegner

Appendix C:

HOW THE SUPREME COURT DECIDES TO REVIEW INTELLECTUAL PROPERTY CASES

BY MATTHEW M. NEUMEIER

INTRODUCTION

The U.S. Supreme Court plays a crucial role in the field of intellectual property ("IP") as the final arbiter of IP rights based on federal law. This means that the Supreme Court provides ultimate guidance in most core areas of IP law, including patents, copyrights, trademarks and trade dress, which are governed by federal statutes. While many states may still have statutes on their books or common law precedents governing IP rights in the fields of patents, trademarks, trade dress and unfair competition, for the most part federal law is clearly dominant in these areas today. Federal IP law is based either on federal statutes providing for exclusive coverage in areas such as patents and copyright, or practical recognition that federal law provides all the relief necessary, making parallel state law claims superfluous. One notable exception to this federal law dominance is the law of trade secrets, but even here, new federal statutes are beginning to encroach in this area by providing alternate bases for protecting against trade secret theft.

Given the Supreme Court's preeminent role the field of IP rights, it is important to understand the basics of advocacy and presentation of cases before the Supreme Court, particularly when dealing with IP cases. For many years now, most of the Supreme Court's case load has been essentially discretionary, based on its *certiorari* jurisdiction. Since the beginning of the Rehnquist Court in 1986, that discretion has been exercised only in limited circumstances. This is reflected in the fact that since the late 1980's, the Supreme Court has only been agreeing to hear argument in roughly seventy-five to eighty cases each Term, rather than the 150 or more that were typically reviewed each year during the Burger Court years. In the past decade, a total of fewer than twenty-five of these cases involved IP rights in some fashion or another. That means the Supreme Court hears argument, on average, in only two or three IP cases each year, with no cases being heard in some years.

How the Supreme Court goes about deciding which cases to hear when dealing with issues involving IP rights requires an understanding of the Supreme Court's review process, together with a brief review of some of the cases it has heard in this area. This article provides practitioners with some guidance in the area of Supreme Court review of IP cases.

I. THE BASIC CERTIORARI PROCESS

Since the essentially exclusive vehicle for obtaining Supreme Court review for a case involving federal IP rights is by means of a *writ of certiorari*, one of the best references for guidance on this process is the Court's own established Rules, which set forth in detail the procedures for going about seeking *certiorari* review. Under the Rules, an aggrieved party in a lower court must file a petition seeking leave to appeal, using a very strict format for the submission. Although the details of briefing and presenting a *certiorari* petition are beyond the scope of this paper, it is imperative to keep in mind that the Court does not simply grant broad appeals of decisions below, but instead only grants review of specified "issues" that are presented for review. The crafting of these "questions presented" is an art form in itself, requiring careful consideration to attract the Court's attention, as discussed *infra*.

The Court reviews *certiorari* petitions at its weekly conferences when the Court is in session, based on the question or questions presented. Prior to consideration by the Court, law clerks assigned to the Justices will typically have reviewed the petition and any related responses or *amicus* briefs. As part of this process, law clerks will review the lower court opinion and any cited conflicting decisions and generally try to determine what precise issues are being raised by the parties. In other words, they will not simply rely on the issues as framed by the petitioning party, who in many cases may be appearing *pro se*. Based on their preliminary review of the case law and facts as set forth in the parties' submissions, the law clerks will prepare memoranda for their Justices summarizing the case below, including the issues presented, their thoughts on whether the issues were properly preserved for appeal, and their recommendation on whether or not to grant *certiorari*. The Justices then consider the petitions at their conferences, based on these summaries and their own review of the parties' submissions. But unless a Justice specifically requests to place a particular petition on the list for discussion, there is no actual "consideration" of the petition at the conference, with the presumption simply being that the petition will be denied. In those instances where a Justice has flagged a petition for review (which is the clear exception, and not the rule) the Justices will at a minimum affirmatively vote on whether or not to grant *certiorari*, and possibly discuss the case at some length. A petition ultimately will be granted only if at least four Justices vote to hear the case.

II. FACTORS INFLUENCING CERTIORARI REVIEW

The Supreme Court's Rules provide a glimpse of how the Court proceeds in determining what its docket will look like based on its jurisdiction on *writ of certiorari.* This snapshot is set forth in Supreme Court Rule 10, which is set forth below in its entirety:

> Rule 10. Considerations Governing Review on *Certiorari*
> Review on a *writ of certiorari* is not a matter of right, but of judicial discretion. A petition for *writ of certiorari* will be granted only for compelling reasons. The following, although neither controlling nor fully measuring the Court's discretion, indicate the character of the reasons the Court considers:
>
> (a) a United States court of appeals has entered a decision in conflict with the decision of another United States court of appeals on the same important matter; has decided an important federal question in a way that conflicts with a decision by a state court of last resort; or has so far departed from the accepted and usual course of judicial proceedings, or sanctioned such a departure by a lower court, as to call for an exercise of this Court's supervisory power;
> (b) a state court of last resort has decided an important federal question in a way that conflicts with the decision of another state court of last resort or of a United States court of appeals;
> (c) a state court or a United States court of appeals has decided an important question of federal law that has not been, but should be, settled by this Court, or has decided an important federal question in a way that conflicts with relevant decisions of this Court.
>
> A petition for *writ of certiorari* is rarely granted when the asserted error consists of factual findings or the misapplication of a properly stated rule of law.

Based on this guidance, it is clear that there are only a few categories of cases which the Supreme Court is interested in hearing:

1) Cases involving conflicting decisions on the same legal topic;

2) Cases which have "departed from the accepted and usual course of judicial proceedings," such that the Supreme Court should exercise its supervisory powers to correct the error;

3) Cases in which a lower appellate court has decided an "important question of federal law" that should not await further review by other lower courts; and

4) Cases in which it appears that a lower appellate court has failed to adhere to the Supreme Court's past precedent.

The next section discusses in turn how the Supreme Court has applied its review process to IP cases that fall within categories 1, 3, and 4. A departure from the accepted course of judicial proceedings has yet to be an issue in an IP case.

III. APPLICATION OF THE COURT'S REVIEW CATAGORIES IN IP CASES

A. CONFLICTING DECISIONS BELOW

The need for resolving conflicting lower appellate court holdings on identical issues of federal law, such as the interpretation of the scope of a federal statute on patent or copyright topics, is obvious. If the notion of having a federal system in certain areas of IP law is to have any meaning, it is critically important that the law be clearly articulated without conflicting interpretations among the various federal circuits. Given today's global economy, authors and inventors need to know what their federal IP rights are. In addition, competitors need to know the limits of federal IP rights for these authors' works and inventors' patents. Unfortunately, the Supreme Court does not hear every case in which a conflict is evidenced, even on what many practitioners may consider to be important federal questions. The trend since the Burger Court of reviewing far fewer cases has included a decline in the number of *certiorari* grants in pure conflict situations.[i[13]]

Two recent examples of conflicts at the federal appellate level that have led to Supreme Court review in IP rights cases are illustrative. In *Traffix Devices, Inc. v. Marketing Displays, Inc.*, the Court determined the scope of trade dress protection for a traffic sign design that was the subject of expired utility patents. The federal circuits had split on the issue whether an expired utility patent foreclosed the possibility of trade dress protection for the product's design. The Court noted that the party asserting trade dress protection must demonstrate that the matter sought to be protected is not functional, and in the case of a design claim, the fact that the design had once been the subject of a utility patent is strong evidence that the features claimed for the design are functional. As a result, the Court put the burden on the party claiming protection to demonstrate that the feature is *not* functional. In so holding, the Court chastised the Sixth Circuit for misinterpreting trade dress principles generally on the topic of protection for designs, which the Court then undertook to summarize in some detail.[ii[18]]

The Supreme Court's level of unhappiness at the lower court's reasoning in *Traffix Devices*, and its desire to grant *certiorari*, was likely influenced by the fact that the Court had only recently addressed the scope of trademark and trade dress protection in three separate cases, reflecting an extraordinary level of scrutiny by the Court for this narrow topic. Of these three cases, *Qualitex* also involved a conflict among the federal circuits. In *Qualitex*, the Court faced the issue whether a party could register a trademark based solely on the color of the product. The Court held that color alone could serve as a trademark, to the extent that customers identified the color as Qualitex's (such that it had developed secondary meaning), and the color did not serve any other function. This resolved a conflict among at least four federal circuits that had emerged over the previous decade.

Of course, in the area of patent law, there is considerable uniformity in appellate rulings based on the simple fact that the Federal Circuit has exclusive jurisdiction over cases "arising under" the federal patent laws. What that means is that in cases in which a patent holder sues for infringement, or in which a declaratory judgment action is brought to determine whether or not a party's conduct infringes or the patent is invalid, the appellate court will be the Federal Circuit, applying what hopefully will be its own uniform precedent. But even here, there is not 100% uniformity, because it remains feasible for a patent claim to be raised in certain circumstances – such as by way of a counterclaim in an otherwise non-patent case – that will give rise to appellate review by a federal circuit other than the Federal Circuit. This is because the federal statute granting appellate review on patent matters to the Federal Circuit was not drafted to encompass all potential scenarios, as the Supreme Court pointed out in one of its most recent pronouncements in the area of IP law, *Holmes Group, Inc. v. Vornado Air Circulation Systems, Inc.*

B. "IMPORTANT QUESTIONS"

The Supreme Court will not hesitate to grant review in cases raising what the Justices perceive to be issues of significant importance warranting their immediate attention, rather than waiting to see how lower courts wrestle with the issue over a reasonable period of time. These types of cases frequently involve legal disputes that have been on the front pages of the news for some time as they percolate their way up to the Court. A good example involved the publication by the *New York*

Times of the Pentagon Papers, and whether the Executive Branch could enjoin such publication based on national security grounds. As technology advances at an unstoppable and increasingly rapid pace, cases involving IP law are beginning to emerge as more likely candidates for this type of early review. The Justices read the national newspapers, and generally follow trends in the economy and broad areas of technological innovation just like many other readers of these publications. It does not require a genius to recognize a significant and newsworthy ruling below by the time it reaches the Supreme Court. Not only are the issues presented in the media, they are flagged for attention on arrival at the Court by the frequent submissions of numerous amicus briefs by major business, academic, and public interest organizations. And in many cases, there are additional submissions by the Executive Branch, expressing the "official" views of the United States government on the topic at hand. Indeed, when a major issue surfaces without any federal government amicus filing, the Court will often affirmatively request that the United States government express its views.

Based on the Supreme Court's record in the past several years, the "important question" basis for review appears to underlie the granting of *certiorari* petitions more often than conflicts among the federal circuits, particularly in the field of IP law. Important questions, of course, can fall within several different categories, some of which have more attraction for the Court than others. These categories can be roughly segmented as follows: (1) broad constitutional questions, (2) jurisdictional questions, (3) procedural questions, and (4) basic substantive law questions, which typically include issues of statutory interpretation or potential conflicts among statutes.

1. Constitutional Questions.

Questions raising constitutional issues of significance can be counted on to attract the interest of the Supreme Court. Because the Court only has the opportunity to shape the Constitution by means of cases that rise to the surface in somewhat random fashion – *i.e.*, the Court cannot simply reach out and decide to resolve an issue that appeals to them that is not raised in a case being appealed subject to a *certiorari* petition – the temptation to grant *certiorari* when such a case is within its grasp is often overpowering.

Broad constitutional questions, while generally rare in the area of IP law, have surfaced several times in the past few years. Most recently, in *Eldred v. Ashcroft*, the Court considered the scope of congressional power to extend the term of both existing and future copyrights by twenty additional years, in the face of the Constitution's language limiting such power to granting copyrights only for "limited Times."

While the Court at oral argument appeared to be skeptical as to the *desirability* of providing such an extension (which although "fixed" in duration reflects, from a practical standpoint, what amounts to a nearly perpetual grant), the Court nevertheless deferred to Congress in the face of clear constitutional language giving it the right to establish appropriate duration limits, as well as long-standing precedent permitting such extensions. In this case, however, there had been no conflicting rulings below, with the Court of Appeals for the District of Columbia reaching the same result that the Supreme Court ultimately reached. Why, then, did the Court grant *certiorari* review in this case? Obviously, the case raised important issues for the business community (leading to widespread media coverage debating whether the copyrights on Mickey Mouse and other well-known works should be extended yet again), as well as issues of foreign affairs, based on copyright terms in the European Union. Moreover, counsel for the opposing parties – Lawrence Lessig and Theodore Olson – were well known to the Court, which undoubtedly helped influence their decision to take the case.

The other recent decision involving a significant constitutional issue is *Florida Prepaid Postsecondary Education Expense Board v. College Savings Bank*, which concerned the ability of a patent holder to sue a state for patent infringement. This case raised issues as to the scope of sovereign immunity and congressional power to abrogate such immunity, a matter which is near and dear to many current Justices. Resolution of this case required interpretation of several clauses of the Constitution, including the Due Process Clause, the Interstate Commerce Clause, the Eleventh Amendment and the Fourteenth Amendment, as well as several federal statutes drafted by Congress in an attempt to provide patent holders with a federal remedy for any patent infringement involving a state governmental authority. Despite the broad power of Congress to grant patents to inventors, and its separate authority to provide remedies for Fourteenth Amendment violations (such as remedying violations of IP rights by a state in contravention of the Due Process Clause), the Court ultimately determined that Congress had acted too hastily in concluding that the States had not provided a constitutionally adequate remedy to an injured patent owner when attempting to abrogate the States' sovereign immunity for patent claims.[iii[38]] That the Court reached this holding is not surprising, given the trend in cases upholding States' Rights over the past fifteen years.

2. Jurisdictional Questions.

Questions concerning appellate jurisdiction in the area of IP law have arisen only infrequently in the past decade. As noted above, in *Holmes Group*, the Court held that the Federal Circuit had overreached its jurisdiction when accepting an appeal in which the initial complaint filed by the plaintiff did not raise a claim "arising under" federal patent laws. This is one of many instances in which the Court has not hesitated to overrule the Federal Circuit, without need for any conflicting decisions below to support a grant of *certiorari*.

In somewhat similar circumstances, the Court had earlier taken the Federal Circuit to task in *Cardinal Chemical Co. v. Morton International, Inc.* for refusing to review a district court's holding that a patent was invalid after affirming the district court's separate holding that the patent had not been infringed. In that case, the Court emphasized the need to resolve issues that had been fully litigated below in order to protect the public against prolonging the life of invalid patents and encouraging "endless litigation" or uncertainty over the validity of a patent. The Court also expressed concern that by treating the patent validity issue as moot, once non-infringement was found, the Federal Circuit appeared to be attempting to deprive the Supreme Court of the ability to consider the validity ruling, thereby limiting the Court's own power. That type of action at the appellate court level is virtually guaranteed to attract scrutiny by the Supreme Court.

3. Procedural Questions.

Procedural questions, while not typically raising issues as controversial as those involving major constitutional questions, are often the grist of appellate rulings and ultimately Supreme Court rulings. Procedure goes to the process of handling litigation in federal courts, and the Supreme Court has expressed a fair level of interest in how IP rights are litigated at both the trial and appellate levels. This includes questions concerning the roles of the trial court and juries in such cases.

Perhaps the most notable procedural case in the area of IP law in recent years is *Markman v. Westview Instruments, Inc.*, which held that claim construction in patent cases was exclusively within the province of the district court, leaving the jury with only the factual resolution of infringement claims, should they survive the district court's "Markman" hearing stage. While the resolution of this case rested on an interpretation of the Seventh Amendment and the respective roles of the trial court and the jury, as a practical matter, the fundamental issue to be decided was whether to treat a patent similar to a contract and apply the longstanding rule that interpretation of a contract raises an issue of law for the trial court. For this reason, this case is better classified as a procedural case rather than a significant constitutional question case.

A similar overlap between procedural issues and constitutional questions arising out of Seventh Amendment concerns was presented in *Feltner v. Columbia Pictures Television, Inc.* In *Feltner*, the issue was who should determine the amount of statutory damages for copyright violations: judge or jury? The Court first determined that the copyright statute did not expressly provide for a right to a jury trial when the copyright owner elects to recover statutory damages; as a result, the Court had to face the constitutional issue. The Court then had little trouble concluding that juries historically have determined money damages claims, and that there was no basis for altering this practice when faced with the assessment of statutory damages.

A recent procedural issue of a more mundane but still important nature concerned the deference that the Federal Circuit is required to give to factual findings made by the Patent and Trademark Office (PTO) when denying a patent application. In *Dickinson v. Zurko*, the Supreme Court reversed the Federal Circuit's holding that a "clear error" standard should apply, instead adopting the more deferential standard required under the Administrative Procedures Act, which permits the appellate court to ignore or set aside an administrative factual finding only if the court concludes that it was either arbitrary, capricious, an abuse of discretion, or unsupported by substantial evidence. While this might be viewed by some as the Court dabbling in an area of little significance, this topic falls squarely within the overall area of separation of powers between the Executive Branch and the Judicial Branch, based on an Act of Congress setting forth the appropriate jurisdictional boundaries, which is an area of key interest to the Court.

4. Basic Substantive Law Questions.

Substantive law questions in the area of IP law typically involve the interpretation of the federal statutes granting IP rights, such as patents, trademarks and copyrights. The Court has granted review of several cases in this area in the past few years even in the absence of any conflict among the federal circuits, particularly in patent and copyright areas. Some of these cases fall within the "significant issue" category based on any scale for measuring significance. For example, in *J.E.M. AG Supply, Inc. v. Pioneer Hi-Bred International, Inc.*, the Court faced the issue whether newly developed plant breeds are patentable subject matter under the statutory scheme for general utility patents. The Federal Circuit had answered this question in the affirmative, and the Supreme Court in turn affirmed. This ruling ultimately upheld the PTO's interpretation of the utility patent statute, when faced with an argument that two narrower statutes governing plant patents should have applied exclusively. Why did the Court grant *certiorari* only to affirm? This case presented potentially conflicting statutes which had been interpreted by an Executive Branch agency acting within its area of expertise. It also presented a matter of major significance to the business community and the public, *i.e.*, the scope of patents covering living matter, which led to the submission of some thirteen *amicus* briefs, including one by the United States. These factors undoubtedly influenced the Court's decision to not leave resolution of this issue to the Federal Circuit alone.

A second patent law example in this category is *Warner-Jenkinson Co., Inc. v. Hilton Davis Chemical Co.*, which upheld the doctrine of equivalents and gave considerable guidance on its proper application in patent litigation. In particular, the Court held that the doctrine of equivalents must be applied to individual elements of a patent claim, rather than the invention as a whole, and that prosecution history estoppel does not apply automatically whenever a patent claim has been amended during the application process, without regard for the reasons for the amendment. For this case, the Court spelled out its reasons for granting *certiorari* with some specificity, noting that the Federal Circuit was having difficulty applying a fifty-year old precedent, as exemplified by three separate dissents below, and that it was generally necessary to clarify the proper scope of the doctrine of equivalents.

The need to clarify prior holdings of the Supreme Court and lower courts adding gloss to a broad statute with little inherent guidance arose again in *Wal-Mart Stores, Inc. v. Samara Bros., Inc.*, which interpreted the scope of trade dress protection for product design under Section 43(a) of the Lanham Act. In this case, the Court adopted a bright-line rule that product design for trade dress purposes is only protectable upon a showing of secondary meaning, with the hope that this would clear up confusion in the courts below and facilitate summary judgment motions. In reaching this result, the Court found it necessary to clarify the interplay between two of its earlier decisions.

Another example in the "significant issue" category, based the widespread ramifications of the decision, was *New York Times Co., Inc. v. Tasini*, which involved the copyright laws. In this case, freelance authors who had written articles published in a variety of periodicals brought copyright infringement claims against the publishers of the periodicals and the owners of certain electronic databases (such as NEXIS®), after the authors' articles were made available in these databases with the consent of only the publishers. The case turned on the construction of a provision of the Copyright Act governing rights in collective works. The Court had little difficulty adhering to the plain language of the statute, which required the database owners to obtain the consent of the freelance authors before including the articles in this database, due to the limited releases obtained by the publishers when the articles were initially written (which in many cases was prior to the existence of electronic databases of this type). But the decision had wide-spread ramifications, because it caused uncertainty in a large business segment, with no means for readily obtaining consents from all the various authors. Nonetheless, the Court was not deterred when ruling for the authors and against "big business," noting that issuance of an injunction against the databases was not necessarily inevitable upon remand, and that authors and publishers had previously developed practical solutions for resolving such disputes, such as blanket licenses in the music industry. Once again, the Court granted *certiorari* when there was no conflict in the federal circuits, reflecting the significance of the appellate court's ruling below to the national media and the rapidly growing electronic media database industry.

Not all cases reaching the Supreme Court garner the attention of the media as much as *Tasini*, however. There are many cases being granted, albeit infrequently, which Court observers who do not practice in the field of IP law might classify as more "mundane" statutory questions. One recent example is *Pfaff v. Wells Electronics, Inc.*, which involved the issue as to when the statutory one-year "on-sale" period is triggered for purposes of invalidating a patent. Under the "on-sale" bar doctrine, an "invention" cannot be patented if it has been "on sale" more than one year prior to filing a patent application. In reaching its decision, the Court had to interpret the meaning of "invention" under the Patent Act of 1952 in order to determine whether an invention could be patented before it was reduced to practice. Noting that the statute did not contain any express requirement of reduction to practice before an invention could be patented, the Court rejected imposing such an additional requirement, based on precedent dating back to Alexander Graham Bell's patent on the telephone. Instead, the Court held that the on-sale bar was triggered once the invention was the subject of a commercial offer for sale and ready for patenting, either by proof of reduction to practice or the preparation of drawings or descriptions sufficient to enable a person skilled in the art to practice the invention.

While *Pfaff* resulted in affirming the Federal Circuit, a Supreme Court grant of *certiorari* in what might be considered by many to be a less significant case more often is based on the Court's intent to promptly overturn what it considers to be a mistaken ruling below. This has occurred in several areas of IP law in the past decade, including copyright and patent cases.

C. FAILURE TO ADHERE TO PRECEDENT

The failure of an appellate court to follow relatively recent Supreme Court precedent renders the likelihood of a grant of *certiorari* quite high. This is evidenced in the Court's recent decision in *Festo Corp. v. Shoketsu Kinzoku Kogyo Kabushiki Co., Ltd.*, which revisited the doctrine of equivalents only five years after the Court's prior decision in *Warner-Jenkinson.* In the course of reversing the Federal Circuit, the Court held, *inter alia*, that prosecution history estoppel may apply to any claim amendment made to satisfy a Patent Act requirement, but that estoppel need not bar suit against every equivalent to the amended claim element. This holding overturned the Federal Court's attempt to impose a bright-line rule requiring the patentee to surrender *all* equivalents to the amended claim element, which the Court viewed as ignoring the "guidance" provided by *Warner-Jenkinson* and "disrupt[ing] the settled expectations of the inventing community."

IV. PRACTICAL CONSIDERATIONS IN SEEKING CERTIORARI REVIEW

Preparing a petition for *certiorari* is not an easy task, and there is no magic formula that guarantees success. This is particularly true in the area of IP law, where the Court grants at most two or three cases a year, with some Terms experiencing a complete dearth of IP cases. Some practical pointers that should be followed in all cases are worth reviewing.

A. NARROW THE ISSUES

It is important to recognize that, like all appellate review, the petitioner-appellant must take the time to narrow the issues on which review is sought. Appeals courts are not interested in reviewing every plausible error below; there simply is no time for a complete retrial on appeal. This consideration is even more important at the Supreme Court level. A petitioner must attempt to narrow the issues presented to one or two, and not pursue multiple issues that suggest a lack of significance, given the unlikely prospect that one case will raise multiple issues warranting *certiorari* review. What this means is that by the time you reach the Supreme Court, you have to recognize that you must drop some issues that you lost below, and try instead to focus on picking one or two potential winners. This is often a very difficult process for a trial lawyer who does not want to relinquish any possible argument, but that is the art and necessity of appellate practice.

B. FRAME THE QUESTIONS PRESENTED

The drafting of the question presented can be a formidable challenge. Good drafting requires the preparation of alternatives that can be eliminated, each of which attempts to phrase the issue for review in a different manner. Simple and easily understood questions that appear compelling in their logic are more likely to grab the attention of law clerks and Justices than complex and poorly worded examples that are indecipherable. Your question should make the Justices want to reach out and grab the issue, rather than dulling their eye as they weigh through a convoluted iteration that is impossible to comprehend. Remember, this is your fifteen seconds of fame as the nine Justices each review your question, which will be presented up front at the very beginning of your petition. Since the Court reviews many thousands of petitions in a given year, you cannot expect them to try and distill what the issues really are on their own; there simply is not enough time or resources available. Once again, the Court provides guidance on this topic in Supreme Court Rule 14, as follows:

> Rule 14. Content of a Petition for a *Writ of Certiorari*
>
> 1. A petition for a writ of certiorari shall contain, in the order indicated: (a) The questions presented for review, expressed concisely in relation to the circumstances of the case, without unnecessary detail. The questions should be short and should not be argumentative or repetitive. . . . The questions shall be set out on the first page following the cover, and no other information may appear on that page. The statement of any question presented is deemed to comprise every subsidiary question fairly included therein. Only the questions set out in the petition, or fairly included therein, will be considered by the Court.

C. DEAL WITH STARE DECISIS

It is hard enough to get the Supreme Court to accept your petition in cases where the Court has not yet spoken. It is even more difficult to get the Court to accept a petition that appears to seek (or expressly seeks) to overturn prior decisions of the Court, particularly if the law has become settled in that area. But it is not impossible, especially if the make-up of the Court has changed over the intervening years, or the economy or other circumstances have changed. One caveat is that the petitioner must not attempt to hide the fact that the petition seeks to overturn applicable precedents, as it is highly unlikely that the Court will overlook them when considering the petition. Any perception that the petitioner is trying to gloss over such precedent will only discredit the arguments presented.

D. EMPHASIZE THE PRACTICAL IMPORTANCE OF THE CASE

No matter what the topic area, the Court is most interested in deciding only significant cases that are worthy of its time and attention.

But since most Justices have little experience as practitioners in any specialty area (or at least, any recent experience), particularly in the field of IP law, it is crucial that the petition explain, in simple terms, why it is so critical to the field of IP law to reverse the decision below. This factor is one that generally favors IP law petitions over many others. The rapid pace of technological change often provides the platform for advocating for new rules to replace or distinguish outmoded doctrines that no longer meet the needs of the current state of technology. Hence the interest of the Court in taking on cases involving patents in new areas (such as patenting life forms) or new forms of copying that suggest the need for addressing older copyright statutory provisions (such as the invention of the VCR and the development of electronic databases, which make it simple and nearly cost-free to make perfect electronic copies of protected works).

The interest of the Justices in a given case is not infrequently influenced at least in part by their law clerks' enthusiasm for a topic. Once again, IP law is one area that gains from this factor. Law clerks frequently are more current on the state of new technology than their employers. They often are attracted to technology cases and thus willing to put in extra effort to dig into the issues presented to see if there are any diamonds in the rough that warrant a strong recommendation for review.

E. SOLICIT HELP FROM OTHERS

There is no need to go it alone in seeking review in many instances. Supporters willing to submit an amicus brief in support of your position should be lined up well in advance of the due date for a petition, as the same due date applies to their briefs. Moreover, if the opposing party does not consent to an amicus brief, a motion for leave to file it will be necessary. One key supporter in many cases is the United States, particularly when questions of statutory interpretation or constitutional issues are presented.

V. CONCLUSION

Advocacy before the U.S. Supreme Court is not an art that is practiced by large numbers of practitioners. Given the limited number of cases in which review is granted each year, the chances of having a petition for *certiorari* granted are quite slim, and even slimmer for IP cases generally. That does not mean, however, that a case that ultimately reaches the federal appellate level is not generally certiorari-worthy. The vast majority of complaints filed in federal courts concerning IP matters are settled prior to trial. Even fewer are appealed after a verdict is reached or a judgment is entered. In those few cases that are the subject of a federal circuit court opinion, the issues raised on appeal tend to be those that are less certain as to their outcome and thus more significant in the eyes of the Court, unless the appeal was taken despite the lack of any support for the arguments presented. As a result, many appellate court decisions, if properly presented, have the potential for selection for review by the Supreme Court. For that reason, close attention to detail in preparing the petition, and especially close attention to the legal argument and prior rulings of the Court in the area at issue, may lead to success even for practitioners who have little or no prior experience before the Court.

---

* This paper was presented at The John Marshall Law School Center for Intellectual Property Law's 47th Annual Conference on Developments in Intellectual Property Law on February 28, 2003 at The John Marshall Law School, Chicago, IL.

** J.D., Harvard University, 1984, Magna Cum Laude, and B.G.S. with Distinction, University of Michigan, 1981.

A